This book offers an original examination of the formation of
the English canon during the first two thirds of the eighteenth
century, looking in particular at the treatment of Shakespeare,
Spenser, and Milton. Through close readings of periodical
essays, editions, treatises, reviews, disquisitions, pamphlets, and
poems, Jonathan Brody Kramnick recounts the origins of
modern literary study and situates the rise of national literary
tradition in the broad context of the making of a public culture.
He argues against the consensus view that locates the beginnings of literary criticism comfortably within the rise of the
public sphere, and suggests instead that the makings of the
canon lie in a combined evolution of publicity and specialization. Much of what we understand as professional criticism,
literary language, and national literary tradition, he proposes,
received its definitive shape during the mid-eighteenth century,
when the century-long effort to define "modern" literature
against the earlier achievements of the "ancients" culminated
with a new idea of national antiquity.

Jonathan Brody Kramnick is assistant professor of English at
Rutgers University..

# MAKING THE
# ENGLISH CANON

*Print-Capitalism and the Cultural Past, 1700–1770*

JONATHAN BRODY KRAMNICK

CAMBRIDGE
UNIVERSITY PRESS

PUBLISHED BY THE PRESS SYNDICATE OF THE UNIVERSITY OF CAMBRIDGE
The Pitt Building, Trumpington Street, Cambridge CB2 IRP, United Kingdom

CAMBRIDGE UNIVERSITY PRESS
The Edinburgh Building, Cambridge, CB2 2RU, United Kingdom
hhtp://www.cup.cam.ac.uk
40 West 20th Street, New York, NY 10011–4211, USA   http://www.cup.org
10 Stamford Road, Oakleigh, Melbourne 3166, Australia

First published 1998

Printed in the United Kingdom at the University Press, Cambridge

Typeset in Baskerville 11/12.5pt   [CE]

*A catalogue record for this book is abailable from the British Library*

*Library of Congress cataloguing in publication data*
Kramnick, Jonathan Brody.
Making the English canon: print-capitalism and the cultural past, 1700–1700 /
Jonathan Brody Kramnick.
p.   cm.
Includes index.
ISBN 0 521 64127 6 (hardback)
1. English literature – Early modern, 1500–1700 – History and criticism – Theory. etc.
2. Shakespeare, William, 1564–1616 – Criticism and interpretation – History – 18th century.
3. Spenser, Edmund, 1552?–1599 – Criticism and interpretation – History – 18th century.
4. Milton, John, 1608–1674 – Criticism and interpetation – History – 18th century.
5. Great Britain – Intellectual life – 18th century.
6. Criticism – Great Britain – History – 18th century.
7. Canon (Literature)   I. Title.
PR421.K73   1998
820.9'005–dc21   98–21089   CIP

ISBN 0 521 64127 6 hardback

*For my parents*

# Contents

# Acknowledgments

I would like to thank the William and Andrew Clark Memorial Library and the Center for the Critical Analysis of Contemporary Culture at Rutgers University for their generous assistance during the writing of this book. I would also like to thank *ELH*, *MLQ*, *PMLA*, and *Profession* for allowing me to reprint material that appeared, in earlier form, in their journals.

I am grateful for the kind guidance of Ronald Paulson, who saw me through early drafts. I am also grateful for John Guillory's reading, inspiration, and friendship. Jonathan Goldberg has been the most demanding of readers and closest of friends; the book has been enriched by both. I began writing this book in the warm and supportive community of Jared Gardner, Elizabeth Hewitt, and Michael Trask. Since then, I've profited greatly from the careful reading and friendly advice of Michael McKeon and Adela Pinch.

Rosalinda Stone has been my soulmate and counsel from the beginnings of this project to its end. My debt to her is inexpressible.

## NOTE ON THE TEXT: EPIGRAPHS

The epigraphs for chapter two are from Max Weber, *Economy and Society: an Outline of Interpretive Sociology*, 2 vols., trans. Ephraim Fischoff *et al.*, eds. Guenther Roth and Claus Wittich (Berkeley, Calif.: University of California Press, 1978) 608; and Georg Luckács, "Reification and the Consciousness of the Proletariat," in *History and Class Consciousness*, trans. Rodney Livingstone (Cambridge, Mass.: MIT Press, 1971) 137.

The epigraph for chapter five is from Laurence Stern, *A Sentimental Journey through France and Italy* (London and New York: Penguin, 1968) 106–107.

# Introduction: the modernity of the past

The English literary canon achieved its definitive shape during the middle decades of the eighteenth century. The idea of national tradition to which we have given a final burial was born at that time from debates over the past. Eighteenth-century literary critics looked to older works in response to a prolonged and pronounced transformation: the opening of the cultural product for a nation of readers. What we have learned to call "the canon" – a pantheon of high-cultural works from the past – came into being as a contradiction. Modernity generates tradition. The swelling of the book trade, the passing of aristocratic authority, the rise in literacy, the prominence of women writers and readers, the professionalization of criticism, together provoked over the course of the century a recourse to older works as national heritage. Canon formation, then as now, partook in wide-ranging debates about the nature of the cultural community. Critics weighed the value of older works and pondered their relation to modern writing. They also contemplated the character of modern readers, and examined how the education, class, and gender of the reading audience had changed over time. The paradoxical establishment of tradition out of a sense of modernity happened when literary culture was seen to be under considerable duress, even in crisis. Whereas the new literary and social world was unpredictable, and readers and genres no longer conformed to a settled pattern, works written before the onset of cultural modernity exhibited a contrasting splendor.

*"identity crisis"*

The decisive reception of the English literary past was settled during the mid-eighteenth century. Years of critical discussion coalesced then into a durable model of literary history and aesthetic value. Consider the following pronouncement by Joseph Warton in 1756: "Our English poets may I think be disposed in four different classes and degrees. In the first class, I would place, first, our only

1

sublime and pathetic poets, Spenser, Shakespeare and Milton."[1]
Warton's canon may now seem rather conventional, but the idea
that older English writers composed a trinity of classics was new to
the mid-eighteenth century. Before then, the literary past was
typically considered a progressively unfolding lineage. One writer
followed another in a steadily flourishing line of achievement. Like
the exuberant economy and military, England's literature improved
with time. For literary critics of the late seventeenth and early
eighteenth century, writers like Spenser and Shakespeare were
rather uncouth. Far from classics, writers from the early ages of
English society were imperfect versions of their modern progeny.
Warton's limpid enshrinement of the English greats was, in this
sense, distinctive and portentous. Midcentury critics had difficulty
sharing the optimism of their predecessors. Modern culture seemed
beleaguered by the book trade, literacy, and rationality. In contrast,
the past shone with value and achievement.

I examine the increasing luminance of the past in the writings of
British literary critics over the first two thirds of the eighteenth
century. My argument is built out of readings of figures like Joseph
Warton, critics whose activity over the period was instrumental to
the reception of older works. Some of these figures are among the
most well-known of the time, Joseph Addison and Samuel Johnson
for instance. Others have faded into near obscurity, William Huggins
and Charlotte Lennox for instance. Still others were as anonymous
to the eighteenth century as they are to the twentieth. The genres
and media in which these critics wrote span periodical essays,
editions, treatises, reviews, disquisitions, pamphlets, and poems. My
use of the term literary criticism to describe these writings and
literary critic to characterize their authors is deliberate but not
anachronistic. I would not want readers to think that I am suggesting
that the eighteenth century knew literature or criticism in the way
that we do now. Nor would I want to suggest that either the noun or
adjective were then fixed. Rather, much of what follows traces out
the varied meanings of "literary," "criticism," and "literature."
Within the shifting meanings, we can detect underlying cross-
currents of change. The first two chapters of this book attempt to
capture the wide inclination of these currents: among them, the turn
from amateur to professional criticism, the shift from the beautiful to
the sublime, the separation of commercial from aesthetic value, the
rise of literary expertise. The second two chapters examine the cases

of Shakespeare and Spenser. The last chapter examines the problem of national literary culture. I remain throughout as it were on the surface of the critical cross-currents. My interest in print-capitalism should not lead readers to expect an empirical sociology of reading.[2] The thesis about modernity, commerce, and print is built, rather, from the inside out, from the wide course of criticism as it variously responds to and maps out the public and the market.

We have inherited a canon formed during the tumultuous decades of the mid-eighteenth century. But this canon was both long in the making and formed out of intricate conflicts about literature, reading, and even history itself. Perhaps the broadest conflict obtained over the nature of the past and its relation to the present. The midcentury's new valuation of historical distance and older writers established itself against an earlier hostility to the crude works of English antiquity. Canonical works were now honored on the terms of their former rejection. The idea of the past was turned on its head. In this sense, canon formation is tied to developments in midcentury culture with which readers will already be familiar: the rise of gothic historicism, for example, or the growing interest in the sublime. But the appearance of these period motifs in this study will, in another sense, be not so familiar. The midcentury's interest in older and sublime forms was profoundly mediated by its own past. The revaluation of English antiquity grew out of a cultural crisis that had been established during the heady days of the early eighteenth century. Critics from that time, so the midcentury complained, had opened up the literary product to polite conversation only to let it descend, eventually, to the level of the market. In response, midcentury writers championed the very terms their predecessors abused. Perhaps the clearest example of this dialectic can be found in the category gothic: first a term of abuse for archaic vulgarity, later a sign of the past's iridescent charm.

Midcentury critics learned to treasure the antiquity of English writers. This idea of English antiquity was patterned on the prior notion of the classical age of Greece and Rome. The present paled in comparison to a golden age of cultural achievement. In this way, the canon grew out of the "battle of the books" and was the battle's most lasting product. It is difficult to overstate either the importance of the "ancient" and "modern" antitheses during the period or the complexity of its long-term development. In the initial fray between Wotton and Temple, the period term "ancient" referred exclusively to Greco-Roman antiquity, whose literary monuments were on all accounts superior to the best of English writing. The entirety of English writing fell under the period term "modern." Within this overarching conception of modern culture – comprising not only Dryden but Chaucer – relatively contemporary writers were closest to the ancients in the regularity and decorum of their verse. The most modern of the moderns were paradoxically the most like the ancients. Even in the early years of the battle of the books, therefore, the antithetical contrast of ancient and modern crept into the discussion of English literary history. Ancients versus moderns reappeared within the category of the modern. The antiquity of older English writers, initially, distanced them in value and form from the antiquity of the classics, whose mannered precision was uniquely like contemporary English. As critics grew concerned about the conditions of literary culture, the disparity between ancient and modern English widened and the scales of valuation began to turn. First, the entirety of English writing was modern. Later, a singularly English antiquity separated from its modern descendant. But now the English ancients were more like the classical ancients than were the English moderns. The criteria of canonicity likewise shifted, from the graceful regularity of the classics to their sublime weight. In the updated battle of the books, English ancients like Shakespeare did battle with English moderns like Pope. In this transposition of terms, an important event in literary culture occurred. Critics established English antiquity as the moment of literary achievement against which all subsequent writing would be measured. A national canon formed on the precedent example of the classical canon took shape. This canon was necessarily old and carried with it much of the aura of antiquity: difficulty, rarity, sublimity, masculinity. In the effort to make the national literature weighty and recondite, canonical English began to take on the qualities of Latin and Greek. A quasi-classical language, canonical English stood apart from the language of trade and commerce.

The endeavor to establish English literature as a world unto itself was paradoxically obsessed with the demeaning argot of polite society and consumer culture. The idea of a separate domain of national, literary treasures went hand in hand with the idea of public culture. In thinking about this puzzling dialectic, I have made recourse to Jürgen Habermas's influential account of the growth of the public sphere.[3] Habermas's analysis has become increasingly central to eighteenth-century studies. This book should be taken as an attempt to reflect critically on his early work. As is now widely familiar, Habermas argues that the discussion of news and books in such places as the coffee-houses and salons, the establishment of the circulating library, and the growth of the popular novel, brought about a "public sphere" involved in "rational critical debate" over cultural and political norms. To this conventional narrative (borrowed extensively from Ian Watt, Richard Altick, and Arnold Hauser), Habermas adds his distinctive twist: the literary public derived from the epochal separation of state and civil society, government and commerce, power and sociability.[4] In a dramatic retelling of the dialectic of enlightenment, instrumental reason springs from the nexus of print and commerce.[5] Stripped of feudal publicity, private classes found in books and news a medium of cohesion against the oligarchic state and for their shared needs. Cultural debate shaped manners and habits suited to the modern regime. The separation of public from private, Habermas points out, was repeated within the private sphere, from the publicly relevant domain of commerce to the public domain of literature all the way to the core of intimacy, the bourgeois family itself.

The attraction of this model for eighteenth-century studies, it seems to me, has been that it places special emphasis on literary culture in the making of modernity. The following chapters share in this attraction, but attempt also to transform the conventional reception of Habermas's narrative. Owing perhaps to Terry Eagleton's influential study *The Function of Criticism* (1984),[6] a prevailing reading of the public sphere has emphasized a bourgeois encroachment on aristocratic institutions. Criticism here was at the vanguard of the middle classes' farewell to elitism, whether in the Church, the Universities, or the Court. The appeal of this narrative for late twentieth-century readers is clear. For a criticism that now sees itself bereft of a public vocation, Eagleton's story provides a contrasting relief. If we are now functionless for the technocratic age, at least we were once an agent of bourgeois hegemony. Against this model, I will argue for the dialectical development of publicity and specialization. Criticism took arms against restricted culture, to be sure. This was the great war waged on "pedantry" throughout the long eighteenth century. Yet a new group of scholars also fought public culture. This was the battle over professional expertise. Struggles between the academy and journalism, sociability and training, are not new to literary criticism or to culture wars. They are, rather, present at the very origins of literary canon formation itself.

It is in this light that I would revise our understanding of the public sphere and literary culture in the eighteenth century. The dialectic of public and private had an agile career. The commerce in books did not just foster rational discussion of matters of taste; it led also to a mordant concern about the dissemination of literary goods. The opening of culture for a nation of consumers joined with the seclusion of older works in a clerisy of experts. These developments were, I argue, importantly modern and set the terms for literary study as we know it. But they are not finally reducible to the rise of the middle class. Critics fond of public culture often dwelled on the mannerly gentility of the elite classes. In contrast, scholarly mandarins were generally opposed to the aristocratic cult of leisurely dilettantism. The development of criticism during the eighteenth century was, in other words, a great deal more complicated than the conventional reading of Habermas might suggest, even if it still followed a discernible pattern. The worry over public culture produced corresponding modes of specialized privacy, whether the rarefaction of delicate taste or the expertise of professional scholars. The idea of the reading audience underwent a corresponding shift: from the crowd of modern consumers to the historical spirit of common English. Forms of public culture discovered they had a specialized component. Modes of specialization took on a public cast.

These variant paths of critical thought converged around the integral unit of the national literature. So much is implied, of course, in the subtitle to this book. The phrase "print-capitalism" comes from Benedict Anderson's seminal study of nationalism, *Imagined Communities* (1983).[7] For Anderson, as for myself, print-capitalism refers at once to the trade in books and to the wider dialectics of modernization brought about by literacy and commerce. Anderson's thesis is now well known. One of the first fully capitalized commodities, print assembled vernacular languages and audiences into nations: "imagined communities" bound by language, territory, and custom. In the climate of contemporary cultural studies, public and nation are often used interchangeably, as they were frequently enough by the critics discussed in the pages below. Still, one goal of this book is to trouble this too easy identification. For eighteenth-century criticism, the public could in fact stand for the nation, just as it could also stand for the polite stratum of educated readers hovering above the toiling masses of vulgar illiterates. Likewise, the nation could mean the imagined community of readers, the plenum of fellow Shakespeare lovers, just as it could also mean an antique heritage expressed in works from the deep past. In its various forms, the canon oscillates between these two models and slowly binds them together. By 1770 the canon alternately "looms out of an immemorial past," in Anderson's words, and expresses the essential Englishness of modern readers.[8] Like the public, the idea of the nation was built out of a complicated tension among different strands of critical thought.

One such tension stemmed from, as it were, the capital of print-capitalism. As critics pondered the imagined community brought together by print, they were not uniformly enthusiastic about the simultaneity of collective reading or about the dispersion of the national literature. More and more, print commodification was seen to have a deleterious effect on cultural value. To understand the impact of the market on the apperception of aesthetic value, I have drawn from time to time on the cultural sociology of Pierre Bourdieu. For Bourdieu, the modern period is defined by the growing market in cultural goods and by a division within that market of high-cultural from mass-cultural products. Bourdieu's varied corpus presents a compelling narrative for students of the history of criticism. As the traffic in literature and art expands, the economic field exerts a pervasively negative influence on the cultural field. Exchange value opposes itself to aesthetic value. The dominant principle of cultural stratification derives from a work's "autonomy" from the pressure of politics and commerce. In this "economic world reversed," symbolic profit and the cash nexus meet each other in continuous reversal. The cultural field splits into two modes of organizing production and reception: the "field of restricted cultural production" and "the field of large-scale cultural production." The "field of restricted culture" is shaped by the rejection of the market of readers, while the "field of large-scale culture" is coordinated to consumption and public demand.[9]

These terms provide a supple means of grasping the eighteenth-century's ambivalence toward the cultural market and the peculiar development in which genres that notionally appealed to a wide readership, like the novel, served to buttress a vision of the past as difficult and unpopular. I have found the idea of "restricted culture"

particularly useful in understanding the growth of critical specialization during the eighteenth century, the emergence of both the
professional reviewer writing for the periodical press and the
philological scholar laboring in the archives. In each case, expert
knowledge authorizes the subject and object of criticism. One must
have an adept sensibility or an exceptional training to apprehend
literary works. These works are deserving of learned treatment.
Either way, canonical texts confront readers with difficulty and
require a system of interpretation. Works of restricted art "owe their
specifically cultural rarity to the rarity of the instruments with which
they may be deciphered."[10]

Still, I would caution against conceiving of midcentury criticism as
a continental rift between restricted and large-scale production.
While such a conception may be intrinsic to the metaphor of field
itself, it seems important to stress that in the period under consideration restricted and large-scale culture were not broken apart into
rigid topographical zones. Rather, the idea of the canon grew out of
the torsion between the two. Restricted culture itself gets accused of
serving the market. This is that peculiar and important contradiction
familiar to students of eighteenth-century culture: the accusation
against the scholarly class that it is part of Grub Street; before Colley
Cibber, after all, there was Lewis Theobald. Large-scale culture
likewise turns out, for some critics, to ensure canonical status. This is
that equally novel development in which consumer culture ceases to
demean aesthetic value but becomes the means of gauging literary
achievement, the very test of time itself. Secured by historical
continuity, reading weaves into the fabric of a work its status as a
permanent artifact of the national culture. Canonical works neither
lose their aura of rarity nor quit receding into the past. According to
this model, cultural consumption transforms into a system of value
analogous to economic consumption. In any case, restricted and
large scale, public and private culture prove to be in dynamic
interaction over the course of the century, with important results:
Shakespeare's unique position in the canon is largely explained by
his simultaneous popularity and antiquity.

In writing the history of canonicity, I have chosen an object now
under considerable duress. As with the eighteenth century, debates
in our time over a wide range of curricular, social, and economic
matters have telescoped into the question of the cultural past and its
allegedly monumental works. The culture wars of the eighteenth

century provided the object, if they did not set the terrain, for the culture wars of the late twentieth century.[11] By treating the English literary canon less as a timeless achievement of a lithesome antiquity than as a symbolic product of the modern age, this book does take an implicit stand in the canon debate, such as it still preoccupies the academy today. Likewise, by tracing the recursive arch in which canonical works recede into the past, the study provides, I think, an historical accounting for what recent criticism has discovered as the exclusion of women writers and others from the canon of literary greats. The intricate and compound turn to English antiquity was the matrix of what from hindsight is somewhat mistakenly perceived as an expulsion.[12] As eighteenth-century critics of all stripes were well aware, older works were necessarily more restricted in the gender and social class of the author. For many critics, this restriction was precisely the point. For others, the opening up of culture to women and commoners augured modernity's laudable triumph. For still others, women readers provided an elegant alternative not just to the boorish past but to the presence of that past in the lower classes. Canonical "exclusion" thus has a more elaborate pedigree than is often presumed. The burden for us is to understand the present without abbreviating the past. Were it not for the contemporary culture wars, of course, this book would probably not have been written, or would have taken a different cast. Today the idea of English antiquity itself seems antique, a relic of a past age. Yet the anachronism of the canon in the twentieth century should not obscure its origins in the eighteenth. The dusk of the canon throws light on its making.

Like everything that passes, the canon is easier to see in its twilight. But the view does change with time. For an influential tradition of left cultural studies growing out of the work of Raymond Williams, the idea of "literature" as a finite category referring exclusively to imaginative works takes shape only in the late eighteenth century. The enlightenment narrowed the term from all printed works to well-written poems, plays, and novels. The categorical tapering of literature and the placement of it in the hands of the educated middle classes was part of the larger shaping and domination of culture by a bourgeoisie ever eager to find an expression of its values and legitimacy. Eventually, literature named a national tradition that loomed above what common people actually read and wrote. For Williams and his students this history sketched a cau-

tionary image of how the idea of literary tradition had been usurped
and deployed by the ruling classes. Their counter-history proposed a
theory of culture premised on a radical popularizing of signification,
an appreciation of the wide variety of writing that composed the real
national heritage. Now, I would not want to dispute the achievements
of this program. Much of the proceeding argument takes off from
Williams's political philology. I am particularly interested in, for
example, the way in which the winnowing of "literature" into works
of the imagination concurrently displaced the older portmanteau
category "poetry" and made it the regal subset verse. The chapters
below document how literature grew to name a domain of imaginative writing within which poetry lorded over the prose works
favored by the public of readers. Still, the present study should be
considered a departure from Williams's school in several important
respects. For Williams, the growth of aesthetic philosophy, professional criticism, and literary scholarship was tied to a common
gentry/bourgeois regime. In the present study, this narrative neither
explains the course of these developments nor charts the relations
among them. The point is not so much to dispute a thesis of social
change as to outline its intricacy, to see how cultural categories
emerge from an abiding sense of dislocation and crisis. It is difficult
to reduce any single position mapped in the following pages to one or
another class. (To whom, exactly, do the scholars speak? What
interest is expressed in deriding their work as pedantry?). But it is not
so hard to detect the period's novel sense of change. In the organs of
national-culture building, the shock of modernity opened the future
only to fall into the past. The first great wave of literary history
writing gave to us progress and nostalgia, dilettantism and expertise.

The revision I propose does not just ask for greater attention to the
effective variations of critical development. It also introduces a thesis
operative at the most general level of analysis: the idea of literary
antiquity was indelibly linked to the institutions of modernity, to the
market, the public, the nation, and the division of labor. This model,
I think, better captures not only the past but also the present crisis.
The tenor and argument of the chapters below derive from a culture
war now shifted into a dramatic new phase: no longer the fight over
the curriculum alone but the effort to sustain academic work in the
face of institutional downsizing and resurgent anti-intellectualism. In
this forbidding and straitened context, struggles to rid ourselves of

canons, to draw up new ones, or to return to them once more seem almost quaint. Our cultural politics, whatever the stripe, have scant purchase in a world with little room for the study of culture in the first place. Thinking about the crisis of the academy and literary study as they head into the next millennium, one is reminded of precedent struggles between the public and the academy during the eighteenth century. I would hope that this study provides not just a history of the canon over which we have debated so heatedly but also an antecedent image of the problems we face in the coming years.

PART ONE

# The structural transformation of literary history

Few notions may appear so essential to a literary canon as the antiquity of its authors. What is a canon, after all, if not a pantheon of older writers and their great works? For much of the eighteenth century, however, the English canon consisted of writers valued for their modernity. This is not to say that antiquity was entirely a late arriving concept. The seventeenth and early eighteenth century had a settled notion of the ancients. But the ancients were writers from the classical age of Greece and Rome: Homer and Virgil in epic poetry, Sophocles in drama, Horace in satire, and so forth.[1] In its initial moment, the English canon consisted of modern authors who were understood to write like their ancient predecessors. Denham and Waller, for instance, composed with a stately decorum akin to the Greeks and the Romans. The idea of a particularly English antiquity, against which modern English pales, developed gradually during the eighteenth century as critics began to think through the conditions of literary culture and society. This chapter explores the transformation in the narrative of English literary history that gave to us the modern form of the canon: a trinity of English ancients. Criticism's lasting idea of English antiquity, I argue, grew out of a prolonged consideration of the contexts of reading: the uneven distribution of print and literacy, the professionalization of criticism and scholarship, the institutions of print culture, and the commerce in books.

## THE CAREER OF REFINEMENT

Like all cultural developments, the formation of the English canon into its canonical form – Spenser, Shakespeare, and Milton – was at once a reaction to immediate concerns and a long and complicated process of abstraction.[2] Critics of the mid-eighteenth century made their own history, as it were, but they did not make it just as they pleased. The terms of midcentury criticism were shaped by previous generations of thinking through the problem of literary change. In the decades before the formation of the canon as a trinity, critics put in place a model of literary history concerned with the progress of major and minor poets across the span of vernacular writing. The progressive narrative focused on the linguistic substance of poetry; the diction and meter of English literature leveled out over time. From the vantage of contemporary refinement, critics viewed the past as the prehistory of the present, roughness the progenitor of eloquence. The prism glass of politeness both presented to the modern age an account of its insuperable progress – the march of national culture through commerce and conquest – and refracted a literary history uniquely suited for the elegant colloquy of the public sphere. For a model so concerned with stability, however, the signal importance of this literary history was actually to transform itself into the discourse of retrospective canon building. Progress and refinement gave way to decline and roughness. Bridging the moment of Joseph Addison to Joseph Warton is an important discussion among critics about the different status of commodity and aesthetic value and about the changing nature of criticism itself.

How did the literary history of England arrive at the model of refinement only to have refinement turn into recession? The making of the English canon occurred against the backdrop of the late seventeenth century's "battle of the books," in which the defenders of Greco-Roman antiquity took on the avatars of modern writing.[3] (In the characteristic opposition, the friends of Aristotle fought off the promoters of Bacon, or the followers of Sophocles stood ground against the party of Jonson.) During the early years of this battle, all writing in English was considered to be modern, insofar as it was not from the classical age. English poets from Chaucer to Dryden stood together as a unit defined in contradistinction to the ancient writers of Greece and Rome. The question for critics was how close did modern poetry approximate the transcendent value of Homer and Virgil and how might one judge the various achievements of modern writers among and against themselves? When Gerard Langbaine's *The Lives and Characters of the English Dramatic Poets* (1691) endeavored to give "a succinct account of the time in which most of the poets lived; the place of their nativity, quality, death, [and] writings," for example, he cataloged and *alphabetically* discussed all hitherto existing playwrights.[4] The "memory of those later writers . . . of our own nation, Mr. Shakespeare, Fletcher, Johnson, Cowley, &c" had the form of simultaneity rather than chronology, an orbit rather than a sequence (4).

When critics did attempt to understand the procession of modern writing and measure its historical evolution they often made reference to a narrative of progressive and unfolding refinement. English literature may not aspire to the same heights as classical literature but it still could promote rational thought and polite language among a nation of readers. We may get a sense of this project in a derisive aside by the prototypical "ancient," Sir William Temple. Midway through the 1691 *Miscellanea*'s essay "On Poetry" Temple switches focus from the formal properties of verse to their elaboration over time: "Instead of critick, or rules concerning poetry, I shall rather turn my thoughts to the history of it, and observe the antiquity, the uses, the changes, the decays, that have attended this great empire of wit."[5] His history charts a predictable decline from antiquity to modernity; but in ridiculing the debased poetry of the moderns Temple also engages what was more and more modernity's central claim for legitimacy:

much application has been made to the smoothness of language or stile, which has at the best, but the beauty of colouring in a picture, and can never make a good one, without spirit and strength; [this] vein has been much cultivated in our modern *English* poetry, and by such poor recruits have the broken forces of this empire been of late made up, with what success I leave to be judged by such, as consider it in the former heights, and the present declines both of power and of honour. (354–355)

The trajectory from ancient to modern poetry limns a descending curve. A near century later, this idea of "decline" will be established within English literary history. At this point, however, modern verse as a unit pales against the long-ago past. Temple's rejection of refinement concentrates on the one obvious claim that the moderns have over the ancients, their composition in the shared language of the nation. The argument that English poetry could bring about a refined and dignified speech, as Temple notes with distaste, was one way in which critics could defend modernity's value without setting it against antiquity. The language of English poetry was the language of polite society. Polite society embodied the nation at its finest hour.

Early models of national literary history made a great deal of discursive refinement. Many turn-of-the-century critics described the English literary past in terms of the successive improvement of modern writers on their own uncouth ancestors. English as both a language and a literature, in this account, culminated with poets like John Denham and Edmund Waller, whose "smooth numbers" marked the arrival of English verse to regularity and the English language to mannered speech. In Thomas Rymer's paradigmatic formulation, "Chaucer found an Herculean labour on his hands; and did perform to admiration [but] our language retain'd something of the churl; something of the stiff and Gothish did stick upon it, till long after Chaucer . . . In Queen Elizabeth's time it grew fine but came not to an head and spirit, did not shine and sparkle till Mr. Waller set it running."[6] In Rymer's account, the English poetic tradition stages unfolding drama of smoothness. The important contribution of this model was not just the idea that the language of the moderns was refined, but that the career of refinement might be understood as a narrative, in which the move from one writer to the next mapped the leveling out of English over time.

By Dryden's *Fables Ancient and Modern, Translated into Verse* (1700) the narrative of refinement had set.[7] In this volume, Dryden defended his "translation" of Chaucer into "modern English" by suggesting that Chaucer's language had become foreign, and that "turning some of the *Canterbury Tales* into our language as it is now refined" presented an improved and readable text.[8] The distance and difference between Chaucer's language and Dryden's is the history of poetry. English poetry is a progressively unfolding lineage. While Chaucer "is the father of English poetry," he "lived in the infancy of our poetry" and "the dawning of our language" (277–278, 281). After this birth, English reached its adolescence with Spenser, Fairfax, and Milton, and then matured with Denham and Waller. Dryden's progressive narrative thus does not hesitate to suborn the father to his offspring: "nothing is brought into perfection at the first . . . we must be children before we grow into men" (281). Seen from the vantage of prosody, the history of English poetry charts the steady civilizing of the native language. Poetry overcomes the roughness of earlier English to arrive at Dryden's moment to a stability of utterance and constancy of measure: "even after Chaucer, there was a Spenser, a Harrington, a Fairfax, before Waller and Denham were in being; and our numbers were in their nonage until these last appeared" (281). Chaucer "first adorned and amplified our barren tongue"; next came "Spenser and Fairfax both . . . great masters in our language . . . who saw much farther into the beauties of our numbers than those who immediately followed them"; after this generation arose "Milton . . . the poetical son of Spenser and Waller of Fairfax"; of the two it is "our famous Waller" who is responsible for "harmony of numbers" (270–271).

For many turn-of-the-century writers, Waller and Denham evinced the arrival of English verse at the regularity of modern form and the English language at the etiquettes of polite speech. In some quarters, the progress of refinement was enough to seal the case for the moderns. John Dennis declared that his design in *The Advancement and Reformation of Modern Poetry* (1701) was "no less than to set the moderns upon an equal foot with even more admir'd antiquity."[9] Dennis uses the term advancement in two senses: his cause is to champion modernity; modernity advances on the past. Both types of advancement turn on linguistic regularity, the very substance of poetry itself.

Before we proceed let us define poetry; which is the first time that a definition has been given of that noble art: For neither ancient nor modern criticks have defin'd poetry in general. Poetry then is an imitation of nature by a pathetick and numerous speech. As poetry is an art, it must be an imitation of nature. That the instrument with which it makes its imitation is speech need not be disputed. That that speech must be musical, no one can doubt: For numbers distinguish the parts of poetick diction from the periods of prose. Now numbers are nothing but articulate sounds and their pauses measur'd by their proper proportions of time. (24)

Dennis's eclectic and brazen claim to be the first critic ever to have defined poetry contains a suggestive sense of the work that the vernacular canon was understood to perform at the turn of the eighteenth century. Poetry equals metered language. Meter should be regular. Regularity is the foundation of national culture: "I am very much inclin'd to believe, that 'tis the polite learning of any nation that contributes most to the extending its language, and poetry is the branch of polite learning which is the most efficacious in it" (7). As the pure form of orderly speech, of abstract equivalence among the members of polite society, poetic refinement "extends" learning across the manifold: "the poetry of that language which is most reasonable and most instructive, must in all likelihood have most attraction for the gentlemen of neighbouring nations; and we have shewn above, that that is the most reasonable and most instructive poetry, which is the most regular" (xviii). The modernity of modern writers lies not in their subservience to the ancients but in their worldly sociability, their utility in establishing civil bonds. Placing the moderns on equal footing with the ancients obliges Dennis, in turn, to repudiate moderns who fail to meet the canons of regularity. These are writers from modernity's own past. While Sophocles's "*Oedipus* is exactly just and regular," for example, Shakespeare's "*Julius Caesar* is very extravagant and irregular" (viii).

The distinction that Dennis draws between the modest regularity of contemporary English and the extravagant irregularity of older English (here, notably, in Shakespeare) turns out to be rather important in the long term making of the canon. As critics considered the progressive evolution of vernacular writing they soon discovered an "ancients and modern" distinction within English literature itself and, in this initial phase, valued modern English writers over their ancient precursors. Consider Edward Bysshe's *Art of English Poetry* (1702). The *Art* was half miscellany, half poetic manual.[10] Passages from English poetry sat next to a handy rhyming dictionary and lists of familiar tropes. Readers were invited to enjoy the great works of English poetry and to try their hand at composition. Both the reading and writing of poetry were understood to be leisurely activities; "this is a book that may be taken up and laid down at pleasure, and would rather choose to lye about in a drawing-room, or a grove, than be set up in a closet."[11] The poetry suitable for such leisurely politeness was uniquely contemporary.

I have inserted not only similes, allusions, characters, and descriptions, but also the most natural and noble thoughts on all subjects of our modern poets; I say of our modern: for . . . the garb in which the ancients (as *Chaucer, Spenser*, and others) are cloath'd, tho' then Alamode, is now become so out of fashion, that the readers of our age have no ear for them: And this is the reason that the good *Shakespeare* himself is not so frequently cited in the following pages, as he would otherwise deserve to be. (3–4)

The English ancients have fallen out of fashion because their language is difficult for modern ears. The reference to aural reception here is not accidental. It exemplifies the importance of the sonorous quality of polite speech for the evaluation of modern writing. One perceives the smoothness and regularity of modern writing in its sound, a sound evidently superior to the rough cadence of the English ancients. This is not to say, however, that Bysshe like Dennis understands the vernacular moderns to take precedence over their Greco-Roman precursors. Rather, this early displacement of the ancients and moderns division onto English literature transforms the value of the division's crucial terms. The English moderns are more like the Greco-Roman ancients than are the English ancients because they write with decorous uniformity. It is this celebration of the vernacular moderns, therefore, that is subsequently reversed by the midcentury revival of the very poets whom Bysshe finds to be lost on the modern world. For critics writing fifty or so years later, the linguistic distance of Shakespeare, Spenser, and Milton (and on occasion Chaucer as well) was an important part of what made these writers "literature." The emphasis falls on the English ancients. Bysshe's preference for modern refinement, however, is characteristic of his period, referring to a common understanding of literary and linguistic *progress*.[12]

Smooth enunciation and uniformity of measure may appear to be curious ingredients for literary canon formation, but we need only glance at the social conditions of early eighteenth-century England to see their logic. Drawn on the largest canvas, the early eighteenth century's semi-official culture of polite speech brought together the reformed aristocracy and the mercantile bourgeoisie into what contemporaries giddily referred to as the "beau monde," "the better sort" or "the public." The collusion or "alliance" of land and commerce after the settlement of 1688 is something of a truism of eighteenth-century studies, as is its shaping by the material culture of reading: the commerce in books and newspapers, the growth of coffee-houses and lending libraries.[13] One important consequence of this alliance was that its linguistic foundation could not be Latin, the cosmopolitan script of the old aristocracy.[14] Print-capitalism fashioned a vernacular culture of broad latitude and duration, and in the small venue of literary history it placed great emphasis on urbane discourse as the shared idiom of the public. This is one way to understand the early formation of Habermas's famous "public sphere": the joining of print and social power.[15] As Habermas's "model case," eighteenth-century England first saw the formation of "public opinion" over matters of literary taste and political judgment.[16] Print abstracted individual readers into an imaginary collective that evaluated art for aesthetic value and politics for civic value.

Habermas's work has occasioned much revisionary work on the social history of print and audience in the eighteenth century.[17] I would emphasize, for the moment, the broad dimension to his

argument. The dialectic of public and private finds its origin in the
separation of state and civil society, the parting of economic
production and the patriarchal family from politics and the court.
Like Hegel and Marx before him, Habermas views this disseverment
as singular to the capitalist epoch and first instantiated in England.
"With the growth of the market economy arose the sphere of the
'social,' which broke the fetters of domination based on landed
estate and necessitated forms of administration invested with state
authority. In the measure to which it was linked to market exchange,
production was disengaged from its connection with functions of
public authority; conversely, political administration was released
from production tasks" (*Structural Transformation*, 141). Habermas's
eponymous public sphere hence carves itself out of the officially
private domain of civil society. The prior division between state and
civil society "was repeated once more within society itself" as
private readers confronted texts understood to be public culture (28).
For Habermas, the dialectical volatility of public and private charts
the course of cultural development in the modern age. Privacy
inevitably discovers a public component; publicity inevitably splits
off a section of the private. We have seen this dialectic already at
work in turn-of-the-century models of literary history. The public
culture of polite speech sheered modern writers from an antiquity
overly bound to the difficult privacy of the "gothic" past.

Readers familiar with *The Structural Transformation* will recall how
Addison and Steele's *Spectator* enjoys a special place in the Haberma-
sian narrative.[18] The *Spectator*'s interweaving of aesthetic discussion
with broadly topical matters represented for Habermas the dual
project of widening the scope of literary culture and refining the
taste of the new reading public. In this account, the emergent book
trade was warmly embraced by Addison and his followers, who
found in the new print institutions a form of sociability not limited
by aristocratic entitlement. Such was at least the crux of Addison's
famous claim, in *Spectator* no. 10, to have brought philosophy down
from the heavens and into the polite quarters of the reading public:
"I shall be ambitious to have it said of me, that I have brought
philosophy out of closets and libraries, schools and colleges, to dwell
in clubs and assemblies, at tea-tables and in coffee-houses."[19]
Addison's claim to be the modern Socrates is inseparable, in his own
estimation, from his being "possessed of the art of printing" and
from his successful sale of his writing: "my bookseller tells me that

the demand for these my papers increases daily"; "my loose tracts and single pieces" are "retailed to the publick, and every page submitted to the Taste of forty or fifty thousand Readers" (I: no. 124, 507–508). The commerce in print allows modern English culture to surpass even the culture of the ancients as it lays the grounds for rational discourse:

Had the philosophers and great men of antiquity, who took so much pains in order to instruct mankind, and leave the world wiser and better than they found it; had they, I say, been possessed of the art of printing, there is no question but they would have made such an advantage of it, in dealing out their lectures to the publick. Our common prints would be of great use were they thus calculated to diffuse good sense through the bulk of a people, to clear up their understandings, animate their minds with virtue, dissipate the sorrows of a heavy heart, or unbend the mind from its more severe employments with innocent amusements. (507)

Here print-capitalism is at one with the standardization and refinement of the social activity Addison terms "conversation." "Knowledge, instead of being bound up in books and kept in libraries and retirements, is thus obtruded upon the publick; . . . it is canvassed in every assembly, and exposed upon every table" (507). Addison's widely remarked extolling of the new reading public is of course not without hesitation. As I shall discuss at greater length in the following chapter, the idea of dispersed reading was a matter of tactical ambivalence for the *Spectator*, the full consequence of which would not be apparent until later in the century. Nevertheless, the disencumbering of culture for what the *Spectator* represented as a nation poised for its perusal was the periodical's favorite mode of self-authorization. Among those given a new entrée into the literary world were women – an invitation subject to pronounced uncertainty. Feminine literacy was something to be contained and educated as well as the herald of egalitarian modernity.[20] The "unaccountable humour in woman-kind, of being smitten with every thing that is showy and superficial" needed the supervisory attention of criticism (I: no. 15, 66). At the same time, the prominence of "gentle readers" from the "female world," whose leisurely domesticity put "so much time on their hands," was an emblem and agent of modern England's polished elegance (I: no. 10, 47).

The opening up of the cultural product for a nation of readers darkened the past, when texts were read by only the literati and when writers composed in an obscure idiom. Like Dryden's "translation" of Chaucer, Addison's essays on wit, the pleasures of the imagination, and the virtues of Milton designed a polite modernity by separating it from a "gothick" prehistory (I: no. 124, 211). Addison's version of the past was by no means isolated. Glancing at older works, many early eighteenth-century critics retroactively barbarized antique English writers, whose versification was rough and diction impolite, whose puerile language troubled the mature flowering of the public. In addition to celebrating contemporary style, many critics revised or rewrote older works so that their rough language or their indecorous bawdiness and violence would better fit modern reading habits. Dryden's "translation" of Chaucer was but one instance of a movement which included, among others, John Hughes's orthographically "improved" edition of Spenser (1715), Pope's laboriously regularized and sanitized edition of Shakespeare and "versification" of Donne (1725, 1735), and Bentley's notorious *Paradise Lost* (1732). Here the present not only produced its own past, of which it was the necessary and healthy descendant, but also fashioned that past in such a way that would persist into the future: whence enchantment, superstition, the mythic, and the gothic.[21]

Against this darkened past, the present shone brightly. Models of the progress of English poetry and the English language often widened themselves to include military triumph, political stability, and economic expansion. "I think Old England to have been in every respect a very indifferent country," wrote Anthony Ashley Cooper, the Third Earl of Shaftesbury, in 1711.[22]

We were [then] . . . under a sort of Polish nobility, and had no other liberties than what were in common to us with the then fashionable monarchies and Gothic lordships of Europe . . . I think Late England, since the Revolution, to be better . . . than Old England by many a degree, and that in the main we make somewhat a better figure in Europe than we did a few reigns before . . . [O]ur name or credit have risen, our trade and navigation, our manufactures or our husbandry [have] been improved. (III: 150–151)

English modernity, in this Whig-celebrant formulation, comprises a broad improvement across culture and economy alike. Like Shaftesbury, the editor of *The Present State of the Republic of Learning* (1728) argues in the inaugural number that "no country in the world furnishes greater plenty of good materials for such a work [as this periodical] than England, as there is none where arts and sciences are cultivated with greater encouragement, or better success." This plenty is a consequence of a vibrant civil society: "'Tis to this happy liberty, both of conscience and the press, so much envied by our neighbours, that we owe those many excellent books that are daily printed in England."[23] Freed from the integument of state authority (in the particular form of censorship and "licensing"), English culture can now flourish along side of its economy. In the words of Edward Young:

> Commerce gives Arts, as well as gain:
> By Commerce wafted o'er the main,
> They barbarous climes enlighten as they run.
> Arts, the rich traffic of the soul
> May travel thus from pole to pole,
> And gild the world with Learning's brighter sun.
>
> Commerce gives learning, virtue, gold:
> Ply Commerce, then, ye Britons bold,
> Inured to winds and seas; lest gods repent,
> The gods that throned you in the wave,
> And, as the trident's emblem gave
> A triple realm, that awes the continent.   (*Imperium Pelagi*, II: 1–2)

Literature, commerce, and nation are reciprocally bound. England's commercial and naval power brings with it a certain cultural imperialism: the illuming of the world with the lamp of its learning. Yet it is also the "arts" of the Britons that subtend the nation's economic and nautical supremacy:

> Hence, Reason, the first palm is thine:
> Old Britain learnt from thee to shine.
> By thee Trade's swarming throng, gay Freedom's smile,
> Armies, – in war, of fatal frown;
> Of Peace the pride, – Arts, flowing down,
> Enrich, exalt, defend, instruct our isle.                    (I: 34)

Commerce and culture form an integral and dialectical unit. The one motors the other only to find that it is itself the other's product. As this dialectic works itself out over the course of the century the interdependence of commerce and national "arts" becomes increasingly fraught. While commerce and culture remain tied to each other's fate, their relation, as we shall see, is more and more conceived in terms of negation. In the writings of early eighteenth-century critics, however, polite speech, regular meter, the refinement of English verse and the like became tied to a national culture of broad scope, an imagined community somehow realized by the even couplet.

One consequence of the nationalist aspect to the discourse of refinement – in which polite society and the *beau monde* become sufficiently abstract to stand for "England," and the latter for glorious power – was that the subordination of England's past as gothic or barbarous carried with it a certain guilt. Almost as soon as it was constituted as "gothic" and superseded by the politeness of the modern age, the English past became the object of nostalgic retrospection. A suggestive example of how the socio-linguistic program of politeness generated both the narrative of refinement and the seeds of its later critique may be found in Henry Felton's *A Dissertation on Reading the Classics and Forming a Just Style* (1718). The *Dissertation* is presented as one long letter from Felton to the young Marquis of Granby (in line to become Duke of Devonshire) on matters of taste and learning, on what sort of culture is appropriate to his breeding. The whole is organized into a familiar tautology, namely, how the members of a class ought to acquire the breeding that they always already have. Yet the tautology is only tautological to the degree to which this audience is, in fact, the recipient of the letter. Once printed, the point is to publicize the culture of aristo-cratic refinement for an audience of readers that, of course, extends beyond the nobility:

Your birth is attended with peculiar advantages of title and estate, or worth and goodness in your ancestors and parents: the honour and dignity of your family; the great examples of virtue in your progenitors for a long descent; and the living and more prevailing example of your most illustrious grand-father and father will fire a soul like yours to a generous emulation; and, I hope, your lordship with *follow them with equal steps, if you do not go beyond them.* So select a conjunction of the happiest circumstances must have a blessed influence on the whole course of your life; and if families are the more noble for being more ancient, your lordship will shine in true nobility, and reflect a luster on all the long *Gallery* of your predecessors. But, my Lord, the fairest diamonds are rough till they are polished, and the purest gold must be run and washed, and sifted in the oar. (5)

Readers of the *Dissertation* are here, with the intermediation of print, let in on a private conversation between a young noble and his rector over the manner of achieving the appropriate polish. The *Dissertation* goes so far as to close with a calculated disclosure of its composition: "I am ashamed to present these thoughts in so ill an hand" (230). Felton's attempt to authenticate the letter with the intimate reference to his penmanship at once reminds the reader of the author's virtuoso dashing off of the pages on one leisurely afternoon and hints at the secret of private correspondence which the consumer of this little duodecimo enjoys. The "polish" of the young marquis is as abstractable as consumption itself, and to that degree the emblem of a certain idealized version of English national identity.

Central to achieving the polish appropriate for an elevated station is the reading of English classics as well as the works of antiquity. Yet, while the version of the English canon that Felton recommends for the young Marquis and which by implication is the sign of cultivated refinement conforms to the narrative of linguistic refinement, it also wistfully glances at the strong works of the past that ought still to be read despite their roughness.

I may recommend Mr. Addison, and Mr. Prior, as perfect patterns of true poetic writing. To these I may add some of a more ancient date, and tho' their style is out of the standard now, there are in them still some lines so extremely beautiful, that our modern language cannot reach them. Chaucer is too old, I fear, for so young a company as your lordship; but Spenser, tho' he be antiquated too, hath still charms remaining to make your lordship enamoured of him. His antique verse has music in it to ravish any ears, that can be sensible of the softest sweetest numbers, that ever flowed from a poet's pen.

Shakespeare is a wonderful genius, a single instance of the grace of nature, and the strength of wit. Nothing can be greater, and more lively, than his thoughts, nothing nobler, and more forcible, than his expression . . .

Milton, my lord, is the assertor of poetic liberty, and would have freed us from the bondage of rhyme, but like sinners, and like lovers, we hug our chain, and are pleased in being slaves . . .

Waller, for the music of his numbers, the courtliness of his verse, the easiness and happiness of his thoughts on a thousand subjects, deserves your lordship's consideration more, perhaps, than any other, because his manner and his subjects are more common to persons of quality, and the affairs of a court . . .

I cannot help inserting into the body of this book that character which I think Sir John Denham so highly deserveth, for his excellent version of the psalms: they are so admirable in our old prose translation, that I despair of ever seeing them equaled in verse; but Sir John, by a noble simplicity of style, by a clearness and easiness of expression, by an exactness and harmony of numbers, hath made them so delightful to the ear, and so pleasing to the reader that as a mere poetical work, it must be read with all satisfaction which pieces perfect in their kind can give us. (215–218)

Refinement oscillates with its own transcendence. Felton outlines a course of vernacular study for his student that dwells on the measured grace and numerical purity of the most modern of the moderns while also pointing to an essential kernel of older English writers whose value depends less on ease than on "charm," "force," "wonder," and "genius." The two scales of valuation exist side by side: the one sees vernacular culture as the instrument of sociable polish; the other (eventually) sees it as the rejection of sociability. Within this oscillation one may detect a conflict between modes of understanding the nature of reading and the cultural economy that will continue to unfold to dramatic affect. Does English poetry continue to improve over time? Did English literature consummate itself in the forceful and wondrous writings of the ancients? Should the language of poetry be the same as polite speech or oppose itself to the language of trade and callings? For many critics, the answers to these questions lay in the very nature of the cultural economy.

## ANTINOMIES OF CULTURAL PRODUCTION

As critics began to rethink the consequences of widespread reading and the trade in books, an affirmative relation to the cultural market became increasingly difficult to sustain. The very "common prints" Addison saw as the condition of rationality soon became the condition of an unstable consumer culture.[24] The earlier emphasis on decorous ease gave way to a revaluing of difficult obscurity. To the degree that linguistic difference still distinguished between ancient and modern English literature it only confirmed for many midcentury critics the valuable distance of older writers from what they took to be the competitive stress of market society, the utility of polite conversation, and the disintegration of literacy.[25] Why did print rationality bring about a nostalgia for pre-rational forms and language? In a suggestive gloss on Walter Benjamin's famous story of the desuetude of art's aura, Habermas describes how the public sphere instituted a crisis at its very meridian:

Culture products no longer remained components of the Church's and court's publicity of representation; that is precisely what is meant by the loss of their aura of extraordinariness and by the profaning of their once sacramental character. The private people for whom the cultural product became available as a commodity profaned it inasmuch as they had to determine its meaning on their own (by way of rational communication with one another), verbalize it, and thus state explicitly what precisely in its implicitness for so long could assert its authority. (*Structural Transformation*, 36–37)

Benjamin's narrative, in this analysis, is ultimately grounded in the social relations of artistic production: the change in producers and consumers over time.[26] The important point for the current argument is not so much the implicitly Whiggish story of art's democratization, however, as the counter-narrative of the aura's phoenix-like rebirth as the aesthetic. The affirmative culture of the market soon produced its antithesis. Literary culture became an object of critical discussion and so formed a public sphere of private subjects; but, at the same time, its sacramental aura was debased by circulation and consumption. Far from disappearing in modern culture, the aura was in fact its product. Habermas's analysis may be rewritten to cover the emergence of English literary history only by turning our attention to that moment in the 1740s and 50s when the earlier emphasis on polite conversation bequeathed a compensatory revaluing of the past.

The first intimations of such nostalgia were virtually coincident with the birth of refinement, typically as a mourning of the loss of the strength of the English ancients (as in the case of Felton but also earlier in such poems as Dryden's "To Oldham" and "To Congreve").[27] Over the course of the century, nostalgia for the literary past gradually combined with a skeptical rethinking of the narrative of refinement. John Oldmixon's *An Essay on Criticism* (1728), for instance, notes how "we in *England* are apt to confound all the various kinds under the general terms of good language, and a fine stile. The sublime, the natural, the didactick, the narrative, the tragick, the comick, the polite, the affected, are seldom rightly distinguished, and the latter very often mistaken for the polite."[28] Politeness is too often "affect," an instrumentalizing of writing for the social agenda of the public. As such, it smoothes over the various achievements of modern verse. "In these things our taste is strangely confined: provided the verses run smoothly, and the language is soft and harmonious, we think it is fine" (70). Oldmixon's argument has two important components that will develop into greater prominence and clarity later in the century: first, that modern habits of reading are themselves lacking; second, that this lack has to do with the composition of the national audience. The slackness of modern reading is revealed by the public's increasing inability to read older English writers: "Several ladies and gentlemen have subscribed for *Chaucer* in the *Christ-Church* edition, but I much doubt whether they understand him or not" (68). The gendering of this imaginary audience will prove to be significant. The often tacit conflation of cultural refinement with feminine taste is made manifest, but in the manner of critique: "ladies and gentlemen who read like ladies are nine out of ten of all readers of poetry" (70). Like many critics who came after him, Oldmixon represents the expansion of the public as the inclusion of women and, as a result, the effeminization of men.

Oldmixon's skepticism of polite reading establishes itself in deliberate contrast to the moment and program of Addison.

The Spectator, with all his Modesty, has discover'd something of this self-love in that of the sciences, and could not help giving into this infirmity. Every one knows what a fine talent he had for writing, and particularly how beautiful his imagination was, and how polite his language. Himself was not a stranger to it; and we therefore read in the Spectator, no. 291; *I might further observe, that there is not a Greek or Latin Critick, who has not shewn, even in the stile of his criticisms, that he was master of all the elegance and delicacy of his native language.* Here does this excellent author forbid any one's claim to the character of a critick, who is not like himself master of the delicacy and elegance of his native tongue. (8)

Oldmixon finds it difficult to imagine that refinement, especially as it becomes in this case a variety of self-advertisement, is itself a sufficient criterion of judgment. Eloquence begins to lose its legitimacy as a means of distinguishing among cultural products. The implication of the *Spectator*'s agenda, Oldmixon protests, was that "no body ought to criticize on that author's writings, unless he could write as elegantly as himself, which effectively cuts off all *criticism*" (15). One ought to judge literary products by criteria relatively distinct from their sociability. The difficult labor of critical judgment need not disguise itself as mannered ease. Yet Oldmixon only partially develops this argument. For all of his resistance to Addison's program, his literary history falls well within the narrative of refinement he critiques. The line of poets from Dryden to Pope charts "the improvement of our tongue 'till the time of the *Spectator*

and the translation of *Homer*, where, I think, it is in the greatest
purity and elegance" (55).

Oldmixon's position on refinement is internally divided: refinement is both an insufficiently rigorous way of understanding the
properties of literature and the activity of criticism, *and* an important
means of appreciating the improvement of English poetry over time.
In subsequent decades these two positions become more clearly
distinct and the critique of refinement begins to produce a countervailing literary historical model. Part of what motivates this shift is
the increasing attention paid to the problem of the cultural market.
We may get a sense of the changing perception of the book trade by
comparing two similarly framed yet starkly opposed observations,
the first by Philip Skelton in his monograph *The Candid Reader* (1744)
and the second by an essayist in the periodical *The World* (1753). Near
the beginning of his piece, Skelton ironically announces a "very
peculiar" pleasure "in beholding the daily and plentiful additions
made to the commonwealth of letters by my contemporary
writers";[29]

I consider the whole body of writings, that have hitherto appeared in the
world, of whatsoever kind, whether philosophical or poetical, historical or
political, moral, theological, or critical; whether they be the performances
of great wits or dunces, of the learned or the illiterate, as one great
community or republic of books, in which every individual performance
hath its own place and use. As in a well regulated commonwealth,
consisting of men, there must be persons for all purposes, some to be
treasurers, and others to be scavengers, some to be judges, and others to be
hangmen; so in one of books, there ought to be some sublime and learned,
others low and illiterate, some, full of sense and life, others, dull and
insipid, some, of a senatorian order, and some other of a plebeian; because,
all books being wrote, if I mistake not, in order for perusal, and all
mankind being either obliged by duty, or moved by inclination, to peruse
some kind of books or other, and there being such an infinite variety of
tastes and capacities among men, prodigious numbers would be excluded
from the great and delectable exercise of reading, were it not for the
plentiful provision made, and laid in, by the writers of past and present
times. We have almost a competency of writings, calculated for all sorts of
tastes, and all degrees of understanding. (227–228)

This passage seems to express nothing so much as confidence about
the abiding regime of cultural and social hierarchy. Every "senatorian" reader corresponds to a "sublime and learned" text, and
every "plebeian" reader a "dull and insipid" text. Skelton's remarks

are remarkable not just in their one-to-one overlaying of the cultural onto the social, but also in their vision of society as a stable, unified, and "well regulated commonwealth." Perennial social order subsumes cultural change; while the commonwealth of letters includes all sorts of books, these books are ranked as rigidly as the "commonwealth of men." High culture bears the same immemorial relation to mass culture as elites do to peasants.

Despite Skelton's apparent equanimity, his canon is notably defensive; it is shaped in response to what he represents as a tide of plebeian books and illiterate readers. The notion of social and cultural stability is rendered with tongue in cheek, or at the least with the sense that both were under significant pressure. When the contributor to *The World* (1753) attempted a parallel "meditation . . . on a library of books" nine years later he was pointedly unable to see them in terms of Skelton's rational and hierarchical order. For this critic, the new glut of books was a primordial chaos:

Before my eyes an almost innumerable multitude of authors are ranged; different in their opinions, as in their bulk and appearance; in what light shall I view this great assembly? Shall I consider it as an ancient legion, drawn out in goodly array under fit commanders? or as a modern regiment of writers, where the common men have been forced by want, or seduced through wickedness into the service, and where the leaders owe their advancement rather to caprice, party favour, and the partiality of friends, than to merit or service?

Shall I consider ye, o ye books! as a herd of courtiers or strumpets, who profess to be subservient to my use, and yet seek only your own advantage? No; let me consider this room as the great charnel-house of human reason.[30]

Literature is here experiencing a crisis of over-production. The excess of books has lowered their overall value; "complete cooks and conveyances; bodies of school divinity and Tommy Thumb; little story-books, systems of philosophy, and memoirs of women of pleasure; apologies for the lives of players and prime ministers; all are consigned to one common oblivion" (153). The essayist does manage to catch a fleeting glimpse of a vanquished high culture within the sepulchral oblivion of the library, but the image is equally telling:

Amidst this army of anti-martyrs, I discern a volume of peculiar appearance; its meagre aspect, and the dirty gaudiness of its habit, make it bear a perfect resemblance of a decayed gentleman. The wretched monument of mortality was brought forth in the reign of Charles the Second; it was the darling and only child of a man of quality. How did its parent exult at its birth! How many flatterers extolled it beyond their own offspring, and urged its credulous father to display its excellencies to the whole world! Induced by their solicitations, the father arrayed his child in scarlet and gold, submitted it to the public eye, and called it *Poems by a person of honour.* While he lived his booby-offspring was treated with the cold respect due to the ranks and fortune of its parent: but when death had locked up his kitchen, and carried off the keys of his cellar, the poor child was abandoned to the parish: it was kicked from stall to stall, like a despised prostitute; and after various calamities, was rescued out of the vender of Scots snuff, and safely placed as a pensioner in the band of freethinkers. (153)

The position of the essay's speaker in this passage is curious, and can be read in at least two ways. The late aristocratic milieu of the Restoration court is either the last redoubt of high culture before the triumph of the market or a farce dressed up in the expired raiment of the sixteenth and seventeenth centuries. Each reading of the passage would imply a different object of nostalgia; the first, a nostalgia for books of poetry that cannot be read by ill-educated moderns (like *Poems by a person of honour*); the second, a nostalgia not so much for the Restoration and *Poems by a person of honour* as the book's genuinely aristocratic and honorable father who cannot even be named because he is so obscured by the tide of print. The one points to an abuse of high culture writ large, the other to an abuse particularly of the English ancients. The essay does not come down on either side but ironically offers both readings as plausible responses to the deathly oblivion of modern culture.

What has transformed the order of culture into a "charnel house"? The swell of books and their readers was, for many critics, evidence of the economy's shadow over culture. In the parodic *Peri Bathous* (1727), Pope's Martin Scriblerus notes that "our wiser Authors have a present end . . . Their true design is *profit* or *gain*; in order to acquire which, 'tis necessary to procure Applause, by administering *pleasure* to the Reader: From whence it follows demonstrably, that their Productions must be suited to the *present taste*."[31] This disavowal of the "present taste" is an early example of an increasingly common mode of critical position-taking. Scriblerus aligns writing with production, reading with consumption and both with the aesthetically devaluing standard of profit. Ironically mimicking the voice of Grub Street, Pope tells what soon becomes a cardinal rule of modern culture building, that market criteria erode the viability of aesthetic experience. Pope's cautionary satire squares well with the sociology of Pierre Bourdieu. The latter's corpus is concerned to watch how the aesthetic separates itself out from politics and develops a peculiar symbolic value inversely proportional to exchange value. In this account of the "cultural field" as an "economic world reversed," the market places insuperable pressure on the relative autonomy of the aesthetic. The value of artistic goods is soon released from the vulgar dominion of commercial sales; the "loser wins." The expert culture of criticism and the academy emerge at this point both to labor on the new sphere of culture and to renew constantly its distance from the idioms of everyday life. The cultural field is forever split between "the field of restricted production" for other artists and cultural *cognoscenti* and the "field of large scale production" for lay purchasers and mass audiences.[32]

Bourdieu's work helps us to examine with greater specificity the idea of the market in the making of the canon. Still, once we bring his terms to bear on eighteenth-century culture, we need to be alert that, for contemporary critics, "large scale" and "restricted" culture were conceived in relation to each other and shaped by the gradually evolving problem of publicity, refinement, and national reading. Critics concerned with public culture and the commerce in books became increasingly moved to distinguish fiscal profit from literary excellence. Consider the anonymous pamphlet *A Letter to the Society of Booksellers* (1738). The *Letter* is written as a critic's friendly admonition to the collected tradesmen and publishers of books, urging them to forge a "due disposal of books," an internally regulated control on the quality of the nation's cultural product. The *Letter* unambiguously frames the problem as a matter of art's new status as a commodity: "Do not all mankind naturally seek their own interest? and I believe it will readily enough be allowed that booksellers do not less consult it than other people. Now if so, it cannot well be deny'd, that, where you can imagine or see your profit, you will readily enough come into it, and consequently without the least difficulty willingly print any such copies, seeing none can be more sensible of the great profits where the copy is good."[33] That booksellers would print what sells is taken as a matter of course. Yet this is an item of some worry. The exchange value of a cultural product is motored by a demand almost appetitive in its intensity: "the good success of a book does not so much depend on the excellency of the performance, as on the necessity, novelty, or the interest it has in our passions which excite us to demand it (tho' it must be confessed, that its excellency or exceeding accuracy enhances its real value)" (25–26). The point of this statement is less to vaunt demand as the measure of genuine literary goodness than to suggest that the aesthetic, "real" value of the product ought to be defined in terms other than profit and economic success. Aesthetic value (what the author calls twice simply "excellency") and exchange value, that is, are shown to be at once inseparable and antithetical categories. Books are commodities with a commercial value and a cultural value. The one is based on the suppression of the other.

The *Letter* hardly blames booksellers for consulting their "interest," but it does remain disturbed by the turning of books into commodities. The author describes, with notable distaste, having stumbled upon "an apple or orange-woman who sold fruit, near the court, one side of her shop being used for that purpose, and the other for the sale of pamphlets, small books, &c, for she likewise followed this business." "The good woman" was "flush'd with the prospect of great success in the bookselling way" (18). Demand and desire cut across food and culture; each are items for purchase, products in a basket of goods. The problem is that demand is an insufficient guarantor of cultural excellence. While our taste for fruit may ensure that the best apple or orange is purchased, our taste for books may ensure that the entire cultural order is overturned. "We find that Robinson Crusoe sells quicker than Locke on Human Understanding, and the Beggars Opera than the best comedy: nay is it not sufficiently known, that some have acquired estates by printing Tom Thumb, riddles, songs, fables, the Pilgrims Progress, and such like common trumpery?" (31).

The resolution that the *Letter* offers to this upside-down world of consumer culture is to distinguish among the distributors of cultural products, to divide "mean peddling traders," like the "aforementioned apple or herb-woman," "from those of capacity, credit and reputation" (40). Booksellers of capacity will, the author hopes, be able to balance aesthetic and exchange value in such a way that ensures profits without debasing the national product. The adjustment of the two systems of value proves, however, to be a difficult act:

I doubt not you will be apt to tell me, that the books which sell best are most for your purpose, and that you need not be solicitous about the intrinsic value of a book, if it does not sell, that being its principal goodness in your estimation . . . I am very sensible, gentlemen, that your business, like all other trades, is to *get money*; yet give me leave at the same time to remark, that this immediate or present gain (so commonly snatch'd at by the unthinking) perhaps, very seldom proves to be their real interest; so that, in my opinion, as honesty is the best policy, and good wine needs no blush, the tradesmen, who take the contrary course, are generally found to thrive most; and, perhaps, it is not once in ten times that it happens otherwise. Accordingly, a bookseller, who takes due care to examine his copies, and prints none but such as truly deserve the notice and esteem of the public, even tho' they should not run off so fast as others, on more trifling, indifferent, or obscene subjects, finds at last that they turn to the best account; for men, in general, entertaining a better opinion of such a bookseller, and consequently of the books he prints; his customers will venture to take 'em on his own word, and even strangers be no way fearful of dealing him, since they know he has an established character, for being concerned in no copies that are not really good. (28–29)

The salutation to booksellers does not attempt to hide the public's preference for literary trinkets, for what we would now call mass culture. But neither does the salutation pretend that booksellers will pursue the cultural profit of marketing wares that won't sell. The dilemma is that the "intrinsic value of the book" may not be expressed in the price it fetches. The pamphlet aims to resolve this problem by reuniting what it had intended to keep apart, exchange and aesthetic value. Establish trust among your consumers, the *Letter* promises, and they will purchase more books; your shop will receive the "best account." How are we to assess this slippage from describing "intrinsic value" against the system of exchange to describing it within that system? The answer, I would suggest, is ultimately historical: the commodification of books generates "intrinsic value" as its own antithesis, as everything that lies outside of and so defines the market. In this version of Bourdieu's "economic world reversed," there is a certain "market" in seeming to be outside of the market. If exchange value generates intrinsic value, the latter can generate former. The pamphlet winkingly suggests to the book-seller that people will want to buy books that appear to be elevated above "trifling, indifferent, or obscene subjects."

It is precisely the antithetical proximity of exchange and aesthetic value that underlies Fielding's ironic description, in *Joseph Andrews* (1742), of how "Homer not only divided his great work into twenty-four books, (in compliment perhaps to the twenty-four letters to which he had very particular obligations) but, according to the opinion of some very sagacious critics, hawked them all separately, delivering one book at a time, (probably by subscription)," and thus "was the first inventor of the art which hath so long lain dormant, of publishing by numbers."[34] The irony lies not simply in the framing of the past through the distorted prism of print categories, but in proposing that "great antiquity" itself has become an instrument to reap a certain kind of profit. Readers trained in confronting printed texts have no other means of situating older works, Fielding suggests; for the same reason, Homer's aura derives from his publication by booksellers. But what kind of profit does Fielding intend to burlesque? The aside that Homer's works were published "probably by subscription" refers to the practice in which sales were contracted in advance, so that the publisher could remit the expenses of printing, in return for the subscriber's name appearing in the inside leaf of the book (exactly the sort of high-cultural publication and quality control the *Letter to the Society of Booksellers* wished to see more of). Subscription publishing ties together economic and cultural capital in an intricate knot: the bookseller receives in advance the price of production, while the subscriber receives the permanent marker of his or her cultivation. The value of this marker depends upon the fragility of the book's strictly economic value, the quantum of anticipated demand. That the book cannot be expected to draw a large audience, that it will probably maintain a distance from the modern public's taste, raises the cultural equity of the subscriber, whose interest in such rarefied material is made visible for the smaller public of elite consumers.

Fielding intends to expose and derive a satiric energy from the situation in which high culture and mass culture are interdependent categories, each within the deformative logic of the cultural market. Such is the wisdom imparted by the bookseller to Parson Adams when the latter tries to sell his ill-fated sermons. Adams

was sorry to hear sermons compared to plays. "Not by me, I assure you," cried the Bookseller, "though I don't know whether the licensing act may not shortly bring them to the same footing; but I have formerly known a hundred guineas given for a play –." "More shame for those who gave it" cry'd Barnabus. "Why so?" cried the Bookseller, "for they got hundreds by it." "But is there no difference between conveying good or ill instructions to mankind?" said Adams; "would not an honest mind rather lose money by

the one, than gain it by the other?" "If you can find any such, I will not be
their hindrance," answered the Bookseller, "but I think those persons who
get by preaching sermons, are the properist to lose by printing them: for
my part, the copy that sells best, will be always the best copy in my opinion:
I am no enemy to sermons but because they don't sell." (*Joseph Andrews*, 78)

Adams's is a compound dilemma. Modernity has stripped "religion"
of its tacit authority and placed it at odds with the profit motive; the
"good" of spirit vies with the "ill" of greed. The message of the
bookseller is also double. Even as exchange has taken over religion,
the aura of theology, as with literature, is negatively bound to
economic profit and the cash-nexus.

  Like aesthetic value, Fielding archly points out, spiritual value is
produced out of exchange as its emollient opposite. Cultural and
commercial value exist in a state of continuous inversion: the greater
the appearance of commercial value, the lower the cultural value,
and vice-versa. For the anonymous author of *Reflections on Various
Subjects Relating to Arts and Commerce* (1752) this doubleness is immanent
to art's peculiar status as a commodity. Books are at once one of the
"manufacturing arts" like silk, wool, table linen, or porcelain and
also constitutively averse to the laws of the market:

Manufactures of moderate expense and quick growth may safely be left to
private adventurers, and run the common chance for success; the *finer arts*
will never flourish but under *public* protection and *noble* patronage; no
encouragement in the hands of private persons are adequate rewards to the
man of *genius*. Money is the pay of common men, as praise is that of heroes;
and honour will ever be found a much stronger principle of fine invention
than gain . . . All that was great and noble in antient wit and art, was
produced by honours, by the countenance of princes, the favour and kind
influence of *great men*.[35]

As in *Letter to the Society of Booksellers*, the market is here understood to
be an insufficient agent of aesthetic value. Art is a commodity, but its
price can never be set by demand because demand amounts to the
lawlessness of the public. The rewards of consumption are adequate
only to common men and common products. "Fine art" requires a
system of valuation that runs in contradistinction to exchange. The
system that the *Reflections* promotes for art is scarcely innovative –
patronage was not only the practice of the ancients, but also a finely
articulated cultural economy in the eighteenth century, itself subject
to criticism during this period.[36] What is more interesting, in this
case, is the way in which "honour" emerges as a type of cultural

wage analogous to but distinct from the vulgar form of money. Exchange value and aesthetic value have moved farther apart than they were in the *Letter*. An art object contains a certain amount of congealed mental labor, while a practical object contains a certain amount of congealed physical labor: "the lower branches of manufacture, wherein the price is paid chiefly to labour, contribute most to the increase of labouring hands. The trades of refinement are no way comparable to these . . . the price of *art* rising above labour in proportion as genius is a scarcer commodity than strength" (*Reflections*, 21). The aesthetic is subject to an economy of genius at variance from an economy of labor. Yet what this passage reveals is that the price mechanism of art is more "comparable" to manufacture than the *Reflections* admits. The emergent labor theory of value is simply stood on its head; the value of art is inversely related to the expenditure of physical labor and thus directly related to the expenditure of "genius." The distance between exchange and aesthetic value here is precisely that of analogy.

The construction of an idea of aesthetic value separate from yet inversely analogous to economic value occurred during the midcentury's prolonged consideration of the book market and public culture. Over time, critics grew concerned that cultural goods were becoming too available to "middling" and "vulgar" classes and too sullied by the leveling system of consumption. An important aspect of this consideration was the notion that the rise of literacy was brought about largely by the inclusion of women readers, that the much celebrated domestic woman was spending her leisure time with books.[37] It is not simply the case, however, that eighteenth-century criticism reacted immediately to contain female literacy. The response to the perception of such literacy was heterogeneous. Women readers were understood throughout the eighteenth century to augur polite culture writ large *or* to vitiate the republic of letters. The elaboration of an idea of feminine literacy had the effect of gradually transforming the self-representation of the cultural community. The shifting representation of women readers, feminine taste, and effeminate culture followed the pattern of dialectical development this chapter has been tracing. Initially, the reading of women illustrated the opening up of national culture for a wider public. Feminine taste would educate the public to enjoy polite subjects instead of the rough matters of older writing. By midcentury, however, the specter of female literacy was often understood to be the beginning of the end of national, masculine fortitude. Critics at this point frequently overlapped or combined the question of women readers and consumer culture: the commodification of culture was metaphorically expressed as its attenuated emasculation while the latter was literalized in the specter of domestic women armed with books. (Recall the image of "prostituted" high culture in *The World* and "trumpery" of bad books in the *Letter to the Society of Booksellers*.) In any case, the problem dramatically telescoped in the discussion of the "romance" and the "novel" (which, in the droll terms of Clara Reeve later in the century, were at this moment "springing up like mushrooms").[38] One would-be preceptor of young female readers meditated at length in *The Present State of the Republic of Learning* (December, 1730), for example, over how the ostensibly progressive and culture building aspects of the reading revolution threatened to devolve into "romantic" mass culture. Written as an admonishing note to a young pupil, the letter may be taken as suggestively transitional in its conception of gender, genre, and public culture. The author begins by warmly espousing reading as a form of cultivation superior to mere coquetry:

> Madam, as I am now corresponding with you in the capacity of a *tutor*, it may not be amiss to begin with giving you my sentiments of *books*; such, especially, as most commonly fall into the hands of young ladies. Whatever you may think of the matter at present, believe me, you'll one day find *reading* more essential to your passing your time agreeably, than any of the *gay amusements*; which cannot always be had, and grow insipid by being often repeated. So that *reading* is certainly one of the most desirable things imaginable, were it only for this one reason, that it enables us to converse with ourselves, and to be satisfy'd sometimes in our own company, which is very terrible to most *beaux*, and many *fine ladies*.[39]

This celebration of reading illuminates an important change in the understanding of sociability. Here reading is valued as a retreat from the public sphere, a variety of solitude that exists apart from the insipid clamor of "gay amusements." Yet, once reading turns from the public back to the private it seems to create a curious hybrid, a form of public privacy in which we "converse with ourselves" and find solitude to be a "company" of one. The suggestion appears to be that privacy is a better form of publicity than publicity itself. From what sort of publicity does this privacy shrink in order to generate a more authentic public out of solitude? The domestic reader ought to withdraw from the salons and balls and masquerades, to be sure, but also from a certain type of literacy: "And now, as to the ladies favourite, *Romances*; it grieves me to say it, they ruin more virgins than *masquerades* or *brothels*. They strike at the root of all virtue, by corrupting the mind: And tho' every *Romance-reading nymph* may not proceed to overt acts, I hope you do not think her excusable" (453). Here "romance" stands for a deleterious form of publicity brought back into the private, where its corrosive effects are magnified by the inventive liberty of imagination: "Romances, and such like books, must needs be very pernicious since they tend to soften and enfeeble the mind when they chance not to produce greater evils, such as raising peoples passions, and encouraging their various inclinations" (453). This is hardly the sort of public private-ness suitable for young women readers; the writer asks his pupil "to judge what an excellent housewife a damsel is likely to make, who has read the *Persian Tales* till she fancies her self a *Sultana* (453).

The problem of romance was thus, as is widely remarked, one way in which critics came to terms with the perceived rise in female literacy, with the new phenomenon of domestic privacy, and with the book trade.[40] (The canonical example is Charlotte Lennox's *The Female Quixote* [1752], discussed in chapter three.) It was also one way in which critics addressed the problem of class culture, in particular the specter of lower class reading. Romances are, according to *The Present State of the Republic of Learning*, "current among the common people"; "every footman or chambermaid are fond of [their] lewd inventions" (453–454). The letter puts forth this notion that the vulgar classes were partly responsible for the romantic vogue with, perhaps, a grain of salt; or rather, the point is just as much to invoke the tastes and habits of the lower classes as analogous to the literary class of the romance as it is to contend that the latter's audience is itself "vulgar." In either case, the specter of common, as well as women, readers became increasingly prominent ways to explain commodity culture. When, for example, William Whitehead com-plains in *The World* (no. 19, 1753) that "the present age is overrun with romances . . . so strong does the appetite for them continue" he distinguishes the venerable writers of old romance, including "Homer and Shakespeare," from the vulgar romance writers of the modern age:

The present race of romance-writers run universally into a different extreme. They spend the little art they are masters of in weaving into intricacies the more familiar and more comical adventures of a Jack Slap, or a Betty Sallet. These, though they endeavour to copy after a very great original, I choose to call our writers *below nature*; because very few of them have as yet found out their master's peculiar art of writing upon low subjects without writing in a low manner. Romances, judicially conducted, are a very pleasing way of conveying instruction to all parts of life. But to dwell eternally upon orphan-beggars, and *serving-men of low degree*, is certainly what I have called it, writing *below nature*; and it is so far from conveying instruction, that it does not even afford amusement.[41]

As opposed to "this sort of trash," Homer and Shakespeare retained a nobility of style even when their subject matter was low (84). Modern writing, in contrast, falls to the level of the common world it depicts. Once more, class is used in a double sense: as the category that describes the object and audience of the romance *and* as the status of the romance within the array of cultural products. According to Whitehead, the eighteenth century is overrun with the low "trash" of the modern romance, or, as he portentiously terms it, "the novel": "There are certain vices which the vulgar call fun, and the people of fashion call gallantry; but the middle rank, and those of the gentry who continue to go to church, still stigmatize them by the opprobrious names of fornications and adultery . . . Why then," he asks "should our novel writers take so much pains to spread these infirmities?" (84).

The question is hardly rhetorical. The institution of criticism should, Whitehead claims, exercise a mimetic version of state censorship: "you should interpose your authority," he implores the editors, "and forbid your readers (whom I will suppose to be all persons who can read) even to attempt to open any novel or romance, unlicensed by you; unless it should happen to be stamped Richardson or Fielding" (85). In this embellishment of criticism into a constabulary of culture, we may note several combined developments that together help reconfigure the canon: romance gives way to the novel, while the latter itself divides into the mass, on the one hand, and the Richardsons and Fieldings, on the other; the novel, in turn, betokens a public culture given to vicious gallantry and licentious vulgarity. In response to this situation, criticism begins to superintend the cultural field, to take on a power analogous to the state. The critic is now not just one reader among the manifold but an "authority." Unlike the cultivated amateurs of the *Tatler*, *Spectator*, or *Guardian*, Whitehead's critic is a professional, a writer whose training and skills set him apart from the lay public of fallible readers. For Whitehead, professional critics have the responsibility to censure and admonish. For others, the professional critic simply possessed superior knowledge, a technical facility akin to the modern sciences. For still others, the development of expert literary knowledge corrupted the literary republic, as critics began to use a language and method estranged from the language of polite society. Criticism became the object of a compound ambivalence about the relation between experts and the public. An important consequence of this ambivalence was a revised understanding of the nation's cultural monuments. Casting about for forms that resist the "trash" of the modern age, critical experts looked systematically to the works of the English past.[42]

## FROM REFINEMENT TO DESCENT

The shrinking away from modern refinement and commodity culture culminated in a dramatic transformation of the English canon: Spenser, Shakespeare, and Milton replaced Denham and Waller; philology replaced modernization, and the narrative of improvement became a narrative of decline. Yet it would be wrong to say that the midcentury simply broke from the norms of the Augustans. Rather, the earlier model of literary historical development – progress toward refinement – was turned on its head; the very past crystallized by the Augustans was dialectically preserved by their successors as the radiant sheen of premodern English culture.

The abuse of modern writing on behalf of the English literature of earlier ages was, in this sense, a further elaboration of the ancients and moderns distinction within the vernacular.[43] Let us consider how this distinction might look over the long term of its development. During the late seventeenth and early eighteenth century uniform Latinity breaks down as the cultural capital of the elite classes and variously cultivated vernaculars take its place. The first such vernacular makes a fetish out of grammar and politeness. Yet once politeness is seen as too common and modernizing, too much like conversation as such, critics discover an abstruse, quasi-Latinate vernacular in older, canonical English. This mimetic transcoding of ancient versus modern inside of modern literature itself proceeds as a shrinking away from the market of cultural goods, a disavowal of "modern" politeness and the novel. The project of surmounting the difficulty and vulgarity of England's past gives way to one of appreciating the linguistic distance and aesthetic difficulty of Spenser, Shakespeare, and Milton.

No longer the answer to social change, in other words, vernacular literacy had become by the midcentury a problem in its own right. One solution to this problem was simply to reverse Addison and return culture to the closets and universities from the salons and tea-tables at which it had been sullied. In the *Adventurer* (1753), for example, Joseph Warton argued that what he took to be his period's corruption of literary value and misreading of literary history were both products of the Addisonian embrace of commodity culture. He characterized the entire project of his periodical, in fact, as a rejoinder to the celebration of print and the reading public found in the *Spectator*:

Addison remarks that Socrates was said to have brought philosophy down from heaven to inhabit among men: "And I," says he, "shall be ambitious to have it said of me, that I have brought philosophy out of closets and libraries, schools and colleges, to dwell in clubs and assemblies, at tea-tables and in coffee-houses." But this purpose has in some measure been defeated by its success; and we have been driven from one extreme with such precipitation, that we have not stopped in the medium, but gone on to the other. Learning has been divested of the peculiarities of a college dress, that she might mix in public assemblies; but by this means she has been confounded with ignorance and levity.[44]

The "engaged and easy" manner of the *Spectator* had the unforeseen effect of degrading the very learning with which it intended to please the reading public (288). Addison is right to suggest that the print market has made cultural goods objects of conversation, but this process has turned back on itself; "instead of learning having elevated conversation, conversation has degraded learning" (290).

A striking feature in Warton's response to Addison is that he makes pointed reference to the "literary," a term and problem not yet defined by the *Spectator*. "I would not be thought solicitous to confine the conversation even of scholars to literary subjects, but only to prevent such subjects from being totally excluded" (291). As we move from Addison to Warton, "philosophy" changes to "literary subjects" and "literary subjects" becomes a category at once in crisis and with an importantly educative effect on the public: "It seems therefore that to correct the taste of the present generation, literary subjects should be again introduced among the polite and gay, without labouring too much to disguise them like common prattle" (290). We know what literature is by knowing what it is not. Because, as Warton bemoans, "the tinsel of a burletta has more admirers than the gold of Shakespeare" we can see the literary value of older texts (291). And because literature is, like gold, a rare substance it "corrects" the common taste. This reversal of Addison's model did not so much abandon the project of the *Spectator*, therefore, as extend some of its fundamental premises to their ultimate negation. According to Addison, the language of the public sphere was the same as that of its canonical authors, indeed was formed by them. Warton's subsequent formulation retains the problem of language, but divides the linguistic into two irreconcilable modes. Public conversation and literary language oppose each other, as the prose essay does the lyric poem or as the novel does Shakespeare. In this opposition to the easy and sociable discourse of the literate public, we may begin to detect some of the characteristic features of what begins to be described as uniquely *literary* language: compression, obliquity, rhetoricity, allusion.

One way of thinking about this transformation is that it represents the coming into discourse of the modern category of "literature." No longer an inclusive term for "good books," literature becomes a restrictive category of the "imagination." The story of the literature's increasing specification in the late eighteenth century is, owing to the important work of Raymond Williams, widely familiar to early-modern cultural studies.[45] As John Guillory and Trevor Ross have pointed out, the reduction of literature to the imagination at once displaces and elevates the older term "poetry." Formerly an inclusive term for creative works, poetry is now winnowed to verse and placed at the pinnacle of the literary hierarchy.[46] The midcentury's elevation of the poetic, in Warton and elsewhere, derived from poetry's allegedly fragile relation to a nation more and more drawn to novels, essays, and polite conversation. Older texts, whose customary modes of expression were understood to defy modern conversation, now embodied a frangible and lyrical negativity. But where did this literary language come from and why was it so difficult to access? The rejection of sociability paradoxically incarnated a wide-ranging investigation into the social origins of literary language. Consider Adam Ferguson's chapter "Of the History of Literature," in *An Essay on the History of Civil Society* (1767). "The language of early ages,"

Ferguson observes, "is in one respect, simple and confined; in other, it is varied and free: it allows liberties, which, to the poet of after times, are denied."[47] The explanation for the peculiarly literary nature of earlier languages turns on the social constitution of language itself.

In rude ages men are not separated by distinctions of rank or profession. They live in one manner, and speak one dialect. The bard is not to choose his expression among the singular accents of different conditions. He has not to guard his language from the peculiar errors of the mechanic, the peasant, the scholar, or the courtier, in order to find that elegant propriety, and just elevation, which is free from the vulgar of one class, the pedantic of the second, or the flippant of the third. The name of every object, and of every sentiment, is fixed; and if his conception has the dignity of nature, his expression will have a purity which does not depend on his choice. (174)

As we look back in time at older societies, we see that their simple mode of organization was united by concrete forms of expression. The language of simple societies has yet to divide and weaken itself into the various dialects and idioms of more associative structures of affiliation. The gap between signifier and signified is threadbare; a given linguistic unit emanates collective pathos and concentrated sublimity. Older poetry is hence the spontaneous material of daily life (as the case is often made not just on behalf of Ossian or the Hebrews but, with more lasting impact, on behalf of Shakespeare as well). In contrast, the privileged discourse of the moderns, "elegant propriety," attempts to forge linguistic homogeneity within a society that no longer produces that homogeneity itself. The diffuse and complex structure of modern societies etiolates their linguistic substance. Spontaneous language becomes less literary the more societies become diverse. The vernacular transforms along with the evolving career of the division of labor:

When men become occupied on the subjects of policy, or commercial arts, they wish to be informed and instructed, as well as moved. They are interested by what was real in past transactions. They build on this foundation, the reflections and reasonings they apply to present affairs, and wish to receive information on the subjects of different pursuits, and of projects in which they begin to be engaged. The manners of men, the practice of ordinary life, and the form of society, furnish their subjects to the moral and political writer. Mere ingenuity, justness of sentiment and correct representation, though conceived in ordinary language, are understood to constitute literary merit, and by applying to reason more than to the imagination and passions, meet with a reception that is due to the instruction they bring. (175)

Ferguson here makes two points that are at once combined and at potential odds with each other. The language of organic society is unmediated concreteness. The language of commercial society is mediated abstraction. Modernity has eroded the basis for literary achievement because it has structured a language that stretches across the division of labor and is perforce rational, detoxified of any rhetorical excess or semantic irrationality. As Ferguson describes the history of literature, a subtle yet important transformation of the meaning of literary language occurs. While in the earlier passage, literary language was the language of simplified and direct communication, here it is the language of diversion and rhetoricity, of all that is not "ordinary." Literary language, it turns out, is the ordinary language of older ages defamiliarized and rendered unordinary by modern social life. It is all that opposes itself to the daily interchange of commercial society.

But what is the status of older, more collective and "authentic" modes of language under the commercial regime? What is, in other words, the fate of "literature" in modernity? The discovery of a certain type of transfigured language secreted by older social formations is coincident with the midcentury's desire to curb the opening up of vernacular learning. While the earlier catholicity of polite "letters" depended upon a relatively confident relation to public reading, the midcentury's increasingly specified focus on "literature" derives from a new skepticism. Literature is now what is dramatically absent from public discourse and private reading. It is the name for a certain learning that has been lost. This rethinking of what public culture has done to the nation's learning is well captured by another midcentury periodical, the *Connoisseur* (1754). In an early number, the journal delivers a mock encomium to the death of "literature" at the hands of instrumental politeness. "When I consider the absurd taste for literature, that once prevailed among our persons of distinction," the essay ironically begins, "I cannot but applaud the reformation which has been since brought about in this article by the polite world."[48] The reformation consists, as is the now familiar complaint, in the substitution of sociability for study: "we, of this generation, are wiser than to suffer our youth of quality to lose their precious time in studying the *belles lettres*, while our only care is to introduce them into the *beau-monde*" (179). Whereas criticism once took *belles lettres* and the *beau monde* to be the same thing – or rather, understood its project to form the two in an interdependent and mutually defining circuit – criticism now takes society to be the death of literature. "Some part of the polite world read indeed," the essay notes, "but they are so wise as to read only for amusement; or at least only to improve themselves into the more modern and fashionable sciences" (179). Modern habits of reading bring together the fallen public and the licentious private into a curious unit, collapsing sociable fashion into solitary amusement. Reading has become a kind of literate illiteracy, in which the program of politeness has so socialized literature that its constitutive autonomy is entirely lost:

I have long observed, with infinite regret, the little care that is taken to supply persons of distinction with proper books for their instruction and amusement. It is no wonder that they should be so averse to study, when learning is rendered so disagreeable. Common creatures, indeed, as soon as they can spell, may be made to read a dull chapter in the Testament; after which, the whole duty of man, or some other useless good book, may be put into their hands; but these can never instruct a man of the world to say fine things to a lady, or to swear with a good grace. (179)

As the *Connoisseur* imagines a national culture given entirely to instrumental politeness, the question of the past's relation to the present becomes hauntingly clear. If the project was in Addison's day to refine the taste of the public and fashion for it a culture that would produce and reflect that taste, the project is now to save literary culture from a refinement that has transformed into mass culture, from a modernity that has so detached itself from the past that it erases its own canonical achievements. In the ironic vision of the *Connoisseur*, the culture of refinement strips away all "learned" and "difficult" resistance and substitutes in their place a "polite circulating library" that makes the entire cultural product service-able to society.

First then, as the musty volumes which contain Greek, Latin, and the sciences, since there is no genteel method of coming at the knowledge of them, I would banish them entirely from the polite world, and would have them chained down in university libraries, the only places where they can be useful or entertaining. Having thus cleared the shelves of this learned lumber, we shall have room to fill them more elegantly . . . Many of my books are entirely new and original; all the modern novels, and most of the periodical papers fall so directly in with my plan, that they will be sure to find a place in my library. (180)

Addison's inaugural disentombment of learning is here redramatized as parody.[49] Learning flies back to the universities as useless knowledge while mass culture – modern novels and periodical papers – saturates the nation. In this parodic opening up of culture, "elegant" conversation is at one with its opposite, bad taste.

The quantitative spread of reading produces a qualitative decay in "learning." Another way of putting this, however, is that vernacular "learning," like "literature," emerges as a concept and problem, emerges as such, only at this point of acute crisis. Learning and its dissolution appear in tandem; fear of the one prompts a refurbishment of the other. When, for example, Oliver Goldsmith declares, in *New Fashions in Learning* (1761), that "I know no country but this where readers of learning are sufficiently numerous to give every kind of literary excellence adequate encouragement" he quickly proceeds to discuss how the "encouragement" of unlearned readers actually debases cultural products:

At present every rank of people become . . . pupils; the meanest mechanic has raised his mind to a desire for knowledge; and the scholar condescends to become his instructor.

We now begin to see the reason why learning assumes an appearance so very different from what it wore some years ago and that instead of penetrating more deeply into some new disquisitions, it only becomes a comment upon the past; the effort is now made to please the multitude, since they may be properly considered as the dispensers of rewards. More pain is taken to bring science down to their capacities, than to raise it beyond its present standard, and his talents are now more useful to society and himself, who can communicate what he knows, than his who endeavours to know more than he can communicate.[50]

"Encouragement" comes to mean demand, the zero degree of consumption that Goldsmith imagines to be holding back the advancement in learning. The reading public may encourage "literary excellence," since "learned readers" are numerous, but, for the same reason, the reading habits of the multitude lower cultural production to the level of the marketplace. Literary excellence is inextricably bound up with literary malaise.

What are we to make of this double movement, in which the emergence of a literati coincides with a wariness of the very institutions of reading themselves? One answer is that the category of "literature" has sufficiently detached itself from "romance," "the novel" and the like in order for it to require a custodial cadre of critics. This cadre is itself internally divided, as we shall see in following chapters. On the one hand, the intellectual culture of the universities re-emerges as the medium to sustain literary knowledge and value, with the important transformation now being that classical hermeneutics and philology have been displaced onto English texts. On the other hand, a new variety of periodical criticism attempts to correct the taste of its public by reinstalling learning in the imaginary center of public culture. In the first case, the critique of the public sphere is undertaken by an invigorated "scholarly" community, which forswears the mass circulated organs of the press for the more restricted institution of the learned essay and which sheds its exclusively Greco-Roman focus for the difficult works of England's past. In the second, the public's own medium attempts to self-correct the dissolution of reading.

Out of this tension between the restricted culture of the academy and the public sphere of journalism emerged a revised narrative of literary history in which modernity breaks from its past in a dizzying career of descent. The idea of literary progress gives way to the idea of literary decline.[51] The English ancients loom out of the past to condemn the English moderns. In perhaps the midcentury's most popular and influential account of cultural degeneration, *An Estimate of the Manners and Principles of the Time* (1757), John Brown imagines England's "national capacity" eroded by corrupt literature and dissolute reading:

A knowledge of books, a taste in arts, a proficiency in science, was formerly regarded as a proper qualification in a man of fashion. The annals of our country have transmitted to us the name and memory of men, as eminent in learning and taste, as in rank and fortune. It will not I presume, be regarded as any kind of satire on the present age, to say, that among the higher ranks this spirit is generally vanished. *Reading* is now sunk at best into a morning's *amusement*; till the important hour of dress comes on. Books are no longer regarded as the repository of taste and knowledge; but rather are laid hold of, as a gentle relaxation from the tedious round of pleasure. But what kind of reading must *that* be which can attract or entertain beyond the languid morning-spirit of modern effeminacy? Any, indeed, that can but prevent the unsupportable toil of *thinking*, that may serve as a preparatory *whet* of *indolence*, to the approaching pleasure of the day. Thus it comes to pass that weekly essays, amatory plays and novels, political pamphlets, and books that revile religion; together with a general *hash* of these, served up in some monthly *mess* of *dullness*, are the meagre *literary diet* of town and country.[52]

This colorful jeremiad was only part of a wide-ranging catalogue of "the false delicacy and effeminacy of present manners" (40), but it illuminates the extent to which the new narrative of literary decline partook of a larger rethinking of international trade, domestic commerce, and, not least, the over publication and sale of books. For Brown, "the exorbitant trade and wealth of England sufficiently account for its present effeminacy" (81). The situation is dire: "we are rolling to the brink of a precipice that must destroy us" (11). It was the duty of the professional critics, according to Brown and others, to correct effeminate reading habits and, thus, to save the character of England; "if, in any nation, the number of these superior minds be daily decreasing, from the growing manners of the times; what can a nation so circumstanced have more to fear, than that in another age, a general cloud of ignorance may overshadow it" (41).

Brown's worry that the number of "superior minds" was being dissolved by the relaxed manners of modern England was his own peculiar way of demanding that experts stop "the decline we are gliding down to our ruin" (74). But the desire for expertise, in *An Estimate* and elsewhere, foundered on a core ambivalence toward specialists removed from the idioms of the public. This ambivalence was expressed preeminently in the specter of the "pedant," caught in the windowless cell of his research and unable to speak with the commonality. I shall return to this specter in the next chapter; I would note here, however, that even the critics who wrote the new literary history of descent viewed the rise of their own profession as the sign of literary infirmity. The study of older works took off when such classics could no longer be produced anew. Warton's words are succinct: "In no polished nation after criticism has been much studied, and the rules of writing established, has any very extraordinary work ever appeared."[53] Like Warton, Goldsmith saw criticism as the end point of "our degeneracy in literature"; in his version of the story, criticism alone could redeem literary culture: "The manner of being useful on the subject would be to point out the symptoms, to investigate the causes, and direct to the remedies of the approaching decay. This is a subject hitherto unattempted in criticism, perhaps it is the only subject in which criticism can be useful."[54] The evaluation of the causes of decline, Goldsmith and Warton seem to suggest, forever cleaves the past from the present, production from consumption. We may understand why we can no longer write like our ancestors, but our knowledge is purchased with distance from their achievement.

The decline from literature to criticism, from great works to studies of those works, was also a decline from poetry to prose. The juxtaposing of poetry and prose became an easy way of lamenting the etiolated language of commerce, the dispersion of learning, and the modern institutions of literacy. The literary language of ancient society was necessarily poetic just as much as the didactic writing of modern commerce is necessarily prosaic. According to Ferguson's speculative "History of Literature", it is this iron law of descent – from poetry to prose – that puts in place the untranscendable figures of the literary canon: "whatever may be the early disposition of mankind to poetry . . . it is a remarkable fact, that not only in countries where every vein of composition was original, and was opened in the order of natural succession; but even at Rome, and in modern Europe, where the learned began early to practice on foreign models, we have poets of every nation, who are perused with pleasure, while the prose writers of the same ages are neglected" (174–175). Just who are these national poets? "We had in England, not only Chaucer and Spenser, but Shakespeare and Milton" (175).

Within prosaic society this canon of older poets takes on a recondite aura, as their language is situated aslant common discourse. Modern readers are averse to the linguistic difficulty and allusive density of "classic" texts. The argument that the world of modern prose was eclipsing the world of antique verse fed into the period's frequent lament that the reading audience for older authors was vanishing. Some of the most insistent paeans to the English canon were mounted on behalf of an avowedly unpopular culture, a culture that was both written in English and resistant to the taste of the multitude. Consider again the striking summation to Joseph Warton's *An Essay on the Writings and Genius of Pope* (1756): "Our English Poets may, I think, be disposed in four different classes and degrees. In the first class I would place, first, our only three sublime and pathetic poets: Spenser, Shakespeare, Milton."[55] Warton aligns older writers into a canonical trinity as a way to measure what he takes to be the rather modest achievement of Pope. The limpid confidence of this declaration leads into a broad condemnation of the poetry and reading habits of the modern age. In contrast to older poets of the first class, writers of what Warton calls "PURE POETRY" (iv), Pope was too satirical and "moral," too close to the rhythms of polite society, and the taste of the public: "a clear head and acute understanding are not sufficient, alone, to make a poet; . . . the most solid observations on human life, expressed with the utmost elegance and brevity, are MORALITY and not POETRY" (iv–v). Modern poetry serves an audience that prefers only to read about itself. Older English poetry is, by comparison, bereft of an audience. Yet this bereavement turns out to disclose the frangible condition of elite culture. "For one person who can adequately relish, and enjoy, a work of imagination, twenty are to be found who can taste and judge of observations on familiar life, and the manners of the age" (v). The lament that readers of Pope or of novels had forsworn older poetry was thus rather calculated; it authenticated the difficult and rarefied value of the past.

The present understands itself in terms of a past from which it has broken and toward which it casts a longing glance. Modernity splits into a golden age of poetry and a commercial age of prose. The battle between the ancients and the moderns, now staged within English culture itself, was settled once more on the side of the ancients. To put it this way, however, is simply to suggest some of the points of debate and friction that impelled the reception of the canonical trinity during the middle decades of the eighteenth century. The following chapters explore the terms in which the canon was described and the process of its formation.

CHAPTER 2

# The mode of consecration: between aesthetics and historicism

The more art becomes an autonomous sphere, which happens
as a result of lay education, the more art tends to acquire its
own set of constitutive values . . . But the conscious discovery of
uniquely aesthetic values is reserved for an intellectualist
civilization.

Max Weber

This is not the place to investigate the ever-increasing importance of aesthetics and the theory of art within the total world-
picture of the eighteenth century. As everywhere in this study,
we are concerned solely to throw light on the social and
historical background which threw up these problems and
conferred upon aesthetics and upon consciousness of art philosophical importance that art was unable to lay claim to in
previous eras . . . What is crucial here is the theoretical and
philosophical importance which the *principle of art* acquires in
the period.

Georg Lukács

The last chapter described how the making of the English literary
canon during the eighteenth century happened in tandem with a
rethinking of public culture and literary works. The midcentury
narrative of recession took over from the preceding narrative of
improvement, I argued, because it more adequately constituted a
domain of high literary culture within the vernacular. This chapter
looks at the categories and methods in which critics elevated texts
during the period. I argue that the canon was formed out of the
interplay and tension between aesthetic and historicist criticism, the
one a mode that emphasized standards of taste and sublimity, the
other a mode that emphasized philological expertise and linguistic
difficulty. In the early years of the eighteenth century, aesthetic
philosophy often distinguished itself from the feckless and "pedantic" seclusion of scholars. Historicist scholars likewise ridiculed the

54

leisurely dilettantism of modernizing aesthetes. Out of the evolving opposition grew by midcentury a shared concern for cultural distance and a shared preoccupation with literary change.

### ACCOUNTING FOR TASTE, SHAFTESBURY TO KAMES

The "rise of the aesthetic" has drawn much attention in recent work on British enlightenment culture.[1] The now familiar insight of this work locates aesthetic philosophy in the crucible of early capitalism.[2] Its conditions of possibility include the second great wave of agrarian enclosures and the revolution in domestic commerce and international trade. While the former rendered the landscape an object of genteel contemplation, the latter turned the public into consumers of culture. Beauty, sublimity, and the picturesque soon became competing modes of representing or reconciling the intricate order of commercial society. The idea of taste was, in this sense, *compensatory*; it was crafted by thinkers as a way to assimilate social and epistemological problems. In the following section, I adopt, critically, this revisionary reading of eighteenth-century aesthetic philosophy in order to see how the shifting itinerary of this philosophy through questions of literacy, sociability, class, and gender grew to frame the national canon.

Eighteenth-century aesthetic philosophy began with a palace coup in the court of epistemology. According to neo-Lockean psychology, consciousness is composed of three interrelated faculties: the understanding, the imagination, and the sensations.[3] Aesthetic theorists suggested that, among these faculties, the sensations and the imagination best represented a compound and manifold society, a society that could no longer be grasped with the more exacting precision of the understanding. Shaftesbury's seminal *Characteristicks of Men, Manners, Opinions and Times* (1711), for example, looked at social modernity as a problem of perspective:

Universal good, or the interest of the world in general, is a kind of remote philosophical object. That greater community falls not easily under the eye. Nor is a national interest, or that of a whole people, or body politic, so readily apprehended . . . For here perhaps the thousandth part of those whose interests are concerned are scarce so much as known by sight . . . Thus the social aim is disturbed by want of a certain scope.[4]

If "so remote a sphere as that of the body politic at large" could neither be immediately perceived nor rationally understood, Shaftesbury argued, it might be vicariously limned by one's sensible interaction with the world (I: 112).[5] The project of the *Characteristicks* is hence "to advance philosophy (as harsh a subject as it may appear) on the very foundation of what is called agreeable and polite" (III: 163). The turn from the abstruse heights of philosophy to the warmer pleasures of sensation wraps itself around an idea of the cultivated life. Not just sensation, but the beholding of works of art, the reading of literary works, and the discussion of beauty in affable and leisurely conversation. To make this point, Shaftesbury invokes a term of increasing prominence and latitude: "nothing which is found charming or delightful in the polite world, nothing which is adopted as pleasure or entertainment, of whatever kind, can any way be accounted for, supported, or established, without the pre-establishment or supposition of a certain taste" (III: 164). Taste abstracts polite affability into a comprehensive view of society. What one beheld in a landscape or a work of art was analogous to the community one inhabited.[6] Art, nature, and society share a balanced and proportioned beauty: "harmony is harmony by nature . . . So is symmetry and proportion founded still in nature . . . 'tis the same case where life and manners are concerned. Virtue has the same fixed standard. The same number, harmony and proportion will have place in morals, and are discoverable in the character and affections of mankind" (I: 353). When Shaftesbury wrote that "what is beautiful is harmonious and proportionable" he meant to describe the contours of a meadow, a painting, and his society alike (III: 182–183). It is in this sense that Terry Eagleton is certainly right to inaugurate a project as grand as *The Ideology of the Aesthetic* (1990) with a reading of the *Characteristicks*.[7] Beauty expresses a compensatory liaison between the cognitive faculties and the social order. Shaftesbury's aesthetic is ideological because the idea of nature and art as harmonious and balanced was put in the service of a theory of social development: it subsumed the early capitalist division of labor writ large under the sign of harmony.

The august serenity of this view was facilitated by a certain reduction. Society was harmonious because its members were few.[8] "To philosophize," Shaftesbury opined, "is but to carry good-breeding a step higher" (III: 161). The appreciation of a beautiful object (whether a landscape, a painting, a poem, or society itself) is ideally undertaken by the "young nobility and gentry"; "whoever has any impression of what we call gentility or politeness is already so acquainted with the decorum and grace of things that he will readily confess a pleasure and enjoyment in the very survey and contemplation . . . of beauty . . . symmetry and order" (III: 179–180). While Shaftesbury does not spare the old and otiose nobility, whose luxurious complacency prevents even aesthetic activity,[9] it is nonetheless landed gentlemen who have both sufficient property and sufficient leisure time to devote themselves to developing "an ear in music, an eye in painting, a fancy in the ordinary things of ornament and grace, a judgment in proportions of all kinds, and a general good taste in most of those subjects which make the amusement and delight of the ingenious people of the world" (I: 135).[10] Among the privileges of the "young nobility and gentry" is the stewardship of aesthetic mediation, a mediation that soon extends – by analogy – to literature. Shaftesbury abstracts aristocratic taste for the new age, allowing for its later detachment from the particulars of class and station and persistence as a model of understanding land and commerce alike.[11]

The idea of taste as wordly philosophy survived its initial, Whig-aristocratic formulation. Important for this survival, as many historians of aesthetics have noted, was an elaborate ethos of disinterest.[12] The proper attitude of the landowning gentlemen was to be detached from and uninvested in the object of contemplation and so mindful of the welfare of his polity. To be disinterested in one's reading or in one's gaze on a natural prospect is to surrender one's appetitive particularities for the good of the community. "A man of thorough *good breeding*" never "considers of the matter by prudential rules of self-interest and advantage" (I: 129). Rather, he "consider[s] the economies, parts, interests, conditions and terms of life, which Nature has distributed and assigned" with "a disinterested view" (II: 293). Free from any singular labor, the landed gentleman gazes across a wide compass. In contrast, individuals who have a specialized profession, or who work a particular task, view through a comparatively narrow aperture.[13] Cast in literary critical terms, the stately equipoise of Shaftesburian disinterest places itself against the "pedantry" of interested and expert reading. A public mode of polite conversation defines itself against a private mode of academic, and therefore purposeless, scholarship .

Shaftesbury's scattered thoughts on criticism and textual culture make a great deal of the idea of disinterest as what distinguishes the polite reader from the pedantic scholar. "Human arbitration and the judgment of the literate world" means that "the reader is still superior and keeps the upper hand" (III: 229). The importance placed on "polite reading and conversation with the better sort" in forging social bonds endows reading with a new prominence, and with a new name: criticism. "I take upon me absolutely to condemn the fashionable and prevailing custom of inveighing against critics as the common enemies, the pests and incendiaries of the common-wealth of wit and letters. I assert, on the contrary, that they are the props and pillars of this building; and that without the encourage-ment and propagation of such a race, we should remain as Gothic architects as ever" (I: 235–236). Disinterested criticism, reading that focuses on the harmonious beauty of texts and not the particular workings of their language, brings English culture out from the mire of the gothic past and into the graceful nobility of the modern age.

This defense of criticism as genteel reading entails a significant *depreciation* of authorship. "I may undoubtedly, by virtue of my preceding argument in behalf of criticism, be allowed, without suspicion of flattery or mere courtship, to assert the reader's privilege above the author, and assign to him, as I have above, the upper hand and place of honour" (III: 244). That the enlightenment issued forth the modern figure of the author is a truism of cultural studies.[14] Shaftesbury on occasion provides evocative material for this thesis, as in his neo-Sidneyan account of how "a poet is indeed a second *maker*, a just Prometheus under Jove . . . [who] imitate[s] the Creator . . . [and] like that sovereign artist, or universal sovereign nature . . . forms a whole, coherent and proportional in itself" (I: 207). Yet, interestingly, Shaftesbury's *author* is less often a vatic demi-urge than, like the scholar, a *déclassé* craftsman or artisan whose view of the social whole is narrowed by his labor. Now, to draw attention to this curiosity is less to reject the well-worn narrative of the rise of authorship in the early modern period than to consider more fully its dialectic. Shaftesbury's anti-authorial theory need not diminish one's sense of the novelty of "the author" at the turn of the century, or of the print relations from which that figure sprang; rather the opposite in fact, since the taking away of the author's authority presupposes a present and felt anxiety, an anxiety not just about lower class writing but also its wider cognates (particularity, labor, pedantry, and anything else that might trouble the formation of the community of taste). For Shaftesbury, the sovereign author, owner of words and arbiter of meaning, was a threat to the republic of letters: "we presume not only to defend the cause of critics, but to declare open war against those indolent supine authors . . . who [make] their humour alone the rule of what is beautiful and agreeable" (III: 165).

Shaftesbury's theory of authorship, criticism, and disinterested reading was of some moment for later criticism. A reader ought not to delve too deeply into the particular components of texts or the conditions of their authorial genesis. Such pedantry can please only the singular individual and not the social whole. The "interests" of writers and pedants were akin to the literal interest of economic and cultural profit. The most remote of scholars joined the denizens of Grub Street. Subsequent debates often turned on this paradoxical combination of print-capital and philology. Neo-Shaftesburians frequently claimed that their "pedantic" opponents were too mired in scholarship or the market to maintain a sufficiently detached vantage. Historicist scholars for their part responded that disinterested taste was itself mediated by commerce since it modernized older works and derived from them only social utility; for many scholars, the alleged disinterest of the reader merely elevated that reader's furtive interest in vaunting his status or masking his ignorance

Shaftesbury was not alone in setting the early eighteenth century's aesthetics of polite reading and taste. But the insouciantly chatty tone of the *Characteristicks* was influential in evoking its subject. In the history of aesthetic thought, Addison's essays on the "pleasures of the imagination" stand alongside Shaftesbury's *Characteristicks* as an early example of the enlightenment's concern to represent taste as a worldly philosophy. Like Shaftesbury, Addison "imagines" a community of readers joined by common politeness. But the shared emphasis grew out of two distinct senses of community: the one a tacitly landed community of genteel statesmen, the other an as of yet undefined community of periodical readers and coffee-house *cognoscenti*. It is a commonplace that Addison's aesthetics includes the urban middle classes along with Shaftesbury's "nobility and gentry."[15] We had occasion to discuss the broad implications and problems of this argument in the last chapter; I would only add, for the present discussion, that Addison's making public of "philosophy" contains an important rethinking of the theory of aesthetic disinterest. Consider the Spectator's self-description in the first paper:

I live in the world rather as a Spectator of mankind, than as one of the species; by which means I have made myself a speculative statesman, soldier, merchant, and artisan, without ever meddling with any practical part in life. I am very well versed in the theory of a husband or a father, and can discern the errors in the economy, business, and diversion of others, better than those who are engaged in them; as standers-by discover blots which are apt to escape those who are in the game. I never espoused any party with violence, and am resolved to observe an exact neutrality between the Whigs and Tories, unless I shall be forced to declare myself by the hostilities of either side. In short, I have acted in all the parts of my life as a looker-on, which is the character I intend to preserve in this paper. (I: no.1, 4–5)

By remaining detached from any particular vocation, the Spectator can survey the whole social order. So much was also the case for Shaftesbury's dilettante/connoisseur, whose authority derived not least from his stately indifference to the circumstantial or instrumental. The important difference is that society now includes a broad range of practical, political, and economic activities, each of which is imaginatively performed by the Spectator.

Disinterest is thus what we, as well as Addison, might call an imaginary relation, a relation of the imagination to the real; the Spectator is a spectator because he can imagine himself to perform an infinite number of practical labors without having his view foreshortened by the actuality of any one labor. The imagination intervenes to dilate his prospect. Addison opens up philosophy to the new world of periodical journalism and coffee-house conversation only to introduce the problem of social diversity. That diversity, in turn, finds a peculiarly aesthetic solution. The various groups to which the *Spectator* lays claim are united in the disinterested experience of beauty, that is, in their taste. Addison defines "taste," as "*that Faculty of the Soul, which discovers the Beauties of an Author with Pleasure, and the Imperfections with Dislike*" (III: no. 409, 528). This is an important point that risks being overlooked: taste describes a mode of reading: "If a man would know whether he is possessed of this faculty, I would have him read over the celebrated works of antiquity . . . or those works among the moderns, which have the sanction of the politer part of our contemporaries" (III: 528). The verdict is then summary: if the reader is "delighted" he possesses taste; if he is not, he belongs to "the tasteless readers" (III: 528). The recourse to reading, of course, makes a certain sense; it is by this means that Addison's audience can imaginatively project itself to the position of

Spectator. Through reading "polite authors," "conversing with men of polite genius," and versing oneself "in the works of the best critics both ancient and modern" (III: 529), the merchant, financier, or tradesman, can maintain the "survey and contemplation" of the gentleman. As with Shaftesbury, then, *criticism* is inseparable from the overall circulation of reading and conversation. To be a critic is not to know more than the public, or to educate its taste; it is, rather, to speak the quintessence of public conversation, to read *with* the grain of the collective.

Addison's use of the term "taste" in the *Tatler* and the *Spectator* works in two directions, a theory of artistic delectation and a theory of social behavior. Appreciation and sociability were combined in an ideal of polite reading.[16] The discussion of taste in the *Spectator* no. 409 concludes by advertising a forthcoming series on the "imagination" which will describe "what it is that gives a Beauty to many passages in the finest writers in prose and verse" (530). The papers "On the Pleasures of the Imagination" (nos. 411–421) were devoted, as is well known, to describing what in art or nature is pleasing to encounter and how that encounter obtains in the specific faculty of the imagination. The initial appeal to reading in the advertisement at the end of the essay on taste is not surprising, since taste mediates a community whose self-identity is based irreducibly in language. This mediation places special emphasis on polite English as an abstract form of uniformity. Addison's preferred texts are thus at once culturally elevated and linguistically homogeneous. *Spectator* no. 417, for example, concludes with a striking overcoming of the classical by the vernacular, the ancient by the modern. After assigning Homer to "greatness," Virgil to "beauty," and Ovid to "novelty," Addison offers that Milton embodies and distills all three categories:

If I were to name a poet that is a perfect master in all these arts of working on the imagination, I think Milton may pass for one . . . [for] what can be conceived greater than the battle of angels, the majesty of Messiah, the stature and behavior of Satan and his peers! What more beautiful than Pandæmonium, Paradise, Heaven, Angels, Adam and Eve! What more strange than the creation of the world, the several metamorphoses of the fallen angels, and the surprising adventures their leader meets with in his search after Paradise! . . . no other poet could have painted those scenes in more strong and lively colours. (III: no. 417, 566)

It has often been observed that Addison wrote with an ease and simplicity rejected by his midcentury successors, an ease that bore a systematic relation to the sort of reading community he imagined for his essays. In this passage, we see this as it were instrumental ease woven into the fabric of Milton's text, as the marker of aesthetic success. *Paradise Lost*'s beauty and sublimity are simple for the reader of taste to enjoy. This enjoyment is uniform among tasteful readers and critics.

As this account of Milton may suggest, "the pleasures of the imagination" have a prominent position in the history of aesthetics in part because they adumbrate the midcentury's trinity of sublime, beautiful, and picturesque (here "greatness," "beauty," and "novelty" or the "uncommon").[17] These categories describe first the pleasure of viewing "nature" and then the reviewing of the natural in the reading of particularly well written texts. "Greatness" is "the largeness of a whole view, considered as one entire piece," a "rude kind of magnificence" that obtrudes itself onto the "imagination" of the subject, who, in turn, "loves to be filled with an object, or to grasp at anything that is too big for its capacity" (540). The "new or uncommon" describes variety and change in a given scene or object, that which "fills the soul with an agreeable surprise, gratifies its curiosity, and gives it an idea of which it was not before possessed"; one finds pleasure "at the sight of such objects as are ever in motion, and sliding away from beneath the eye of the beholder" (541–542). At once the most important and enigmatic category, finally, "beauty" denotes "places or objects" that abound "in the gaiety or variety of colours, in the symmetry and proportion of parts, in the arrangement and disposition of bodies, or in a just mixture and concurrence of all together" (542). Addressing himself to a complex and ramified social order, Addison finds solace in the beauty of a blended compound. Modernity may exceed our rational faculties, but this excess is the condition of a pleasurable aesthetic compensation, a refraction of society's harmony onto nature and art.

As in the *Characteristicks*, this refraction strives to represent and contain the modern order by other means. Addison is to be distinguished, however, for his important and programmatic specification of this containment: his shift from the sensations to the imagination. Addison distinguishes at the outset the "pleasures of the imagination" from both "those of the sense" and "those of the understanding" (536–537). The "imagination" derives from "sight . . . the most perfect and most delightful of our senses" (536). Sight "may be considered as a more delicate and diffusive kind of touch, that spreads itself over an infinite multitude of bodies, comprehends the largest figures, and brings into our reach some of the most remote parts of the universe" (536). Ocular experience then further divides into "primary" and "secondary pleasures of the imagination" those "which entirely proceed from such objects as are before our eyes" and those "called up into our memories, or formed into agreeable visions of things that are absent or fictitious" (537). The aesthetic is not just undiluted sensation but the *recollection* of sensation, the imaginative reviewing of the visual. Between the understanding and the senses lies open the vast, uncharted terrain of the imagination.

Aesthetic pleasure begins to detach itself, partially and with hesitation, from the domain of morality and politics, to reenact the real within the imagination. Unlike the understanding, the pleasure of the imagination is distinct from "knowledge or improvement in the mind of man" (536–537). "We are struck, we know not how, with the symmetry of anything we see, and immediately assent to the beauty of an object, without inquiring into the particular causes and occasions of it" (538). Unlike the pleasure of sensations, the innocent pleasure of the imagination is separable from vice:

There are indeed but very few who know how to be idle and innocent, or have a relish of any pleasures that are not criminal; every diversion they take is at the expense of some one virtue or another, and their very first step out of business is into vice or folly. A man should endeavour, therefore, to make the sphere of his innocent pleasures as wide as possible, that he may retire into them with safety, and find in them such a satisfaction as a wise man would not blush to take. Of this nature are those of the imagination, which do not require such a bent of thought as is necessary to our more serious employments, nor, at the same time, suffer the mind to sink into that negligence and remissness, which are apt to accompany our more sensual delights; but like a gentle exercise to the faculties, awaken them from sloth and idleness, without putting them upon any labour or difficulty. (539)

The idea of the aesthetic in this passage emerges through a complicated, double negation. It opposes itself to rational utility *and* to "vicious pleasure," to the understanding *and* the sensations. In both cases, Addison defines aesthetic experience against what is merely instrumental, whether that consists in the practical or the vicious. For later theorists, the separability of the imagination from the understanding is occasion to celebrate art's disjunction from politics and society.[18] For Addison, however, this division is only partial and contingent. The split of the imagination from the understanding is just as much reason to think of the social order as beautiful as it is to think of beauty apart from society.

The relation between taste and its community, society and the aesthetic, was for Addison much less of a problem than it would be for his successors. Yet the seeds of the midcentury standardization of taste and turn to the sublime were very much sown in the *Spectator*. Let us take a look at a famous passage from the "Pleasures of the Imagination" series in which Addison describes with cogent precision the kind of enjoyment brought by the pleasures of the imagination:

A man of a polite imagination is let into a great many pleasures that the vulgar are not capable of receiving. He can converse with a picture, and find an agreeable companion in a statue. He meets with a secret refreshment in a description, and often feels a greater satisfaction in the prospect of fields and meadows, than another does in the possession. It gives him, indeed, a kind of property in everything he sees, and makes the most rude uncultivated parts of nature administer to his pleasures: so that he looks upon the world as it were in another light, and discovers in it a multitude of charms, that conceal themselves from the generality of mankind. (538)

The passage opens by circumscribing the aesthetic community into a minority of the polite who are set off against the vulgar generality. The latter in turn bracket the paragraph as negatively enabling social coordinates. But the "vulgar" in a certain way also stand for those whose pleasure derives only from the "possession" of land. The aesthetic subject has a "kind of property" in what falls under his gaze, and, in this way, like Addison's readership, can be drawn from a large fraction of society.[19] At the same time that the "kind of property" is a free floating aesthetic object, happily sundered from actual possession in an apparent democratization of disinterest, it also signifies landed capital specifically. Making "the most rude uncultivated parts of nature administer to [one's] pleasures," in the early eighteenth-century context after all, describes the process of enclosure, the steady parceling and cultivating of whatever remained of the rural commons, wastelands, and the like.[20] Addison's aesthetic is both a theoretical version of free trade and described in the language of landed property. It both opens itself to all readers and shuts out the generality. The *Spectator* strives to maintain an aesthetic that is at once simple and elevated, in fact elevated because of its stately simplicity. In one essay, Addison writes that "the pleasures of the imagination have this advantage . . . they are more obvious and more easy to acquire" (III: no. 411, 538). In another, he argues that "several readers" may "have a different relish of the same descriptions" because "this different taste . . . proceed[s] . . . from the perfection of the imagination in one more than another" (III: no. 416, 561). The desire for equivalence, for the aesthetic to form an abstract means of comparability and community, here abuts the desire for differentiation, for the aesthetic to form a concrete means of distinguishing among social actors. The novelty and legacy of Addison's model for his successors lay not so much in one particular side of this opposition, one might say, as in Addison's ability to animate the aesthetic through their unresolved tension.

For Addison and Shaftesbury the categorical validity of taste was less at stake than the process by which it was acquired. During the midcentury, however, aesthetic theorists became increasingly concerned with the problem of taste, in particular whether or not one could speak with confidence of a "standard of taste."[21] When John Gilbert Cooper set out to popularize Shaftesbury's aesthetics in his epistolary treatise *Letters Concerning Taste* (1755), for example, he began with a curiously skeptical proposition: Is it in fact the case, he asked, "that taste is governed by caprice, and that beauty is reducible to no criterion?"[22] Cooper's answer to this question was, of course, not affirmative, and the asking was, in a certain sense, but an entrée into a philosophical set piece inquiring yet again into the properties, dimensions, and origins of taste; but Cooper's question, in another sense, contained a dual and variable mutation in the discourse of aesthetics. First, the very concepts that Shaftesbury and Addison had labored to form are here encountered as full-scale abstractions, as the congealed terms of a discussion spanning a near half century. Second, now that the terms of aesthetic discourse are relatively stable, or abstract, they yield themselves to incipient skepticism and redefinition. Looking back at the *Characteristicks* from a later period, Cooper is more "Shaftesburian" than Shaftesbury himself, and it is this lateness that encapsulates his importantly transitional position in eighteenth-century cultural politics.

Cooper answers the skeptical query by reverting to the Shaftesburian idiom of the inner sense. Lest anyone deny the validity of aesthetic experience, or explain it away as mere caprice, he reminds the reader that "the effect of a *good* TASTE is that instantaneous glow of pleasure which thrills thro' our whole frame, and seizes upon the applause of the heart, before the intellectual power, reason, can descend from the throne of the mind to ratify its approbation" (3). The concise alacrity in which Cooper here describes the primary moment of aesthetic experience retrieves from Shaftesbury an account of the sensations and their pre-rational pleasures that drops the *Characteristicks* more halting and digressive manner. The succinct description easily affords a further specification and subdivision of taste into, respectively, nature, society, and art: the "thrill" happens "either when we receive into the soul beautiful images thro' the organs of bodily senses; or the decorum of an amiable character thro' the faculties of moral perception; or when we recall, by the imitative arts, both of them thro' the intermediate power of the imagination" (3).

Cooper's description strives for a kind of maximum yet beguiling conventionality; witness the account of the effect on the inner sense of a beautiful, natural scene:

A rural prospect upon the very first glance yields a grateful emotion in the breast . . . Suppose you were to behold from an eminence, thro' a small range of mountains covered with woods, several little streams gushing out of rocks, some gently trickling over pebbles, others tumbling from a precipice, and a few gliding smoothly in willow-shaded rivulets thro' green meadows, till their tributary waters are all collected by some river god of a larger urn, who at some few miles distance is lost in the ocean, which heaves its broad bosom to the sight, and ends the prospect with an immense expanse of waters . . . [w]ould not such a scene captivate the heart even before the intellectual powers discover minerals in the mountains; future natives in the woods; civil and military architecture in the rocks; healing qualities in the smaller streams; fertility, that the larger waters distribute along their serpentising banks; herbage for cattle in the meadows; and lastly, the more easy opportunities the river affords us to convey to other climates the superfluities of our own, for which the ocean brings us back in exchange what we stand in need of from theirs. (4–5)

The landscape and its affects are deceptively typical. The lesson to be learned from beholding this "rural prospect," Cooper wants to suggest, is that taste is an irreducible quality and the aesthetic a primary experience, that both take precedence over rational cogitation and practical utility: "nature" may have final causes and may give forth all sorts of bounty, but its pleasures spring first from the unadulterated sight of its beauty. Cooper cannot leave this "rural prospect," however, without complicating the naturalist bias. Nature it turns out is even more beautiful with the superinduction of culture: "Now to heighten this beautiful landscape," Cooper continues the letter, "let us throw in corn fields, here and there a country seat, and, at proper distances, small hamlets together with spires and towers, as Milton describes them, 'bosom'd high in tufted trees.' Does not additional rapture flow in from this adjunct, of which reason will afterwards discover the latent cause in the same manner as before?" (5). Cooper's typicality here betrays a striking instability; the conventionally natural topoi of mountains, streams, and meadows need to be heightened by the social arrangement of tillage, manors, and villages and then by the cultural emolument of Milton. That the allegedly natural is, in fact, always already cultural should come as no surprise; yet one may still be struck by the clarity in which Cooper renders social relations and, finally, literature as the necessary conditions of nature's intelligibility. The "rural prospect" transforms into the rustic village of customary squiredom, the nature of which resembles nothing more than Milton's Paradise.[23]

Society mediates the rural prospect. Yet when Cooper turns from the aesthetics of the landscape to that of its avowedly social analogue, the stability of society itself is found to be mediated and partial. For Shaftesbury, the idea of social "harmony," like that in nature and art, gave sensible form to the unimaginable complexity of modern commerce and civil society. With Cooper, social harmony amounts to a rather different and distinct aesthetic: "Here I appeal to your own breast," he writes to Euphemius,

and let me continue the appeal by asking you concerning another science analogous to [the unerring dictates of nature], which is founded upon as invariable principles: I mean the science of living well, in which you are as happily learned as in the former. Say then, has not every amiable character, with which you have been enamoured, been proved by a cool examination to contain a *beautiful* proportion, in the point it was placed in, relative to society? And what is that constitutes moral deformity, or what we call vice, but the disproportion which any agent occasions, in the fabric of civil community, by a non-compliance to the general *order* which should prevail in it? (*Letters*: 5–6)

The aesthetics of sociability in this passage both remain with and depart from their Shaftesburian precursor. The analogue to natural order, as in the *Characteristicks*, resides in the fabric of society, into which any given individual must fit. Yet *beauty* does not so much lie with the rational order of society as it does with the fit between the individual and the social. If the order of society is beautiful, that beauty can be sensed only through the proportion between the singular part and the larger whole. Cooper's aesthetics exhibit, in this respect, a significant narrowing and sharpening of scope, an emphasis on the part, the fragment and the particular that will soon begin to dominate the discussion of taste. Likewise, the "society" that is abstracted from the individual begins to take on a monolithic and numinous obscurity characteristic less of the beautiful than, as we shall see, of the sublime.[24]

It thus falls to art to redeem the partiality of society and, as with Milton, to "heighten" nature. Cooper's description of "the arts of painting, sculpture, and poetry" is again manifestly conventional; they have no "primary beauty in themselves but derive their shadowy existence in a mimetic transcript from objects in the material world, or from passions, characters, and manners" (7). The unsurprising role given to mimesis accounts, however, for art's singularity and importance. Among the three realms of the aesthetic – nature, society, and art – art's relation to taste is the most immediate because, paradoxically, the least direct: "that internal sense we call taste . . . has as quick a feeling of this secondary excellence of the arts, as for the primary graces; and seizes the heart with rapture long before the senses, and reason in conjunction, can prove this beauty by collating the imitation with their originals" (7). Art's secondariness proves to be its route around the difficulties associated with the primary pleasures of nature and society. Nature is more rewarding viewed through Milton, as we have seen; what is also the case, however, is that the individual better fits into society with the help of art.

This is the vocation, in Cooper's *Letters*, of the Shaftesburian connoisseur, the gentleman of polite learning and sophisticated breeding. Taste fits the individual part to the social whole. Cooper recounts, for instance, in a letter to Euginio, how Euphemius is

blessed with a grace in conversation, and a *taste* in society, superior to any man with whom I ever had the happiness of being acquainted. There arises from the vivacity of his fancy, the delicacy of his sentiments, and the beautiful tho' unaffected arrangement of his words, delivered with a freedom of countenance and sweetness of voice, such an inexpressible charm as pleasingly bewitches the attention of all who hear him. He can descant upon serious affairs with the most becoming air of gravity and consideration, without the least mixture of austerity or philosophical affectation; and in the more easy hours of social pleasure, he can raise innocent and instructive mirth from the slightest accident that happens, and convert the most common subjects into a thousand turns of wit and humour. One would imagine that Shakespeare had been acquainted intimately with such a man . . . (107)

This description is neatly fetched from the *Characteristicks* and, as in Shaftesbury's text, the universal individual is taken from a particular class – "the easy air, the happy sprightliness, and elegant turn of expression in the compositions of the former, discover the man of the world educated in courts, and polished by that advantageous collision with the brightest part of our species" (110). Here the *Letters* seem to suggest, as with their precursor, that the provenance of taste is with "the young nobility and gentry." Yet, unlike Shaftesbury, Cooper does not comment extensively, beyond this passage, on the rooting of taste in social status. This change is owing, I would suggest, to the fact that Cooper fashions his late Shaftesburian connoisseur in such a manner that will resolve the dilemma of social proportion. The argument that the man of taste is drawn solely from the elite classes runs the inevitable risk of foreshortening the socially harmonizing effect of taste. The implicitly aristocratic basis of taste is something of a discursive remainder, the importantly residual element of an older aesthetic system.

A key symptom of this lateness may be detected in Cooper's strategic substitution of gender for class as the emblem of social refinement. In the place of courtly education and aristocratic breeding he puts "frequent conversation with women" (25). It is the "habitual intercourse with these polishers of our sex" that gives to men the "constant idea of delicacy and softness" (25–26). What obtained under the sign of aristocratic status in the *Characteristicks* here proceeds as the "harmonizing" affect of femininity: "I have often observed, that this enchanting turn in conversation prevails only in those of our own sex, who have conversed much with the more sensible part of the other . . . for let a man's erudition be ever so profound, his fancy lively, and judgment solid, this grace, which is not to be described, will be wanting, if his soul has not been refined, and his tongue attuned to this sweet melody by an habitual intercourse with these fair preceptors" (108–109). In passages such as these, Cooper simply takes the qualities of Shaftesbury's "young nobility and gentry" and displaces them onto men educated by the delicate conversation with women.[25] The compensatory gendering of Cooper's *Letters* will have a pronounced influence on later writers in the aesthetic tradition, such as Burke (and more obliquely on the entire tradition of male sensibility of which Cooper is a part); it also helps to explain the historicist revolt against "effeminate" culture. For our current purposes, we may note how the idea of gendered refinement attempts to reimagine the aesthetic community of Shaftesbury once the social coordinates of that community have faded from view.

This particular lateness is refracted onto another, namely, Cooper's relation to that central Shaftesburian preoccupation called "criticism." Looking back at a different predecessor, Cooper observes that the "worthy man and amiable writer Mr. Addison, was no *great* Scholar; he was a very indifferent critic, and a worse poet; yet . . . he was blessed with a taste truly delicate and refined. This rendered him capable of distinguishing *what were* beauties in the works of others, tho' he could not account so well *why they were so*, for want of that deep philosophical spirit which is requisite in works of criticism" (28). This recollection of Addison imagines criticism to be something distinct from "delicate and refined" taste. Cooper reads Addison's project in terms of a categorical partition that, in fact, post-dates the *Spectator*. For Addison, as for Shaftesbury, criticism and reading with "a taste truly delicate and refined" were very much the same thing. Like other writers of the 1750s, Cooper distinguishes the critic from the common reader. He retroactively invokes these now fully abstracted categories to assess their prior meaning in Addison.

Cooper's peculiar lateness, however, has him disavowing as he announces the split between reading and criticism. Addison's great failure is also his great success: the choice of the warmer pleasures of elegant taste over the colder philosophy of critical reading. Here Cooper veers into a discussion taken, as we shall discuss below, from the quarrels with historicism: the critique of pedantry. Reading with taste may not be criticism, strictly speaking, but it is closer to the feminizing and socializing program he imagines for art; hence "more taste and elegance in writing is to be acquired in a circle of beauties at Paris, than in a learned society of Capuchins" (110). Even as he charges Addison with being a lax critic, then, he aligns himself with the "delicate and refined" and against the "scholarly" and "philosophical," or rather, he blends the tasteful and the critical into a combined mode of reading:

There is something so repugnant to the pride of mankind in general, something so detractive from the supposed sagacity of every reader to pretend to inform by the dry method of precept, that except an author has all the delicacy and artful address imaginable, to seem to *accompany* the judgments of those he writes for, rather than to *lead* them into discoveries, in such a performance, he will meet with that kind of contemptuous treatment, which those good-natured people receive, who are ready to give their unasked advice in the common concerns of life upon every occasion. It is highly necessary therefore, in such kind of writings, to *sacrifice liberally to the Graces*, without whose inspiration learning will there degenerate into pedantry, and the precepts of wisdom pass unrelished. (118–119)

The feminine sacrifice that Cooper enjoins on criticism marks his tentative solution to the problem of art and the social. To a society whose "harmony" may no longer be tacitly assumed, Cooper prescribes a "graceful" aesthetic. The combination of femininity and sociability is important for the negative definition of high canonical works, as we shall see. Of equal importance to this definition is the growing concern over the status of taste itself. Cooper's *Letters* has the air of received wisdom, a genteel conversation over agreed upon matters of taste. What it both reveals and leads into, however, is anything but consensus.

Consider David Hume's famous essay *Of the Standard of Taste* (1757). Hume begins with a proposition: "the great variety of Taste, as well as opinion, which prevails in the world, is too obvious not to have fallen under every one's observation."[26] Taste here is less the agent of harmony than of diversity and, implicitly, dissension. The problem of this diversity is indeed pronounced, owing to the empiricist argument that taste is neither derived from a priori principles, nor reducible to objective reality itself, but rather validated by experience. Aesthetic categories inhere in the mind of the subject: "no sentiment represents what is really in the object. It only marks a certain conformity or relation between the object and the organs or faculties of the mind . . . Beauty is no quality in things themselves: It exists merely in the mind which contemplates them" (231).Yet what then happens, Hume is left to ponder, when the minds that contemplate objects cease to concur, when judgment yields difference rather than identity? "There must be," Hume responds, a "species of common sense" that "opposes" or "serves to restrain" the aesthetic relativism of "the great variety of taste" (232). Hume's example of pernicious aesthetic leveling is quite suggestive:

"Whoever would assert an equality of genius and elegance between Ogilby and Milton, or Bunyan and Addison, would be thought to defend no less an extravagance, than if he had maintained a molehill as high as Teneriffe, or a pond as extensive as the ocean" (230–231). In this sentence, Hume neatly encapsulates the emergence of high culture and mass culture, ancient and modern, within English literature. The opposition amounts to a distinction between two types of texts and two types of reading: whence Milton against Ogilby, the translator of classical literature, and, along with Addison, against Bunyan the popular novelist. To explain the disparity between canonical and noncanonical literature, Hume must come forth with an *a posteriori* "*Standard of Taste*; a rule, by which the various sentiments of men may be reconciled; at least a decision, afforded, confirming one sentiment, and condemning another" (231). Once we arrive at such a standard, Hume promises, the "principle of the natural equality of tastes" is "totally forgot" (229).

This standard is predicated on the fact that even if beauty inheres in the mind, the "particular forms or qualities, from the internal fabric" that induce it exist in objects; thus, following "experience" and "the observation of the common sentiments of human nature" the critic can isolate beautiful objects according to a rule (232):

allow [a person] to acquire experience in those objects, his feeling becomes more exact and nice: He not only perceives the beauties and defects of each part, but marks the distinguishing species of each quality, and assigns it suitable praise or blame. A clear and distinct sentiment attends him through the whole survey of the objects; and he discerns that very degree and kind of approbation or displeasure, which each part is naturally fitted to produce. The mist dissipates, which seemed formerly to hang over the objects. The organ acquires greater perfection in its operation: and can pronounce, without danger or mistake, concerning the merits of every performance. (237)

Readers are thus not fated to poor judgment; good aesthetic habits are vouchsafed by experience. Yet the sort of experience that Hume has in mind in the essay is of a rather narrow and exacting sort. Following the rescuing of taste from the grip of aesthetic relativism, Hume assumes the labor of describing by what process a critic can read or view properly. Good taste derives from travel, education, property, and the absence of interested "prejudice." Such experience enables one to maintain the suitably disinterested relation to the arts; it fosters the "strong sense, united to delicate sentiment, improved by practice perfected by comparison, and cleared of all prejudice" (241). Among the "great variety" of readers, therefore, there are a scant few who qualify as arbiters of taste: "though the principles of taste be universal, and nearly, if not entirely the same in all men; yet few are qualified to give judgment on any work of art, or establish their own sentiment as the standard of beauty" (241).

One reason that "taste" appears to be the province of the privileged here is that Hume has moved the discussion away from the "reader" toward the "critic." Like Cooper, Hume prizes out and refigures certain elements of the extant discourse of aesthetics in order to come to grips with a relatively new problem, the "great variety of taste." While Cooper was ambivalent about the split between reading and criticism, Hume celebrates the divorce of the critic from the body of the reading public:

Where are such critics to be found? By what marks are they to be known? How distinguish them from pretenders? . . . It is sufficient for our present purpose, if we have proved, that the taste of all individuals is not upon an equal footing, and that some men in general, however difficult to be particularly pitched upon, will be acknowledged by universal sentiment to have a preference above others. (242)

Given the program he has outlined for the acquisition of taste, this statement would seem to designate emphatically the aesthetic object as cultural capital and taste as a marker for entitlement and prestige. So much was of course contained in Shaftesbury's model too. The important difference is the notable defensiveness of Hume's posture, a defensiveness that produces a certain theoretical position-taking. Hume's aesthetic sheds the generalizing function of the earlier understanding of taste and the imagination; for the generality has, according to Hume, "various" and misguided taste. No longer the fulcrum of social harmony, taste is a rarefied faculty. The standard of taste is the standard of a certain minority, a minority that reflexively declares a sparse fraction of the cultural product to be valuable. The reader that Hume calls a critic involves himself with what we would now call canon formation. By way of arriving at cultural forms that have, in their "internal fabric," the "forms and qualities" that produce beauty, against those like Bunyan that bespeak a debased taste, Hume selects works of historically "durable admiration" and beauty, works whose charm has exerted itself on multiple ages of readers (247). The standard of taste falls on a standard of pastness, on the durable beauty of such writers as Milton and Homer.

The same year as Hume's essay on taste, Edmund Burke published his influential aesthetic treatise, *A Philosophical Enquiry into the Origin of our Ideas of the Sublime and the Beautiful*. The treatise contained a powerful case for the priority of the sublime and for rethinking that category as a particularly literary experience of obscurity and terror.[27] The shift of emphasis from the beautiful to the sublime here implies a shift in the understanding of culture and society. In Shaftesbury and Cooper, the "beauty" of society in one way or another lay in its harmony. So much is the case for Burke; "I call Beauty a social quality," he writes; "good company, lively conversations, and the endearments of friendship, fill the mind with great pleasure."[28] Cooper's sense of the problem of bringing the part together with the whole, and the corresponding narrowing of the aesthetic *mise-en-scène*, however, reappear in Burke as a consoling interest in solitude, where the dual question of society and effeminacy, the enervation of social intercourse and the difficulty of harmonizing the intricate networks of commerce and exchange, are displaced and resolved by the sublime.

The shift to the sublime entails a significant reconsideration of reading and textuality alike, a turn from sociable conversation to private affect. Burke discusses at some length the social pleasures of the beautiful, but these are rarely imagined to be derived from texts or exemplified in poetry. One finds the quintessence of the sublime, by contrast, in written objects. This is a point which Burke elaborates not just in the recurrent citations of *Paradise Lost*, but from the *Enquiry*'s opening pages on "obscurity" onward: "It is one thing to make an idea clear, and another to make it affecting to the imagination . . . [T]he most lively and spirited verbal description I can give, raises a very obscure and imperfect idea of such objects; but then it is in my power to raise a stronger emotion by the description than I could do by the best painting. This experience constantly evinces. The proper manner of conveying the *affections* of the mind from one to another, is by words" (60). The importance placed on "obscurity" within Burke's aesthetic system can hardly be overstated; it is the key attribute of "terror," itself the "common stock of every thing that is sublime" (64). For our current purposes, we might note how the aesthetics of obscurity lead into a new way of reading English classics. Addison found Milton's sublimity (deriving from his divine subject, his language, or his descriptions)[29] to lie visibly on the surface of the text. The clarity of literary objects enabled the cultivated ease and refined grace of their reading. Burke claims that a central component of Milton's sublime, and the sublime itself, is its obscurity.[30] The obscurity of literary objects enables the coarse terror and agitated force of *their* reading.

No person seems better to have understood the secret of heightening, or of setting terrible things, if I may use the expression, in their strongest light by the force of a judicious obscurity, than Milton. His description of Death in the second book is admirably studied; it is astonishing with what a gloomy pomp, with what a significant and expressive uncertainty of strokes and colouring he has finished the portrait of the king of terrors. (59)

Eight lines from book 2 of *Paradise Lost* follow, and Burke concludes "In this description all is dark, uncertain, confused, terrible, and sublime to the last degree" (59).

In the discussion of the sublime, the figure for sociable ease is not found in texts. Rather, limpid tranquillity is associated with painting. It is in this sense that we may understand the *Enquiry*'s seemingly idiosyncratic hostility to the visual arts. Painting and sculpture are too clearly representational, the simplicity of their viewing drained of the sublime obliquity of verse; thus, Burke continues, "it is in my power to raise a stronger *emotion* by the description than I could do by the best painting" (60). Burke replaces Addison's model of *ut pictura poesis*, or the literary canvas, with one of obscure poetry. The displacement of painting as a metaphor for textuality, of course, only goes so far; in the description above, Milton's poem is a "portrait" with "strokes and colouring." Burke has not so much departed from aesthetic discourse, in other words, as he has revised its terms, like Addison bringing in the language of nature, landscape, and affect to discuss texts, but dismissing the customary twinning of poetry and painting as sister arts. Poetry's sororicide is the condition of its obscurity. The force and terror of the sublime is fundamentally linguistic and textual. It is worth emphasizing here a point that risks being taken for granted, namely, that Burke's example of sublimity is more often than not Milton, the *Enquiry* reading at times like a commonplace book on *Paradise Lost*: "We do not any where meet a more sublime description than this justly celebrated one of Milton, wherein he gives the portrait of Satan with a dignity suitable to the subject" (61). Eleven more lines from book 1 of the poem follow, from which Burke concludes "Here is a very noble picture; and in what does this poetical picture consist? In images of a tower, an archangel, the sun rising through mists, or in an eclipse, the ruin of monarchs, and the revolutions of kingdoms. The mind is hurried out of itself, by a crowd of great and confused images" (62). In readings such as these, Burke's Milton is the cynosure of art itself; it incorporates the entire system of affect imagined by earlier theorists for nature and painting. One's mind is hurried out of itself when reading *Paradise Lost* because the poem is a better painting, a "poetical picture" brushed with obscure "strokes and colourings." What would negate this aesthetic affect is the limpid pleasure of "Knowledge and acquaintance" (61). The pre-aesthetic domain of history writing or philosophy thus becomes the social grace of the beautiful and turns back on painting as its inherent flaw.

The preference of poetry over painting in Burke's model suggests a shift in aesthetic discourse from a visual to a textual understanding of affect, or rather the absorption in the discussion of textuality of terms first developed to describe visual objects. In this sense, Burke may be said to adapt aesthetics to print culture, rendering the eighteenth century's dominant cultural form the paradigm and matrix of artistic experience. Yet Burke's rejection of painting as the foundation of the sublime is not founded on print's more universal accessibility. Rather the opposite is manifestly the case. It is the abiding clarity and accessibility of painting that marks its inferiority to poetry. And it is the abiding obscurity and difficulty of good poetry that marks it a source of the sublime. This distinction is crucial for critics who adopt the Burkean understanding of the sublime to distinguish among cultural goods. For many such writers, the novel and other written forms of mass culture, as it were, take over from painting to oppose themselves to the sublimity of poetry. The pre-aesthetic clarity of painting turns into the novel's emphasis on quotidian experience.

The move from an aesthetic of accessibility to an aesthetic of difficulty is thus connected to other developments during the mid-century. As a positive quality of aesthetic distance, "obscurity" intersects with what we shall see as the antithetical historicist position concerning the distance of older cultural products. Likewise Burke's emphasis on "difficulty" (section XII) coincides with emergent philological and critical notions of literary language. Burkean aesthetics and historicist criticism together posit a break in the cultural continuum, between the obscure and the clear, the old and the new, the poetic and the prosaic, the high and the low. It is from this perspective, therefore, that we may understand the conditions of Burke's social discrimination and gendering of high culture and mass culture. While Burke prefers sublime to modern forms, he also complicates Hume's grafting of cultural onto social hierarchy. The former's alignment of obscurity and difficulty with older cultural products includes popular ballads and tales. Obscurity attracts and moves the common or excites their taste: "the common sort of people" are moved by "the ballads of Chevy-Chase, or the children in the wood, and by other little popular poems and tales that are current in that rank of life" (61). The idea that sublime obscurity dwells in folk culture hints at the high-cultural appropriation of antique common forms, a move that is picked up by Richard Hurd, as we shall see, and canonized in such anthologies as Percy's *Reliques of Ancient English Poetry* (1765). Burke's tendency to aestheticize a mythic popular culture is held back, however, by his simultaneous tendency to discriminate among levels of obscure forms and their respective values. A taste for "poetry with all its obscurity" runs across what is ultimately a hierarchy of genres and authors, from Milton down to the "vulgar" where "the best sorts of poetry, are not understood" (61). A similar complication obtains in Burke's gendering of the aesthetic. His version of the sublime and the beautiful has been understood traditionally to rest on a prior distinction between the "masculine" and the "feminine," solitude and society.[31] I am less interested in this truism, however, than in the way in which Burke's understanding of Milton's sublimity, as a rethinking of the English literary past, revises Addison's notion of Milton's "manly beauties." For Addison, Milton's beauties were instrumental to composing a polite and sociable masculinity, in contrast to the vulgar gothicism of Donne or Chaucer. Like Cooper, Burke reimagines what was earlier a class community as now one of gender, but only in order for that community to be overturned in favor of a tenacious solitude. For Burke, Milton's sublimity decomposes the mass culture of effeminate taste. Milton is reinvented within a larger system of cultural antitheses: the masculine, "noble," and poetic, on the one hand, and the feminine, middling, and novelistic, on the other.

The *Enquiry* is, in this sense, preeminently concerned with ranking literary texts and discriminating among their readers. For this reason, perhaps, Burke saw fit two years after its publication to add a new "introduction on taste" as a response to Hume's essay. Burke's central distinction from Hume is his opposition to the latter's inaugural claim that the world contains a "great variety of taste" and conclusion that, therefore, genuine taste is both rare and a marker of social distinction. Burke argues, rather, that considered philosophically, that is, within the totality of human faculties, taste is consistent, fixed, and ubiquitous. The "standard both of reason and Taste is the same in all human creatures"; it follows "invariable and certain laws" (Burke, *Enquiry,* 11). Burke is concerned, as is Hume, with the unhinging cultural effects of social change, and likewise attempts to redefine and rescue taste: "my point in this enquiry is to find whether there are any principles, on which the imagination is affected, so common to all, so grounded and certain, as to supply the means of reasoning satisfactorily about them. And such principles of Taste, I fancy there are; however paradoxical it may seem to those who on a superficial view imagine, that there is so great a diversity of Tastes both in kind and degree, that nothing can be more indeterminate" (13). Whereas Hume sees taste, properly defined, as the possession of a small minority, Burke makes the counterintuitive claim that differences in preferences and habits still bespeak an identity of taste. This point is managed through an inductive reasoning up and out of "the pleasures and the pains which every object excites in . . . mankind" (13). It is only "on a superficial view" that Hume's prognosis would obtain, because seen empirically the "diversity of Tastes" resolve themselves into so many versions of the same. Tastes differ in degree not kind. The reader of Bunyan has the same kind of taste as the reader of Virgil, but less of it. This seemingly minor distinction allows Burke to define taste against Hume in relatively inclusive terms: "the pleasure of all the senses, of the sight, and even of the Taste, that most ambiguous of the senses, is the same in all, high and low, learned and unlearned" (16); "So far as Taste is natural, it is nearly common to all" (20). As Frances Ferguson has noted, this statement posits an aporia in which "Burke is constructing a version of scientific empiricism which violates its own basic tenets, because contradictory evidence, indeed, all evidence, is taken always to point toward the existence of common, universal faculty of taste . . . [thus] invalidating empirical evidence and turning conflicts about taste into mere linguistic quibbles."[32] I would suggest that what Ferguson notes as aporetic in Burke can be understood, in historical rather than philosophical-rhetorical terms, as the contradictory labor of constituting an abstract and anthropological model of taste that, in the end, coincides with Hume's attempt to recast taste on normative cultural coordinates. The "invalidation" of cultural contest and "turning conflicts" into "mere linguistic quibbles" are the means by which the "diversity of tastes" confirm a graduated cultural and social taxonomy: Virgil and Milton for the "high" and "learned," Don Bellianis and Bunyan for the "low" and "unlearned." The sublime and the beautiful represent aesthetic qualities admired by a reader who has cultivated taste, taste that in its own substance, however, is indistinct from that of the reader who lacks cultivation and reads poorly.

The sublime that so characterizes Milton's powerful triumph over visual art and, as we shall see, Shakespeare and Spenser's awesome difference from modern writing was one of the eighteenth century's more notable symbolic products and attests to the importance of its sense of cultural transformation. Neither the problem of taste, nor that of the sublime to which it is so closely allied, concluded with Burke. Before closing his two-volume, thousand page long aesthetic treatise, *Elements of Criticism* (1762), for example, Henry Home, Lord Kames found it necessary to add a final chapter on the "Standard of Taste." The opening of the chapter, like its title, echoes Hume: " 'That there is no disputing about taste,' . . . is a saying so generally received as to have become a proverb."[33] In aesthetic matters, Kames goes on to suggest, this proverb has led to the mistaken sense among some readers that "every man's taste is to himself an ultimate standard without appeal; and consequently that there is no ground of censure against any one, if such a one there be, who prefers Blackmore before Homer, selfishness before benevolence, or cowardice before magnanimity" (488). The recourse to Blackmore over Homer, as the *reductio ad absurdam* of literary leveling, is certainly revealing of the origins of aesthetic discourse in debates over the ancients and moderns. But the quarrel is immediately updated and nuanced by the problem of aesthetic standards: "is not every man equally a judge of what ought to be agreeable or disagreeable to himself? Doth it not seem whimsical, and perhaps absurd, to assert, that a man *ought not* to be pleased when he is, or that he *ought* to be pleased when he is not?" (488). Once more, taste transforms from the font of consensus to the sign of instability: how do we come up with a philosophical basis for ranking the arts, Kames asks, for

declaring that some are better than others, without seeming exces-
sively authoritarian? As Kames pursues this question, he discovers
that a theory of taste must bridge what it also seeks to keep apart:
the distinct fields of the cultural and the social.

The first answer to the question of taste's standard turns on a
revised understanding of literature's order. The relativist proverb,
Kames suggests, contains a degree of truth: *within* the various
cultural ranks one is free to follow whim and fancy, while *between* the
levels of the cultural field one is prevented from crossing. In other
words, one may be free to choose, say, Ovid over Virgil but not
Blackmore over Homer.

We are only sensible of the grosser divisions, comprehending each of the
various pleasures equally affecting; to these the proverb is applicable in the
strictest sense; for with respect to pleasures of the same rank, what ground
can there be for preferring one before another? If a preference in fact is
given by any individual, it cannot proceed from taste, but from custom,
imitation, or some peculiarity of mind. (489)

Kames's opening gambit is, in a certain sense, a sophistication of
Burke's point about the universality of taste: every one has "taste"
and taste naturally conforms to a standard; all disagreement or
discord can be resolved as matters of custom. Kames appropriates the
subjectivist proverb literally to "naturalize" the "grosser division"
between high-cultural and mass-cultural texts. If we all agree that
Homer is better than Blackmore, then we all have the same taste, and
then taste is natural: "for what is universal, must have a foundation in
nature," and – here the project of Kames's chapter – "if we can reach
that foundation, the standard of taste will no longer be a secret."
(490). But on cultural grounds alone this search is fatally tautological,
presupposing a taste that is so "obvious" that no one would dispute its
standard, leaving it impossible to surmise, for instance, the popularity
of such writers as Blackmore. Where does the "obviousness" of the
standard of taste find its reflection and analogue?

Having tentatively established a cultural hierarchy, an order of
literary texts, Kames turns to its allegedly more concrete image in
the social world. Where writers like Cooper looked to art as a
harmonizing support to a fragmented society Kames invokes social
stratification as the mirror of culture's standard.

Nature, in her scale of pleasures, has been sparing of divisions: she hath
wisely and benevolently filled every division with many pleasures; in order

that individuals may be contented with their own lot, without envying that of others. Many hands must be employed to procure us the conveniences of life; and it is necessary that the different branches of business, whether more or less agreeable, be filled with hands: a taste too refined would obstruct that plan; for it would crowd some employments, leaving others, no less useful, totally neglected. In our present condition, lucky it is that the plurality are not delicate in their choice, but fall in readily with the occupations, pleasures, food and company, that fortune throws in their way; and if at first there be any displeasing circumstance, custom soon makes it easy. (490)

The evident reality of social division stabilizes the murkier and more puzzling reality of cultural division. The "reasoning" here is both analogical – the "ranks" of art are as much a matter of necessity as the ranks of social labor – and causal; a provident nature engenders the peculiar pleasure we call "taste" out of the infinitely ramified social structure. No one would suggest that the "grosser division" between the plebeians and patricians is spurious; after all, someone has to do the manual labor. And the same natural division among classes explains the natural division among tastes: a delicate taste is the inevitable consequence of a delicate employment, and vice versa. In this formulation, the standard of taste is doubly supported by the standard of labor; it both mirrors and is produced by society.

But as soon as cultural standards achieve a stabilizing ballast from the obvious and necessary division of labor, the very instability of taste seems, as it were, to infect the image of social consonance. Class society is itself discordant and needs the harmonizing influence of the aesthetic:

The separation of men into different classes, by birth, office, or occupation, however necessary, tends to relax the connection that ought to be among members of the same state; which bad effect is in some measure prevented by the access all ranks of people have to public spectacles, and to amusements that are best enjoyed in company. Such meetings, where every one partakes of the same pleasures in common, are no slight support to the social affections. (496)

The very social division that had shorn up aesthetic division is here held together by the aesthetic. Taste acts as a kind of social solvent. Yet not quite in the same manner as Addison. For Kames, the public sphere amounts to a partial and "supporting" edifice to society, a means of overcoming the "relaxing," "bad effects" of class structure. Yet the emphasis on social deportment and publicity, in this passage, also moves the discussion away from Hume's critical aristocracy. The aesthetic is less cultural capital than a social balm, less what one class wields over another than what holds together a fractured society. To a society whose divisions are disaffecting, Kames prescribes aesthetic publicity. To an aesthetic whose standard is partial and authoritarian, Kames prescribes social division. It is the dialectical vocation of taste to draw out of this contradiction a viable standard.

The search for taste's standard thus begins and ends with the wisdom that the category has a reciprocal dependence on two spheres in evident crisis. Having turned from the cultural to the social and then back again, Kames quickly delineates the standard with summary clarity: "Thus, upon a conviction common to the species is erected a standard of taste, which without hesitation is applied to the taste of every individual . . . We have the same standard for ascertaining in all the fine arts, what is beautiful or ugly, high or low, proper or improper, proportioned or disproportioned: and here, as in morals, we justly condemn every taste that deviates from what is thus ascertained by the common standard" (496). Having discovered the philosophical basis for the standard of taste in the reflexive harmonizing of culture and society, the next question is how are we to know what the standard is, who speaks for the "common nature," "what is truly the standard of nature, that we may not lie open to have a false standard imposed on us . . . what means shall be employed for bringing to light this natural standard?" (497). We must rely, Kames answers, on human judgment: "However languid and cloudy the common sense of mankind may be as to the fine arts, it is notwithstanding the only standard in these as well as in morals" (499). Since the answer lies in humanity, and not in the formal properties or dimensions of objects, one returns to the question of social division. Kames here re-introduces the fact of class, about which he may now be said to entertain a suggestively obsessive degree of concern. In selecting the standard bearers, one must discount the "votes" of the working classes: "Those who depend for food on bodily labour, are totally void of taste; of such a taste at least as can be of use into the fine arts. This consideration bars the greater part of mankind" (499). The common turns out to be a rather thin layer of the populace; yet it is not just the laboring classes that are excluded: "and of the remaining part, many by a corrupted taste are unqualified for voting. *The common sense of mankind must be confined to the few that fall not under these exceptions"* (499–500). In a dramatic reversal of the Shaftesburian tradition, Kames places the aristocracy among the unqualified:

Let us next bring under trial, the opulent who delight in expense: the appetite for superiority and respect, inflamed by riches, is vented upon costly furniture, numerous attendants, a princely dwelling, sumptuous feasts, every thing superb and gorgeous, to amaze and humble all beholders: simplicity, elegance, propriety, and things natural, sweet, or amiable, are despised or neglected: for these are not appropriated to the rich, nor make a figure in the public eye: in a word, nothing is relished, but what serves to gratify pride, by an imaginary exaltation of the possessor above those who surround him. Such sentiments contract the heart, and make every principle give way to self-love: benevolence and public spirit, with all their refined emotions, are little felt, and less regarded: and if these be excluded, there can be no place for the faint and delicate emotions of the fine arts. (500–501)

This casting out of the opulent and great from art's domain represents one aspect of taste's dialectic: the emollient of society's wounds, the "support for social affections." That the self-love and greed of the aristocracy results in an ultimately *aesthetic* failure (their inability to feel the "emotions of the fine arts") demonstrates how the cultural field intervenes in society. The division of labor is less the precondition of the order of culture than the image of aesthetic displeasure.

Yet Kames's concept of the aesthetic is dual and holds that taste is as much a reflection of a prior social structure as it is the dissolution of that structure. He thus traces the standard of taste to its origin in a specific class:

The exclusion of classes so many and numerous, reduces within a narrow compass those who are qualified to be judges in the fine arts. Many circumstances are necessary to form such a judge: There must be a good natural taste; that is, a taste approaching, at least in some degree, to the delicacy of taste above described: that taste must be improved by education, reflection, and experience: it must be preserved in vigour by living regularly, by using the goods of fortune with moderation and by following the dictates of improved nature, which give welcome to every rational pleasure without indulging any excess. This is the tenor of life which of all contributes the most to refinement of taste. (502)

It is a commonplace of the history of aesthetics – as a microcosm of modernity writ large – that it is something like the *Weltanschauung* of the rising middle classes, that, in a recent formulation, "the category of the aesthetic assumes the importance it does in modern Europe because in speaking of art it speaks of other matters too, which are at the heart of the middle classes' struggle for political hegemony."[34] Kames's concluding description of the class to whom the "standard of taste" belongs, with its serial invocation of educated moderation, disciplined rationality, and regulated pleasure, certainly tempts such a commonplace reading. Kames finds the middle classes to be the harbingers of taste's standard; at the same time, he finds that taste reciprocally negates the opulence of the great, the vulgarity of laborers, and the dissonance of division. Yet the standard of taste turns as much on exclusion and antithesis as on consumption, politeness, or sociability. A model of affect is exchanged for one of work. The aesthetic is not the reflection of consumer society, then, but of its dialectical twin, that secularized calling we term labor. At the very point at which Kames concludes his long treatise with the uniting of social and artistic harmony in a "standard of taste" he also reveals a new instability at the center of the aesthetic. With Kames, aesthetic discourse separates out a category of high-cultural goods founded on a "middle class" assumption of profitable ascesis.

Beautiful harmony gives way to sublime obscurity only to have the latter reintroduce the problem of labor, the very problem, in the end, of social division that it had set out to resolve. Kames's final appeal to the tenacious fortitude of a middle class audience succumbs to a peculiar fatality; judgment is grounded in a "tenor of life" that also confounds the project of judgment. Or, to put it another way, by Kames's moment, aesthetic discourse learns to turn the problem of sociality into its own solution. The court of appeal is the very condition of loss and negativity that prompts its own aesthetic rationale. This is less aesthetic discourse turning full circle, however, than an attempt to imagine modes of cultural apperception more lithesome than neo-aristocratic disinterest. But the full meaning of this transformation may only be clarified by turning to aesthetics' major antagonist in the field of criticism during these years, a method which from its beginning joined cultural valuation to readerly ascesis.

## ALWAYS HISTORICIZE!

The Weber quote in the epigraph to this chapter concluded on a curious notion: that the emergence of aesthetics is simultaneous to that of "an intellectualist civilization." I shall now argue that the idea of the aesthetic and the idea of intellectual labor during the eighteenth century were both tied together and opposed.[35] Over the course of the century certain critics challenged the dominance of aesthetic modes of reading by focusing on the textual and cultural specificity of high-cultural authors. Reading older texts, they claimed, required training and knowledge beyond the leisurely habits of the "young nobility and gentry." Historicist criticism during the period was developed first in Greco-Latin philology and Biblical commentary (the two crucial figures being respectively Richard Bentley and Bishop Lowth); it was then adapted, in the midcentury, to English texts. Literary historicism in the eighteenth century consisted of a diverse number of practices that together emphasized distance of the past and the insuperable break between it and the present. Many of these practices were developed in material relation to the text: editing or elucidating in a way that focused on cultural, linguistic, and textual distance and difference – the otherness of references, diction, or meter, difficulties of trans-mission, the absence of regularized printing techniques and so forth. In opposition to critics who saw the cultural present in broad continuity and conformity with the cultural past, historicist critics insisted that older texts were in some fundamental sense severed from their modern reader.[36]

Historicist modes of textual studies first gained critical prominence during the late seventeenth century's "battle of the books." As Joseph Levine has recently described, much of the quarrel between the ancients and moderns obtained over particular methods of reading and editing.[37] The moderns (who here include not only William Wotton, but more importantly Richard Bentley and then later Lewis Theobald) aimed to scientize older methods of humanist exegesis and so crystallized a new method of textual reading involving the twin interpretive modes of *philology* (tracing the meaning of words, passages, and phrases through cross referencing within the text, the author's oeuvre, or period production at large) and *antiquities* (contextualization with reference to the extra-textual culture of coins, busts, frescos). This method sought to make the classics a field of scholarly endeavor by situating them within a determinate time and place. Understanding the classics demanded a particular and laborious knowledge. The historicist editor collected all extant copies, emended corruptions, glossed obscure words and

phrases, and described metrical patterns and variations. Emenda-
tions were usually justified in footnotes, and thus placed side by side
with readings from the different variants, glosses, cross references,
vituperative swipes at other editors and the like. Hence the growing
prominence of annotation. The most controversial of these practices
was Bentley's notorious "conjectural emendation," which, in the
absence of manuscripts and autographs, attempted to divine through
collation and comparison what the "original" might have said.[38]

The Bentleyan method engendered a number of important con-
troversies. In the turn of the century debate over the authenticity of
Phalaris's *Epistles*, for example, Bentley's philology pitted itself
against the classicizing aesthetics of Sir William Temple and his
defenders Swift, Francis Atterbury, and Charles Boyle. This debate is
germane for our current purposes because both its terms ("pedantry" vs. "ignorance") and methods (modernization vs. philology)
reappeared later in the century during the discussion of English
texts. While the moderns employed their editorial practice to prove
the *Epistles* a sophist forgery, the ancients insisted the *Epistles* fit the
standards of taste and decorum.[39] The debate soon replayed itself in
much the same fashion over Pope's Homer. There the issue was less
one of authenticity than scholarly inattention and historical insensi-
tivity. Bentley and others charged that Pope's modernization of
meter, tone, and content showed his ignorance of classical culture
and language. The Bentleyan method crafted both a method and,
from the empyrean height of Trinity College, its community of
academic specialists. The ancients responded by deriding what they
saw as an assault on classical culture, and, what is equally important,
as a pedantic and parochial scholasticism. From their perspective,
classical texts belonged to the lay public as much as to the academy.
From the Bentleyan position, by contrast, the ancients read through
the distorting lens of modern taste and refinement. In terms that
would ironically return to describe Bentley's work later in his career,
the moderns found the ancients to be anachronistic. The charge of
anachronism grew out of a relatively novel understanding of literary
history. Arising from a new sense of the period location of classical
texts, the accusation seemed alien to aestheticist ancients, for whom
Homer or Horace transcended the ruck of the historical.

The moderns pointed to the distance of antiquity largely by
returning, over and again, to the difficulty of classical languages.
Consider Bentley's point-by-point rejoinder to Charles Boyle in the

revised edition of the *Dissertation Upon the Epistles of Phalaris* (1699). Phalaris's diction, idiom, and meter betrayed the *Epistles* a forgery from a later age and betrayed their advocates as poor readers. Here is Bentley, discussing Hellenic meter, pausing to note his enemies' linguistic ignorance:

A man that does not only *cast an eye on* but thoroughly reads, the books that he pretends to discourse of, would have been able to bring several seeming examples, where an anapaestic is terminated with a trochee, or a tribachys, or a cretic. This I was aware of, when I published my observation: and yet I entered no caution about it to the reader, but left the thing entirely to his own judgment and sagacity; supposing that, if he took notice of any such exceptions, he would be able of himself to give an account of them. But now, because this observation of mine has been openly assaulted, and lest any body should think, that not its own truth and solidity, but the weakness of the assailant, may be the reason of its holding out; I will here produce every single exception that I can meet with in the three Greek tragedians, and Aristophanes, and Seneca; and shew they are all errors only, and mistakes of the copiers. And the very facility and naturalness of every correction will be next to a demonstration to an ingenious mind, that the observation must needs be true.[40]

Like other matters of linguistic substance, anapestic meter and its variations are part of what constitutes the historical horizon or age of certain classical texts. Periodizing the classics divides inattentive, leisurely reading from the expert rigor of the academy. Expertise proves itself in method: separating out errors of copiers and printers; pointing out corrections; displaying exemplary and parallel texts.

There are a number of ways of understanding these practices and debates in the context we have been tracing. For one, the Bentleyan method was impelled by the early eighteenth century's sense of print regularity.[41] A self-consciously modern ideal of print changed the criteria of textual validity in such a way that previous texts were seen to be obscure, unreliable, and in need of scholarly administration. The vocation of the textual critic turned to providing a regular and error free version of the past. (Indeed, the idea of the manuscript, the autograph, and the original, so crucial to Shakespeare criticism in particular, became more important over the century as critics and editors jostled among themselves for the most accurate edition.) At the same time, the stabilization of typeface allowed, and was often conflated with, the elaborate apparatus of footnotes. In Swift's *Battle of the Books* (1704) and later more markedly in Pope's *Dunciad* (1728, 1743), for example, obtrusive annotation was taken as a sign of the "darkness" wrought by the peculiar combination of Grub Street commerce and pedantic scholarship. According to Pope and the Scriblerians, the Bentleyan text was a threat to classical culture in two ways. By one measure, it is steeped in the emergent market of books. Philology is merely a cover for bookselling and modernity, for the opening of culture to the vulgar. By another measure, the Bentleyan text obscures the public nature of the classics. The "pedantry" of annotation bespeaks the parochial vocation of scholars, one that falls far short of polite conversation and genteel disinterest.

In their hostility to scholarship, the Scriblerians were by no means alone.[42] Literary criticism throughout the eighteenth century was haunted by the figure of the pedant. In a typical example, Felton's *Dissertation on Reading the Classics and Forming a Just Style* (1718) argues that "The present age seemeth to be born for carrying criticism to its highest pitch and perfection" because "many ingenious hands have concurred to rescue it from pedantry, dulness, and ill-nature" (xiv). Even in the enlightened age that has emerged out from under the darkness of scholasticism, the "dangers of pedantry," the "faults of pedants and sententious writers! that are vainly ostentatious about their learning," still obtrude on polite reading (78). The making of polite critics involves a never-ending struggle against the enigmatic and baleful temptation of pedantry. Criticism "is no longer a dry, sour, verbal study, but claimeth a place among the politest parts of learning";

a critic should lift up his head with an easy, cheerful air, and not be distinguished, as the tribe hath generally been, by the wrinkles on his brows, but as men of candor and ingenuity ought to be, by the good-nature, freedom and openness of his countenance. Critics are apt to talk in a supercilious, magisterial way, to obtrude their sentiments on the world, and maintain every singular opinion with stiffness and ill manners. But if they would soften the rigor of their pen, and offer their notions in a modest affable address, their civility and complaisance would take off those prejudices, with which pride and positiveness are generally entertained. (xiv)

Criticism is here the work of a graceful stratum of readers whose relation to society is unequivocally positive. Yet the very emphasis on critical grace and ease, its fulsome overcoming of past ages of scholasticism and dulness, exhibits the refusal of pedantry and philology to die a quiet death, or rather the way in which the ideal of refinement continuously reinvented the specter of the pedant as part of its evolving constitution.

Why such hostility to philology? The answer, I think, lies in the institutional location of historicist practice and the cultural meaning of historicist method: the clergy and the academy were bereft of the open and worldly language of the periodical and the salon. The idea of a clerical-academic enemy was marshaled to the formation of a public culture of novel latitude. The anti-intellectual charges of pedantry, obscurantism, bookishness, and the like served to outline a contrasting domain of rational and general conversation. Consider Addison's description of the musty textualist "Tom Folio" in *Tatler* no. 158 (1710). Addison describes Folio as "a broker in learning," a "learned idiot," and of course, a "pedant."[43]

He is an universal scholar, so far as the title-page of all authors, knows the manuscripts in which they were discover'd, the editions through which they have passed, with the praises or censures which they have receiv'd from the several members of the learned world. He has a greater esteem for Adus and Elzevir, than for Virgil and Horace. If you talk of Herodotus, he breaks out into a Panegyrick upon Harry Staephans. He thinks he gives you an account of an author, when he tells you the subject he treats of, the name of the editor, and the year in which it was printed. Or if you draw him into further particulars, he cries up the goodness of the paper, extols the diligence of the corrector, and is transported with the beauty of the letter. This he looks upon to be sound learning and substantial criticism. As for those who talk of the fineness of style, and the justness of thought, or describe the brightness of any particular passages; nay, though they write themselves in the genius and spirits of the author they admire, Tom looks upon them as men of superficial learning and flashy parts. (384–385)

The same critic who will shortly become the celebrant of print in the *Spectator* here abuses historicist critics for their overweening interest in the condition of books and the printed page. The particular or vocational interest of "editors, commentators, interpreters, scholiasts, and criticks . . . in short all men of deep learning without commonsense" offsets Addison's disinterested interest in matters of aesthetic judgment: "fineness of style" and "justness of thought" (386). As for the editors and scholiasts, Addison closes, "their works sufficiently show they have no *taste* of their authors" (387). On this account, Addison's ambition to bring "philosophy out of the closet and libraries, schools and colleges" is negatively bound to the project of emergent historicism. While the position of the scholar within literary culture becomes more specified during the midcentury, the specter of the pedant also resides at the origin of the public sphere, as nothing less than its negation.[44] The authority of disinterested learning positions itself against the pretension of inter-ested philology.

The attempt to disentangle criticism from pedantry survived even the skeptical rethinking of the politeness from which it was born. We saw in the last chapter that John Oldmixon was weary of Addison's version of polite language. He was at greater pains to distinguish his idea of the critic from the laborious antiquary:

antiquaries . . . have no fund of their own, they must therefore borrow from those that have. It is necessary that there should be such men, but the dryness and barrenness of their studies are inconsistent with a lively fancy and a good taste; and I know not which of the antiquaries deserve to be rever'd by us, those that would restore lost words, letters and points, or those that would recover lost fable or history. To know exactly where *Brute* built his *Palace Royal*, where *Bladud* set up his *Laboratory* would be something; as also to prove, that *Cassibelan* lived where my *Lord Essex* now does at *Cashionbury*; or that *Constantine the Great* was a *Yorkshire* man; which Things have been attempted, would be as much to the glory of the students of antiquity, as to find out a lost *Comma*, or restore a letter to a word that was robb'd of it 1500 years ago. But as for our monkish antiquaries, and the monastic learning, it seems to be reserv'd for the improvement of those whose minds, like barren soils, will never bear without dunging. (Oldmixon, *Essay*: 78)

The effort of statements like these is to represent the antiquarian work of historicists as itself antiquated, as a dirty remnant of a now vanquished restricted culture. Historicists desire to be like their priestly ancestors but, in this age of general knowledge and polite-ness, come across as pedants. The scouring of culture by the open discourse of the public paints restricted knowledge as soiled; the head of the latter-day scholar is made of dung. What was once the seat of learning, of abstract knowledge split from the labor of the body, is now rematerialized in excrement *and* in labor. Philological expertise is, in the end, simply too particularizing and difficult; it is a knowledge so cut off from society as to turn into ignorance:

But since their writings prove nothing but their ignorance and superstition, I believe men of taste and genius will be so generous as to leave such hidden treasures to enrich those, whose invention and judgment lie under the calamity of the most extreme poverty. There is nothing but labour and patience requisite to acquire a mastery in these studies, whether the matter collected be good or bad, 'tis the same thing if it be old, if it be *Teutonic* or

*Runick*, *Danish* or *Saxon*, that's sufficient. A man who has any warmth in his imagination, and any delicacy in his taste, cannot be always raking in the rubbish of barbarous ages, and groping in *Gothic* darkness. (78)

Philology is as "gothic" as the very past to which it is indissolubly linked. Its fate is thus tied to the strange career of the gothic as it makes its way from a term of abuse for older English culture to the name of the latter's sublimity and value. Scholarly reading blocks the communicative rationality of the coffee-house. Later, this gothic blockage takes on the value of national antiquity.

The historicist project crystallized in the 1750s and 1760s out of preceding decades of critical debate. The central texts of this project are the subjects of later chapters. I would like to discuss now two important studies that led into the scholarly constitution of the canon: Lewis Theobald's 1733 edition of Shakespeare's *Works* and John Upton's *Critical Observations on Shakespeare* (1746, 1748).[45] Theobald and Upton were both classical editors by training; Theobald was responsible for a collection of Greek drama, Upton for Arrian's *Epictetus*. When they turned to Shakespeare, therefore, so began the full scale treatment of English texts as classics. Shakespeare both needed and was deserving of the apparatus one gives to antiquity. Theobald and Upton's only antecedent in the application of classical hermeneutics onto English texts was Bentley's 1732 edition of *Paradise Lost*. Bentley's Milton is most interesting, however, in its dramatic failure to inaugurate historical, textual studies to English literature, and its parallel exposure of just how close historicist and aestheticist assumptions about high culture could be. In the notorious edition, the process of "emendation" extended until it seemingly capsized under its own weight, correcting to a point where the claims no longer appeared to be historical, but rather, from the eyes of Pope no less than Bentley's disciple Theobald, to be anachronistic and capricious.[46] After the controversy surrounding his *Paradise Lost*, Bentley's name became associated as much with obtrusive modernization as pedantic scholarship. His fate shows pedantry converting to anachronism by the sheer weight of its insistent application. Method transforms into its opposite; but the important point is that from either side of this peculiar unity Milton was the cherished artifact of English antiquity.[47]

Out of the ashes of Bentley's Milton emerged the revisionary historicism of Lewis Theobald.[48] Theobald, of course, achieved lasting notoriety himself as Pope's first choice to lead the Dunces in the *Dunciad*. Pope's nomination, though, has more to it than simple animosity toward Theobald's excoriation of his edition of Shakespeare in *Shakespeare Restored* (1727). In that study, Theobald attacked what he saw as Pope's anachronistic modernization of Shakespeare's texts and delivered a point by point exposure of editorial blunders. In the 1733 *Works*, he attempted to correct the course of Pope's edition by employing classical hermeneutics, which would be, he insisted, the first time that such methods were applied to English texts: "Shakespeare's case has in a great measure resembled that of a corrupt classick," Theobald writes in the preface, "and, consequently, the method of cure was likewise to bear a resemblance"; "to that end I have ventured on a labour, that is the first of the kind on any modern author whatsoever."[49] Theobald's method gives the scholarly apparatus and authority to Shakespeare that had previously adhered to "ancient writers" (71). He distinguishes his method from both Pope's Shakespeare and Bentley's Milton. Pope and Bentley exhibit different versions of the same problem: inattention to the historical and textual specificity of the author. The harshest words are for "Mr. Pope" who "pretended to have collated the old copies, and yet seldom has corrected the text but to his injury"; Pope "has frequently inflicted a wound where he intended a cure," Theobald continues, and "has attacked him like an unhandy slaughterman; and not lopped off the errors, but the poet" (68–69). Pope's violent mishandling of the text derives from his ignorance, for "he who tampers with an author, whom he does not understand, must do it at the expense of his subject" (68). Theobald does not spare his mentor Bentley either; Bentley intends "to correct and pare off the excrescencies of the 'Paradise Lost' . . . to show the world, that, if Milton did not write as he would have him, he ought to have wrote so" (72). Pope and Bentley's editorial errors coincide in their inattention to period specificity: the foisting of contemporary words or syntax into the text and the evaluation of plays according to present standards of taste and decorum.

In contrast to Pope and Bentley, Theobald intends to recover the "original purity" of the absent but "genuine text" (72). His method amounts to a return to Bentleyan classicism shorn of the "conjectural emendation" that marked the apparent "excesses" of the latter's *Paradise Lost*. Notwithstanding Theobald's uneven reputation over the century, the method had remarkable endurance from

William Warburton through Johnson up to Edmund Malone: "The science of criticism, as far as it affects an editor, seems to be reduced to these three classes; the emendation of corrupt passages; the explanation of obscure and difficult ones; and an enquiry into the beauties and defects of composition" (73).[50] The editor has a kind of practical and technical skill exclusive to him, particularly "the two former parts" of the formula which rely less on general aesthetic judgment than on "diligent and laborious collation." The third, aesthetic function "lies open for every willing undertaker" (73). The division of labor here is remarkably proleptic: criticism splits from its unity with polite reading; the critic as a reader with taste parts from the editor as a scholar-technician; the English literary past becomes historically distinct and distant from the present.

For all of its precocity, Theobald's project has difficulty combining the classical and the scholarly. The edition is split between an intellectual and public understanding of its audience, in a manner, moreover, that we may understand as importantly transitional. Shakespeare is a "corrupt classick" and once his texts regain their "purity" he will achieve the classical status of a Homer. The "editor's labour" is undertaken "with the hopes of restoring to the publick their greatest poet" (73, 72). At the same time, the attempt to rescue Shakespeare from "a condition that was a disgrace to common sense" and to assert the "science" of the editor between the "publick" and "their greatest poet" asserts Theobald's professional expertise. For editors after Theobald, this project proceeded under the assumption that the composition and taste of the public could no longer assume tacit authority. For Theobald, however, the "publick" still retained enough authority to dictate taste and method.

The peculiarly transitional situation of Theobald's Shakespeare can be detected in its prevalence of aesthetic categories. Theobald begins by likening Shakespeare to "a large, a spacious, and a splendid dome" where one sees "a thousand beauties of genius and character"; he continues that the "prospect is too wide to come within the compass of a single view; it is a gay confusion of pleasing objects, too various to be enjoyed but in a general admiration" (51). Shakespeare exhibits here, respectively, the beautiful, the sublime, and the picturesque. Theobald draws on metaphors taken whole cloth from the discourse of aesthetics to authorize his own project and elevate Shakespeare. While the trajectory of Theobaldian method is to disengage the aesthetic from criticism, and the latter from editing, these binarisms are not as much realized in Theobald's project as retroactively discovered by his followers. This is not to suggest that Theobald's successors were immune to the language of aesthetic discourse – I argue in subsequent chapters that they frequently drew on such language, especially that of the sublime. It is, rather, to note how Theobald's aesthetic categories were at an imbalance with his editorial categories, that the two had yet to come together through the suturing of sublimity, antiquity, and obscurity one finds in, say, Thomas Warton. Discussing the broad goals of his edition, for instance, Theobald writes that "to point out and exclaim upon all the beauties of Shakespeare, as they come singly in review, would be as insipid, as endless; as tedious, as unnecessary" as trying to imitate them; but, he continues, "the explanations of those beauties that are less obvious to common readers, and whose illustration depends on the rules of just criticism, and on exact knowledge of human life, should deservedly have a share in a general critique upon the author" (64). The persistence of aesthetic discourse has the negative function of describing the editor's vocation (aesthetic judgment largely resides outside of, and so defines, his erudition). Yet the predominance of Shakespeare's "beauties" and Theobald's occasional claim to be a "reader of taste" signals an ambivalent relation to expertise (66).

Theobald's understanding of literary historical distance is similarly fraught. His method aligns cultural consecration with an understanding of Shakespeare's "obscure" periodicity. The "obscurities" wrought by Shakespeare's cultural and linguistic distance from the present are editorial problems and unavoidable components of the reading experience. The job of the editor is to explain the historical context and rehabilitate the text. This drawing of the analogy to the historical rootedness of the classics left Theobald open to the charge of pedantry formed during earlier debates over Greco-Roman culture. Whereas Theobald views Shakespeare's context necessary to understanding his plays, for example, Pope viewed Shakespeare as a genius who managed to overcome his barbaric culture. If context plays a role, in Pope's account, it is to off-set the splendor of Shakespeare's achievement, his proximity to modern politeness, which might be fully achieved once the editor has taken out all of the antique vulgarity: "The Audience was generally composed of the meaner sort of people; and therefore the images of life were to be drawn from those of their own rank"; he "writ to [these] people, and writ at first without patronage from the better sort, and therefore without aims of pleasing them."[51] The low culture of the Elizabethan theater presents a stark antithesis to modern politeness. Social class also explains the occasional difficulty of reading the text, not only the "vulgarity" which Shakespeare was forced to include in order to please the rabble, but also the unreliability of the Folio and Quartos, debased as they were by the mass-reproduction of the printing presses and the influence of lower class actors:[52]

the judgment, as well as condition, of that class of people was then far inferior to what is in our days. As then the best playhouses were inns and taverns (the Globe, the Hope, the Red Bull, the Fortune, etc.) so the top of the profession were then mere players, not Gentlemen of the stage: They were led into the Buttery by the Steward, not plac'd at the Lord's table, or Lady's toilette: and consequently were entirely depriv'd of those advantages they now enjoy, in the familiar conversation of our nobility, and an intimacy (not to say dearness) with people of the first condition. (469)

Pope is here momentarily concerned to mobilize a notion of Shakespeare's context and of historical development, but these are put in the service of constituting the present as an alliance of the "nobility" and "people of the first rank," an alliance defined by a difference from the barbarous past. History is the familiar progress toward refinement. And refinement determines the role of the editor, which is to demote and excise the vulgar moments of the text into footnotes or brackets. In contrast, Theobald's hostility to such modernizing editorial practices reconsiders the antiquity of cultural objects, a knowledge of which he considers to be crucial for understanding the text. Reading is intellectually demanding (hence the charge that Pope "does not understand" Shakespeare). Theobald also finds the distance of Shakespeare from the present to command, in its own right, a sort of value and authority. Words have fallen out of usage; allusions to events, ideas, or texts are lost. "There are obscurities in him which are common to all poets of the same species; there are others, the issue of the times he lived in; and there are others, again, peculiar to himself" (76). Obscurity arises from the simple alterity of the past: "owing their immediate birth to the peculiar genius of each age, an infinite number of things alluded to glanced at, and exposed, must needs become obscure" (76).

While Theobald's *Works* is moved by both intellectual and public, philological and aesthetic concerns, John Upton's *Critical Observations* (1748) is, by its own estimation, manifestly scholarly. Like Theobald and both the Wartons, Upton was a classical scholar who then turned his attention to vernacular texts, to Shakespeare and then Spenser. The central debate motivating Upton and his colleagues in the late 1740s and 1750s was over William Warburton's 1747 edition of Shakespeare. Warburton's edition attempted to expand on Pope's, and was, according to many critics, guilty of the same modernizing and intrusive errors. The most extensive response to Warburton came from Thomas Edwards in *The Canons of Criticism, Being a Supplement to Mr. Warburton's Edition of Shakespeare, Collected from the Notes in that Celebrated Work, and Proper to be Bound Up With It* published in 1748 and revised and expanded seven times over the following seventeen years. Edwards, like Theobald before him, offered a point by point response to Warburton's work, detailing specific instances where, he argued, the editor surreptitiously altered the text or blundered in a note. Upton published the second edition of his *Critical Observations* that same year, with an added preface and comments echoing Edwards. Warburton and Pope, Upton argued, "indulg their over-refining taste, and pay greater compliments to their own guesses, than to the expressions of the author" (173).

Before detailing Upton's objection to "over-refining taste," one might note a certain continuity between the *Critical Observations* and midcentury aesthetics. Consider the commonality of its opening gesture with that of Hume, Kames, and others. Discussing Shakespeare, Upton suggests, is a way to engage skeptically the problem of taste, its validity, provenance, and scope:

Perhaps all attempts, to reduce so irregular an art [as the vague and licentious spirit of criticism] to any regular method, might deserve a place among the many impracticable schemes with which our nation abounds. But yet when I perceived critics so numerous, (for who more or less does not criticize?) and found every one appealing to a standard and a taste, where could be the absurdity of enquiring, whether, or no, there really is in nature any foundation for the thing itself; or whether the whole does not depend on mere whim, caprice, or fashion?[53]

Upton's interest in specifying the foundation of taste proves upon further reading to be nil – or rather, to happen by other means – and this gestural opening but evidence of a shared ground of discourse between two dissimilar theoretical traditions. Still, the peculiar

collision of motifs is testimony that, despite their frequent opposition, aesthetic and historicist approaches to literary texts both
emerged together and shared many concerns.

Upton's tarrying with the problem of taste soon turns into a
mordant indictment of standardization as such. Popean/Warburto-
nian error and modernization, he argues, come from reading the
past through the standard of the present's taste.

> Besides I began to be apprehensive for the fate of some of my most
> favourite English authors; we have few books in our language that merit a
> critical regard; and when by chance any of these have been taken out of the
> hands of mere correctors of printing presses, and esteemed worthy of some
> more learned commentator's care and revisal; the commentator, by I know
> not what kind of fatality, has forgot his province, and the author himself has
> been arbitrarily altered, and reduced to such a fancied plan of perfection,
> as the corrector, within himself, has thought to establish. (v–vi)

The desire to find the origin of taste's standard here gives way to a
censuring of the way in which other critics read Shakespeare.
Upton's persistent term for this mistake is "correction." The
problem with Warburton and his ilk is that they see fit to refurbish
older texts. Upton takes from the aesthetic tradition the notion that
certain texts are especially deserving of critical "merit" (a claim that
is also implicit in his very method of reading), but he also replaces
the pursuit of taste with the program of scholarship.

This recourse to scholarship and to the past is elaborated in a
particular method of reading. Warburton's deficiency is above all
linguistic; he has "gone out of his way to show his readers, how little
he knows of the English, how less of the Latin, how nothing of the
Greek languages" (xlvi). Upton's charge presumes a relatively new
understanding of "English." Warburton's error does not consist in
low diction or poor grammar, but rather in "the want of scholarship" (xlv). To gauge the novelty of this accusation we need only
recall the turn of the century's notion of "English." Upton might
agree with, say, Edmund Bysshe that Shakespeare's language is
sharply distinct from contemporary language but less to celebrate
the politeness of the modern idiom than to enjoin the critic to know
something of linguistic history. Warburton and Upton's criticism
presuppose divergent linguistics: grammatical correctness versus
grammatical history, ease versus difficulty, speech versus writing,
and, ultimately, the present versus the past. Warburton's investment
in the first half of each of the preceding couples marks his fidelity to

Pope and to the tradition of literary "improvement" of which the latter's Shakespeare partook. Upton understands this fidelity to be the sign of negligent reading skills; Warburton has "launched forth on the immense ocean of criticism with no compass or card to direct his little skiff; and tho' perhaps he may blind the eyes of the less-observing reader . . . all this fig leaf covering will be but the more severe to discover the nakedness of the commentator to the discerning eye of the real critic" (xlvi). Here we are given two varieties of readers: true scholars and lax correctors, "discerning eyes" and "less-observing" eyes. Warburton's edition will be, Upton promises, "despised by the real scholar" (xlvii). And it is "real scholars" who form the intended audience for Upton's study. Readers of the *Critical Observations* are, if nothing else, "learned." Now, this particular term was already prevalent in the earlier notion of cultivated politeness, where it was nearly synonymous with breeding and refinement. By the time of the *Critical Observations*, learning amounts to scholarship; it is less the genteel capital of the polite, less a sort of aristocratic connoisseurship, than the expert knowledge of the critic. With Upton, then, we witness a sharp narrowing of the audience for high-cultural texts to the intellectual class of university dons and clerics; "without learning," he dryly notes, Shakespeare "cannot be read with any degree of understanding or taste" (11). The audience of mere correctors undergoes a corresponding shift, expanding to subsume not only the Popes and Warburtons of the world but the wealth of untrained and common readers.

Before examining this peculiar and significant transformation – in which the public sphere of refinement turns into the specter of mass culture – we might examine the specific assumptions and material practices of Upton's method of reading. Although not an edition, *Critical Observations*, like Theobald's *Works*, adapts the method of Bentleyan philology to English classics. Since Shakespeare left no manuscripts or autographs, his texts, like Homer's, need to be reconstructed through collation, through painstaking archival reconstruction of parallel texts and sources. And since Shakespeare's time is not ours, his texts need to be read with a knowledge of history, whether social (the otherness of political allusions, customs, and consciousness), literary (the otherness of textual references, genre, and convention), or linguistic (the otherness of usage, meter, and grammar). By means of this scholarly ascesis, the critic can arrive at the "genuine text"; for "how is his genuine text to be discovered and retrieved? how but by consulting the various copies of authority? by comparing the author with himself?" and by "knowledge in ancient customs and grammar[?]" (ix, 137). Theobald's ambivalent blending of historicism with deference to the public and politeness alike here yields to a confident historicist method announced in limpid prose:

We are to proceed with caution, with doubt and hesitation . . . 'Twere well therefore if a careful and critical reader would first form to himself some plan, when he enters upon an author deserving a stricter inquiry: if he would consider that originals have a manner always peculiar to themselves; and not only a manner, but a language: if he would compare one passage with another; for such authors are the best interpreters of their own meaning: and would reflect, not only what allowances may be given for obsolete modes of speech, but what a venerable cast this alone often gives a writer. I omit the previous knowledge in ancient customs and manners, in grammar and construction; the knowledge of these is presupposed; to be caught tripping here is an ominous stumble at the very threshold and entrance upon criticism; 'tis ignorance, which no guess-work, no divining faculty, however ingenious, can atone and commute for. (135–138)

What is striking in this passage is not just Upton's succinct and methodical deployment of historicist method, but the working up of this method into a near aesthetic in its own right. Scholarship is attentive labor. In order even to think of reading Shakespeare, one must possess all sorts of working knowledge, of language and history, of text and context. As a necessary corollary to this idea of critical labor, the literary text is dramatically shorn from the present: "originals have a manner always peculiar to themselves; and not only a manner, but a language." The philological turn in midcentury criticism is, thus, preeminently *periodizing* in method and influence.

If this model of reading begins to sound literally ascetic, that is because Upton is here bringing in the language of scriptural commentary as well as that of classical philology. In fact, he adopts for literary reading the methodical restraint Bentley had reserved for scriptural reading alone. For Bentley, editing Horace or, eventually, Milton involved frequent emendation. But editing the Bible was a different matter; "The author is very sensible," Bentley writes, "that in the sacred writings there's no place for conjectures or emenda-tions. Diligence and fidelity, with some judgment and experience, are characters here requisite. He declares, therefore, that he does not alter one letter in the text without the authorities subjoined in notes."[54] Upton's adoption of scriptural method embellishes that method's rhetoric. The "careful and critical reader" arrives at the Shakespearean text with tremulous hesitation and modest self-doubt. Clerical/critical readers are trained in eminently Protestant restraint and fortitude. Warburtonian readers, by contrast, bear the taint of a familiar hermeneutical and religious laxity; they demonstrate, according to Upton, how "mystical and allegorical reveries have more amusement in them, than solid truth; and favour but little of cool criticism, where the head is required to be free from fumes and vapours, and rather sceptical than dogmatical" (145). The blending of classical and biblical hermeneutics into a combined historicist program is but one aspect of the overall secularizing motion of midcentury criticism, which both adapts spiritual language to literary texts and also brings in the old anti-Catholic charge against mysticism and allegory to abuse overly aestheticizing and modernizing reading. Upton's reader is much like a cleric approaching a sacred text, a text which – like the Bible – is the best interpreter of its own meaning, is deserving of enquiry, and is endowed with a "venerable cast." If Shakespeare is like Homer, then, he is also like scripture, and again in two different and related manners: the way that he is read and the aura he casts. This is "English literature" as secularization in a double sense: first, as a mode of hermeneutical reading and second as a mode of aesthetic value. What brings them together in Upton and other historicists is the notion of literary critical reading as difficult and demanding, as a kind of work.

The central venue for this work is linguistic. Upton's emphasis on the oldness of Shakespeare's language – the distance of its cadence and rhythms – led him to devote a third of the treatise to analyzing Shakespeare's diction and defending the author's original scansion. This idiomatic and metrical alienation of the text from the language of contemporary readers both rejected the model of refined speech and marked linguistic learning as a key element of scholarly diligence: "The third book . . . as it treats of words and grammatical construction, is very dry, (as 'tis called) and will scarcely be read, but by those, who are willing thoroughly, and not superficially, to understand the diction of our poet. Every rule, there drawn up, is Shakespeare's rule; and tho' visibly, and apparently such to every scholar-like reader, yet there has not been one editor of our poet, but has erred against every one of these rules" (lxi–lxii). Here the accusation of pedantry is a welcome sign of the scholar's success, the rejection by the "mere correctors" an emblem of the critic's learning. At the beginning of the book on "words and grammatical construction," Upton sizes up the opposition: "a piece of idle wit shall laugh all such learning out of doors: and the notion of being thought a dull and pedantic fellow, has made many a man continue a blockhead all his life" (295). The laugh of the anti-pedant only serves to outline the vocation of the scholar. Knowledge of Shakespeare's "grammar and meter" is, in the end, presupposed for any attentive reading of Shakespeare. To read like a scholar is to place a text in its own language world, not to bring it into one's own; reading in this manner, "we shall be less liable to give a loose to fancy, in indulging the licentious spirit of criticism; nor shall we then so much presume to judge what Shakespeare *ought to* have written, as endeavour to discover and retrieve what he *did* write" (296).

The ascetic focus on Shakespeare's grammar means that the proper readership for his works is scholarly and that another type or group of readers is incapable of reading well. These are the correctors and modernizers, readers more interested in the "ought" of politeness than the "did" of historicity. The weight placed on sociability had produced, on Upton's account, a distorted account of literary history and the national canon. Taking account of Pope's errors, he writes,

The misfortune seems to me to be, that scarce anyone pays a regard to what Shakespeare *does* write, but they are always guessing at what he *should* write; nor in any other light is look'd on, than as a poor mechanic; a fellow, 'tis true, of genius, who says, now and then, very good things, but wild and uncultivated; and as one by no means proper company for lords, and ladies, maids of honour, and court pages, 'till some poet or other, who knows the world better, takes him in hand, and introduces him in this modern dress to *good company.* (16)

Rejecting the model of refinement, Upton maintains in this passage that a rational approach to the artifacts of the literary past consists in acknowledging their periodicity. This is the approach, furthermore, of the specialist critic/editor and not that of the dilettante "poet or other" like Pope. The periodizing move of the specialist supervenes a kind of high-cultural aura to literary texts as they fade into English antiquity, valuing older works to the degree to which they are difficult to assimilate into the community of modern readers. The reversal of the modernizing narrative is thus also, like the midcentury sublime, a rejection of sociability, of the remaking of literary texts to suit the designs of readers who would define themselves against the past.

As Upton looks back at the way in which Pope tailored his edition for the public, he registers the social composition of that public, its confinement to "lords, and ladies, maids of honour, and court pages," to the elite classes. Now, one might wish to suggest that Upton either longs for the restriction of that audience or, in contrast, celebrates its democratic overcoming. More to the point, I would argue, is that Upton acknowledges that audience itself has become a problem, that the stately equanimity he imagines for Pope is increasingly difficult to conceive. Upton may have no nostalgia for the refined public of "lords and ladies," but neither does he embrace the newly established public of common readers. Rather, he folds the two into a single condition from which the "real scholar" shrinks. This is a crucial move of later historicist criticism: the public has forgotten how to read older texts. The national canon needs to be secured by a group of specialist critics. As is often the case with social critiques of audience in the eighteenth century, the representa-tion of cultural degradation is provocatively gendered: "How far the corruption of even our public diversions may contribute to the corruption of our manners, may be an inquiry not unworthy the civil magistrate," Upton avers; "matters of these concernments are now left to the management of our women of fashion: and even our poets, whose end is *profit* and *delight,* are exceeding cautious how they incur the censure of these fair umpires and critics" (17). The culture of refinement to which Upton responds is no longer simply Warbur-tonian taste-mongers; rather, it is now a female conspiracy, a public managed by women. The gendering of refinement, in passages such as these, is of a piece with Cooper's later refurbishment of gentle-manly breeding as feminine sensibility; it registers a similar trans-coding of class problems onto those of gender. Where Cooper celebrates the stately conversation of women as the mode of refine-ment for his post-Shaftesburian age, however, Upton finds the management of female readers to be "death and destruction to the little taste remaining among us" (11). If refinement is the re-emergence of Pope's polite audience under the guise of a female stewardship, then, it is also the figure and symptom of diluted culture. Encapsulating the degeneration of the public's reading habits, Upton writes that "it seems no wonder, that the masculine and nervous Shakespeare, and Milton should so little please our effeminate tast. And the more I consider our studies and amusements, the greater is the wonder they should ever please at all" (15). Looking at the past through the lens of gender, Shakespeare and Milton are strikingly embodied, not just manly but nervous, their very distance from modern, mass-cultural products reified in the strength and resiliency of their corporal fibers. But Upton may be understood, as well, to be suggesting "nervous" in the modern sense of anxious: Shakespeare and Milton look to the present and see their eclipse by effeminate, mass culture. The past viewed from the present proleptically worries over its demise. In either case, the notion that the "manly" Shakespeare and Milton "little please" contemporary readers genders the midcentury's increasingly familiar sense that the reading audience for Elizabethan poetry is vanishing. For Upton, Pope, and Warburton's modernizing of Shakespeare demonstrates how criticism can mirror the slack effeminacy of modern reading. Fixing Shakespeare's text is, after all, putting him in "a modern dress."

If *Critical Observations on Shakespeare* draws out positions already nascent in Theobald, Bentley, and elsewhere, we shall see that the extremity of Upton's thesis undergoes important modulation and revision, not least in his own subsequent work on Spenser, or in the persistence of the aesthetic. Even at this early stage, however, Upton's work shows how aesthetic and historicist discourse shared some core assumptions. They both imagined distance as, in one way or another, a constitutive feature of the reading experience. The distance that historicist critics impart to texts places a break in the cultural continuum and, with it, a claim for canonical status on behalf of works whose value has endurance but needs to be recovered or rehabilitated. This is not so far from the distance implied by disinterested contemplation, nor from the way in which Hume and others (markedly Johnson, as we will see) value objects according to historical survival. The aesthetics of obscurity in turn lends itself to philological criticism and its investigation into the history of the language. Obscurity forms a unity between a text's sublimity and its recession into the dimness of the past, whether this be a function of the oldness of the language, or of genre, or of the empirical instability of the text itself.

To the degree that midcentury historicism joins with aesthetic discourse around several crucial categories and concepts, however, it is also a mode of consecration in its own right, the period's most significant mode of critical expertise. As we have seen, the development of this form of expertise had two phases: first, the growth of scholarly modes of textual interpretation and editorial practice roughly coincident with the early eighteenth-century moment that sees them as anathema; second, the application of such method to English classics by critics looking to correct, educate, or disavow the nation's taste. Intrinsic to the philological model of historicist criticism is the assumption that older English writers are textually and historically difficult and obscure, and for that reason that they resist the reading habits of the multitude. The application of hermeneutical methods specific to classical texts onto vernacular texts, finally, is an important moment in the elevation of the English literary past. Midcentury historicists drew an analogy between the Greco-Roman ancients and the English ancients at the level of textuality. "Spenser, Shakespeare, and Milton" presented the same difficulties as their classical predecessors. The classical works of the national canon were no longer modern.

Historicist and aesthetic models of the canon evolved together and reached an important level of tension during the middle decades of the century. It would be, perhaps, nicely "historicist" to argue that this shifting itinerary simply charts the working out of contingency, the tossing of the dice of historical chance. Yet this argument would leave historicism itself unmediated, shorn equally from its own uneven development and its combined evolution with aesthetics. I shall attempt to outline, in the chapters below, the pattern that unifies the historical manifold.

PART TWO

PART TWO

# CHAPTER 3

# Novel to lyric: Shakespeare in the field of culture, 1752–1754

The previous chapters argued that the description of the literary past evolved by the midcentury to an opposition between aesthetic and historicist discourse, and that this transformation emerged out of a prolonged consideration of the literary public sphere. This chapter follows this development into the treatment of Shakespeare during the early 1750s. The eighteenth century's peculiar interest in Shakespeare is well documented, as is the process, over the *durée*, in which Shakespeare became not just a precious oddity of the cultural past (an artless genius) but *the* national poet.[1] What I would like to explore in this chapter is a particularly important episode in the century-long canonization of Shakespeare. I shall discuss how Shakespeare's unique status in the national canon – first among the trinity – came about because of the way his texts seemed to answer to a cultural dilemma: the relation of public culture to literary genres and language and to the past as such. For critics of the early 1750s, it was possible to imagine that Shakespeare was both antithetical to the market and a favorite of the nation's taste. The allure of Shakespeare for midcentury criticism (even for critics like Charlotte Lennox who used Shakespeare as the negative example to advance her case for the novel) derived in no small degree from the wealth of discussion surrounding his relation to contemporary readers. Once the model of refinement had passed out of fashion, or rather could no longer answer the social problems it had set out to resolve, Shakespeare was both rediscovered as neglected and revalued as "literary." Criticism does not so much finalize Shakespeare's canonical status during these years, however, as set it in motion. It is a series of debates and conflicts – between publicity and scholarship, commerce and culture, the domestic novel and lyric poetry – that put in place the terms for Shakespeare's definitive reception as "sublime" and "transcendent" and his sensibility as "human."

## SHAKESPEARE'S "BEAUTIES"

William Dodd's *The Beauties of Shakespeare* (1752) is an early instance of what would later become a common mode of anthologizing English authors: a selection and compilation of exemplary passages from the plays gathered under topical headings (running the gamut from "action, the power of it" to "youth, pert and bragging").[2] Dodd's *Beauties* delivers two volumes of excerpted lines, an elaborate theoretical introduction, and regular forays into textual annotation. That Dodd cannot seem to decide if his work is an anthology, a treatise, or an edition speaks less to his own personal confusion, however, than to the fact that these three practices had not yet separated into a sphere of critical autonomy.[3] While his anthologizing impulses point him in the direction of the public, his editorial practices speak to "scholars"; between these two antithetical positions lies the province of the sublime.

Dodd places on the title page, as the epigraph to the *Beauties*, six familiar lines from *A Midsummer Night's Dream*:

> The poet's eye, in a fine frenzy rowling
> Doth glance from heav'n to earth, from earth to heav'n,
> And as imagination bodies forth
> The forms of things unknown, the poet's pen
> Turns them to shape, and gives to airy nothing
> A local habitation and a name.

As hackneyed as these lines may seem to us, for the eighteenth century such was not yet a common notion of poetic production. (We might consider the eighteenth century the long moment of their banalization.)[4] In their immediate context, the lines form something of a polemic against abiding notions of taste, akin in certain ways, as we shall see, to Joseph Warton's critique of polite verse and Augustan refinement. These lines also signal a specifically aesthetic understanding of the poet and poetry. Dodd refers the reader of the epigraph to page eighty-seven of the first volume which then repeats the lines under the heading of "The Power of Imagination." Intended as the general rubric for the *Beauties*, Dodd's emphasis on the imagination firmly situates Shakespeare's texts within the aesthetic tradition that Addison had carved out for Milton and the classics. Whereas Addison's "Pleasures of the Imagination" series had prioritized beauty in the trinity of aesthetic qualities, however, Dodd's interest in Shakespeare's "beauties" leads him paradoxically in the direction of the sublime. The general effect of this shift is to amplify the rhetoric of cultural consecration. "I shall not attempt any labour'd encomium on Shakespeare or endeavour to set forth his perfections, at a time when such universal and just applause is paid him, and when every tongue is big with his *boundless fire*" (v).[5] This "collection of *Beauties* cannot be paralleled from the productions of any other single author, ancient or modern" (vi). Indeed, the "weight" of Shakespeare's "bullion lines" is equivalent to gold itself (xviii). The intensity of these claims made on behalf of Shakespeare rest on the frequent invocation of Longinus and the sublime, most commonly through the figure of flight. Shakespeare's "boundless fire . . . shines unrivaled, and, like the eagle, properest emblem of his daring genius, soars beyond the common reach, and gazes undazzled at the sun" (vi).

Dodd's recurring metaphor of flight describes a relation of cultural hierarchy. Shakespeare flies over criticism in a relation of authoritative subordination: "His flights are sometimes so bold, frigid criticism almost dares to disapprove them; and those narrow minds which are incapable of elevating themselves to the sublimity of their author, are willing to bring them down to a level of their own" (vi). This placement of literary priority in authorial production (as sublime and demiurgic) at the expense of critical consumption (as "frigid" and "narrow") is intended to reverse an earlier understanding of the relation between poet and critic. Whereas Shaftesbury, for example, circumscribed poetic production with critical consumption, considering the former to be a *déclassé* and private craft and the latter a public vocation of taste, Dodd has the poet fly over the critic. This reversal is undertaken, however, by recasting the content of the poles of production and consumption as they had appeared in earlier criticism. Dodd's poet becomes the medium of *public* sublimity and the critic the medium of *privatized* scholarship:

How many fine passages have been condemned in Shakespeare, as Rant and Fustian, intolerable Bombast, and turgid Nonsense, which, if read with the least glow of the same imagination that warm'd the writer's bosom, wou'd blaze in the robes of sublimity, and obtain the commendations of a Longinus. And unless some little of the same spirit that elevated the poet, elevate the reader too, he must not presume to talk of taste and elegance; he will prove but a languid reader, an indifferent judge, but a far more indifferent critic and commentator. (vii)

In this passage, the reader's identity with the critic only underscores the latter's failure to raise himself to the position of the author. Reading is criticism, as Shaftesbury and Addison had argued, but this now means that criticism is, paradoxically, not writing. Dodd's assertion of the authority of the author rethinks the meaning of authorship itself. According to Shaftesbury, critical reading was fundamentally genteel. Reading led to a community of polite taste. In contrast, Dodd claims that the author of a sublime work unites an internally divided public under its "glow." Shaftesburian proportion and harmony are ill-suited to describe modern cultural relations. As Dodd reconsiders the relation among criticism, reading, authorship, and aesthetics, he comes up with a two-fold transformation of the earlier model. Firstly, the "upper hand" of the reader-critic cedes authority to the sublime poet. The authority of the author, in this case, is the precipitate of the authority of the reader-critic, now understood to be an untrustworthy guarantor of taste. Secondly, social order is no longer beautiful but must be held together by the sublime.

Like the historicists, Dodd is hostile to the "elegant" rejection of Shakespeare's gothicism. Yet he is also hostile to the historicist emphasis on "learning," hence his inaugural claim not "to attempt any *labour'd* encomium." Shakespeare sublimates modernizing taste *and* pedantic scholarship. Dodd's aesthetic and his editorial practice are staked against post-Theobaldian hermeneutics, recapitulating certain key features of the anti-scholarly critique of "pedantry" but from a remodeled aesthetics of the sublime. Among "Shakespeare's commentators" are found

many ingenious men, whose names are high in the *learned* world . . . yet this much, in justice to the author, must be avowed, that many a critic, when he has met with a passage not clear to his conception, and perhaps above the level of his own ideas, so far from attempting to explain his author, has immediately condemned the expression as foolish and absurd, and foisted in some footy emendation of his own. (vii)

Dodd takes from the anti-scholarly polemic the notion that historicist critics are, in fact, baleful pedants. Accordingly, he echoes the notion that these "very dabblers in learning" use a language and method too removed from the reading habits of the public. Dodd's sublime is opposed to the attempt by scholars to make Shakespeare a form of intellectual capital, a position that he discloses in a telling anecdote:

Shakespeare was ever, of all modern authors, my first and greatest favourite: and during my relaxations, from more severe and necessary studies at college, I never omitted to read and indulge myself in the rapturous fights of this delightful and *sweetest child of fancy*: and when my imagination had been heated by the glowing ardor of his uncommon fire, have never failed to lament, that his BEAUTIES should be so obscured, and that he himself should be make a kind of stage for bungling critics to shew their clumsy activity upon. (xv)

Milton's encomium from "L'Allegro" ("sweetest Shakespeare, fancy's child," 133), in this reading, describes Shakespeare's sublimity as a compensatory repose from the buffeting winds of scholarship. Historicist method represents something like a return of the re-pressed, in which the very scholarship from which the reader seeks relief enacts its revenge on the aesthetic object. As if to discount strenuously and distance the threat of scholarship on aesthetic autonomy, Dodd concludes his memory by analogizing such editors to the original players of Shakespearean drama, the "clumsy" and "bungling" actors supposedly responsible for the very textual errors on which editors focus. He then contrasts his editorial method to the classicizing philology of the "learned":

It would have been no hard task to have multiplied quotations from Greek, Latin, and English writers, and to have made no small display of what is commonly called *learning*; but that I have indistinguishably avoided; and never perplexed the reader (or at least as little as possible) with the learned language, always preferring the most plain and literal translations, much to his ease, tho' (according to the manner in which some judge) less to my own reputation. (xviii)

Here the scholarly interest in the history of the English language, which sought to alienate Shakespeare from the language of the public sphere, is countered by the "ease" of Dodd's translations. The linguistic capital of the scholars (both foreign and domestic) obtrudes on the aesthetic experience of the reader, who is denied the "fire" of Shakespeare by the encroachment of difficult annotations.

Dodd's sublime is thus professedly public, if in a different sense from that of the earlier eighteenth century. Indeed so much is implied by the rewriting of critical consumption as privatized scholarship and poetic craft as sublime exuberance. Publicity is inscribed in the very texture of sublime poetry. "Longinus tells us that the most infallible test of the true sublime, is in the impression a performance makes upon our minds, when read or recited"; hence, "in a word, you may pronounce that sublime, beautiful, and genuine which always pleases and takes equally among all sorts of men" (xvi–xvii). Here Dodd anticipates the line of argument given in Burke that a taste for sublime obscurity is uniform among readers, a fact demonstrated above all by the overarching "human" preference for Shakespeare: "This fine observation of Longinus is most remarkably verified in Shakespeare; for all humours, ages, and inclinations, jointly proclaim their approbation and esteem of him" (xvii). Sublimity names the aesthetic condition of poet and of reader, the former lit with a "boundless fire," the latter "warm'd" with a "glow of the *same* imagination." The diversity of reading habits, and of readers, are held together by the uniformity of sublime experience; for Dodd at least, it is impossible to say if Shakespeare's sublimity is before or after the "impression . . . upon our minds," as it is the reader's "tongue" that is "big with [Shakespeare's] boundless fire." Production here is always already consumption. Like "bullion," Shakespeare acts as an abstract cultural equivalent, a form of "common" currency which is at once the quintessence of value and of general uniformity.

Dodd's grounding of the sublime in the coincidence of authorial production and readerly consumption would also underlie his sense of the form of *Beauties*, which is designed to facilitate the demand of readers, from "the old, the grave, and the severe," to "the gay, the young, and the passionate" (xvii). "It was my *business*," he writes in this vein, "to collect for readers of all tastes, and all complexions, let me desire none to disapprove, what hits not with their humour, but to turn over the page, and they will surely find something acceptable and engaging" (xviii). For as much as Dodd's claims for Shakespeare are cast in the high-cultural discourse of the sublime, then, he also imagines an authoritative grounding in the market as a constitutive element of his engagement with intellectualist critics. (Gold is, after all, a commodity like all others.) "It is in my opinion no small affront to the world to pester it with our *private* and insignificant animosities, and to stuff a book with querulous jargon, where information is paid for, and justly expected" (xiv). Dodd here squares the recourse to the reader, as the test of true sublimity, with the traffic in cultural goods, momentarily elevating the purchasing of his text to the site of sublime "approbation" and deflating editorial practice as the "private" and "querulous jargon" of scholarship. He continues Shaftesbury's assertion of the "reader's privilege," while departing from the "argument on behalf of criticism," and so finds himself the advocate and theorist of cultural demand. Shakespeare is the uniquely sublime *and* marketable poet, both "beyond common reach" and "for all readers." This combination is managed by the unity of Shakespeare's sublimity with its effect on the reader. Disencumbered from the particularities of scholarship and appealing to "all sorts of men" across the span of "humours, ages, and inclinations," Shakespeare becomes synonymous with "literature" and the critical assault on sublimity one on *"literature in general"* (xiii).

This conception of literature and the market is to be distinguished from the earlier "beautiful" model of Shaftesbury and Addison insofar as it does not imagine a polite community of taste but rather projects a striated and antagonistic readership held together by the power of the sublime. Dodd's endowment of "literature in general," and Shakespeare in particular, might explain why he claims that "the text of the author is a *sacred* thing" (vii) and that the contents of his book are "so much good *divinity*" (xvi). Dodd's rendering of Shakespeare as a sacrament demonstrates in the most strident metaphoric sense the process of vernacular elevation underway at the midcentury, imagining Shakespeare to fly over the world in a manner that conflates him with the sacred. "Literature" vies to supplant "divinity" in providing a common sense of belief through a consecrated order of texts. Dodd's Shakespeare exemplifies, in a concrete dynamic, what has become something of a commonplace of cultural theory, namely, the historical emergence of aesthetic discourse at the interface between literature and religion.[6] If we are to consider the rise of the aesthetic in mid-eighteenth-century England as inseparable from secularization and modernity, then Dodd's Shakespeare partakes of the struggle in which "art" begins to supplant "religion" as the mediating form of spiritual values, and the vernacular begins to supplant Latin as the vehicle for collective imaginings.[7] The conjoining of the sacred and the economic in Dodd's notion of literature explains how Shakespeare can at once be seen to fly over the world and be in the mouths of all its people, and how Dodd can find cultural value in the very market against which other critics redemptively fashion Shakespeare. The worldly purchasing and reading of texts structures a sublime relation between the audience and the poet (the consumer and product) akin to the now supplanted and outmoded form of belief called "divinity." Shakespeare is inserted into a circuit of exchange that has already absorbed the beliefs of the older religious system. No longer a threat to faith, the market has become a reinvented religion in its own right; for the reputation of Shakespeare this is nothing less than the condition of sublime. Shakespeare replaces "sacred" material by means of the very system of exchange that constructs "literature" as its other.

For as much as the break between "divinity" and "literature" (or the structural supplanting of divinity by literature, in which the latter attempts to occupy the former's collective function through the displaced mechanism of the print market) provides the strong claim of Dodd's argument, however, it also marks the condition of its ambivalence. The sacredness of Shakespeare's texts endows them with a sublimity capable, in its more utopian moments, of stitching together the imaginary body of readers. But their divinity begins to make Dodd anxious about how anti-religious his version of literature is. He concludes the preface to *Beauties* by claiming:

> For my own part, better and more important things henceforth demand my attention, and I here, with no small pleasure take leave of Shakespeare and the critics; as this work was begun and finish'd, before I enter'd upon the sacred function, in which I am now happily employed, let me trust, this juvenile performance will prove no objection, since graver, and more very eminent members of the church, have thought it not improper employ, to comment, explain, and publish the works of their own country's poets. (xviii)

Dodd here refers to the fact that at some point during the previous year he had been ordained a deacon and attained the curacy of West Ham, Essex, a development that he represents as a career change from "literature" to "the sacred function."[8] No longer identical, the two represent points along the axis of maturation. The relocation of "sacred" material from cultural to theological texts reimagines what was literally an attempt to consecrate Shakespeare as now just a "juvenile performance." Dodd's ambivalence over the secularizing power of sublime "literature" in other words is revealed by the emergence of his biography at the end of the preface, which represents his own response to sublimity as a shrinking back into the clergy. Yet this clergy, he claims in order to defend his previous activity, is also involved with the very literary project by which it is threatened. If this discussion appears relatively abstract, we need only assert that Dodd is referring to a very concrete institutional phenomenon, namely, that literary culture is already entirely permeated by the clergy (who perforce comprise university faculty and who historically have a monopoly on exegesis). Dodd's aside that his literary critical practice is defensible on the grounds that it is shared by other clerics, therefore, points to the interpenetration of theological and literary culture in the construction of high-cultural texts, both in the generally uneven process of secularization, and in the particularly institutional convergence of criticism and theology in the university. Dodd's ambivalent understanding of this convergence should not detract from the importance of his notion of literary sublimity; rather, it should illuminate the historical conditions and cross-currents that gave a sanctified cast to the national canon.

## SHAKESPEARE'S NOVELS

It is part of the larger argument of this book that midcentury aesthetic accounts of Shakespeare, especially as they take Dodd's strongly sacerdotal form, often draw the line of distinction at the formal level of prose versus poetry. Dodd's "collection of Poetical Beauties" is composed, not surprisingly, almost entirely of selections in verse (*Beauties*: xv). According to the form of the anthology, these selections are lifted from the context of the play from which they are taken. Dodd constructs "literature" as the sublime passage, which stands apart from "the plot and characters" (xx). Why such trepidation in the face of prose and narrative? This question is best answered by turning to another critical text, parallel in many ways to Dodd's, which illustrates with unique clarity the mid-eighteenth-century's concern to distinguish Shakespeare from narrative and, in particular, the novel. Alone among midcentury Shakespeare studies, Charlotte Lennox's *Shakespeare Illustrated* (1753–1754) endeavored to resist the aura of the Elizabethan past. Lennox is most famous as a novelist, as the author of *The Female Quixote* (1752) in particular.[9] She was also, however, a friend and colleague of Johnson and part of the circle he dominated.[10] Commissioned by Johnson and Lord Orrery, *Shakespeare Illustrated* offered the first major translation and summary of the dramatic sources.[11] Across three long volumes, Lennox presented the translated source (including, for example, the entirety of Plautus's *Menaechmni*) side by side with Shakespeare's redaction and then followed both with "critical comments."

The form and method of the study are that of midcentury philology.[12] Here is one of Lennox's few general statements of

method: "in order to make a true estimate of the abilities and merit
of a writer, it is always necessary to examine the genius of his age,
and the opinions of his contemporaries."[13] For all of its bland
typicality, this declaration of intentions places Lennox's historicism
well within the larger patterns of midcentury criticism, including the
discovery of older texts and the granting of antiquarian esteem to
manuscript culture. Often overlooked in the histories of Shakespeare
scholarship, Lennox's project contained two important innovations.
Both arose from the idea of source. Shakespeare's debt to continental
narratives fleshed out the period circumstances of his work. His
dramatic evocation of English history and fable – in the Henriad
and *Lear* – tied period specificity to a vision of national culture.

The forgetting of Lennox's work in the recitation of eighteenth-
century Shakespeare scholars, on further reading, is neither surprising nor without consequence.[14] Lennox's philological project –
the job for which she was hired – is the cover and vehicle for an
altogether different project. By the publication of *Shakespeare Illustrated*, Lennox was already the well-known author of two novels;
indeed the title page advertises that the volumes are "by the author
of *The Female Quixote*." Lennox repeatedly terms the sources she finds
"novels and histories," and follows each translation with "observations on the use Shakespeare has made of the foregoing novel" (or
"history"). The term "novel" of course was hardly settled during the
period. Lennox's career exhibits a growing preoccupation with
defining the word. In *The Female Quixote*, she is concerned with
nothing as much as the question of that text's own genre, placing the
implacable romanticism of Arabella (the eponymous heroine) and
the quotidian realism of her suitors into an interminable struggle
bereft of a common set of conventions or terms.[15] Two years later, in
*Shakespeare Illustrated*, Lennox precociously describes "the novel" as
an imaginative and fictive, but "probable," prose narrative.[16]

The venue for this precocious definition is the philological
comparison of Shakespeare's plays to the "novels" that are their
sources. The comparison invariably prefers the source. Bandello's
"novel" is superior to *Twelfth Night* because "the novelist is much
more careful to preserve probability in his narration than the poet in
his action: The wonder is that Shakespeare could task his invention
to make those incidents unnatural and absurd" (Lennox, *Shakespeare
Illustrated*: 245). Lennox evaluates the plays and their sources according to the efficient unfolding of the narrative and the believable

delineation of character, both of which are combined in the concept of probability. In contrast to the novelists whose stories he drama-tizes, Shakespeare fails to deliver a credible and meticulously constructed narrative. As with *Twelfth Night*, *Measure for Measure* worked better as a novel: "There are a greater diversity of characters and more intrigues in the fable of the play, than the novel of Cinthio; yet I think, wherever Shakespeare has invented, he is greatly below the novelist; since the incidents he has added are neither necessary nor probable" (i: 21, 24). The same case is made on behalf of Boccaccio's "novel" over Shakespeare's *Cymbeline*: "the catastrophe of the story, though the same in the play as the novel . . . is very differently conducted in each: there is more probability in the incidents which lead to it in the novel, and more contrivance in the play" (i: 146).

Lennox's critique of Shakespeare by the source – or, as it soon becomes apparent, the antique "romance" by the modern "novel" – is given perhaps its most evocative delivery in the discussion of *The Winter's Tale*:

> In the novel the accidents that happen to the exposed infant are governed by chance; the boat into which it was put being left in the midst of the ocean, is driven by the winds to the coast of Bohemia, and being spied by a sheaperd is drawn to Land.
>
> In the Play, Antiginous, who is bound by oath to leave the child in some desert place quite out of his father's dominions, is warned in a dream to call the infant Perdita, and carry it to Bohemia, and there leave it.
>
> Antiginous obeys, and this done, it is absolutely necessary he should not return to Sicily, otherwise it may be discovered where the Princess is left, and all the future adventures would fall to the ground; therefore a bear rushes out of the woods and devours him; the good natured bear, as it should seem, resolved not to spoil the story, passes by the little princess, who is to make so great a figure hereafter, and a violent storm arising, splits the ship in which she was brought thither, so that all the sailors perishing, though they were near enough the shore to have saved themselves, no one is left to carry back any account of the affair to Sicily, and thereby prevent the adventures which are to follow.
>
> All this is very wonderful: Shakespeare multiplies miracle upon miracle to bring about the same events in the Play, which chance, with so much propriety, performs in the novel. (ii: 80)

This passage delineates with mordant clarity the evolutionary scheme governing the whole of *Shakespeare Illustrated*: the modern novel tells stories in the secular idiom of probability, chance, and propriety; the older romance tells stories in the mystical idiom of dark complexity and miraculous intervention.[17] The trick of this progressive narrative is that the modern form exists prior to the antique form: Shakespeare antiquates the novel and makes it romance. Lennox's unique and at first glance puzzling literary history has the form of a metalepsis, a reversal of cause and effect. The chronological sequence of source to text ("novelle" to "play") is overwritten and replaced by the sequence of Shakespeare to Novel. Before Shakespeare is the very genre that other critics find not only to come after Shakespeare, but in fact to bespeak his canonicity.

The heterodox distinction Lennox draws between the novel and Shakespeare, prose and poetry, or probability and romance, persists even into the discussion of the history plays. Here the source texts are works like Holinshed's *Chronicles* and Hall's *Union of the Noble and Illustre Families of Lancaster and York*. Discussing *Hamlet* in the second volume, Lennox notes that "the Danish history of Saxo-Grammaticus" is "a story so full of incredible fancies, wild and improbable circumstances [that it] has more the appearance of *romance* than historical fact" (II: 267). Yet, she continues, "the historian, romantic as his relation seems, has the advantage of the poet in probability" (II: 269). Lennox's equivocation over the source's factual status is resolute in the categorical boundary it establishes between novel and history: the one offers probabilistic stories; the other sets forth demonstrative facts. The two orders of discourse require two orders of judgment. *Richard II*, for example, contains

> several . . . instances in which Shakespeare's inattention to the history is plainly proved; and is therefore the less pardonable, as the subject of it is not one entire action, wrought up with a variety of beautiful incidents, which at once delight and instruct the mind; but a dramatic narration of historical facts, and a successive series of actions and events which are only interesting as they are true, and only pleasing as they are gracefully told. (III: 109)

Here Lennox invokes two narrative paradigms, first the novelistic "one entire action," and next the historical "narration of facts"; held to the latter's strictures, Shakespeare fails in comparison to the source (moderately in the Henriad, extensively in *King Lear*). This failure is a departure from "fact" that bears the name "fiction." Lennox remarks that the manner of the Duke of Suffolk's death in *Henry VI*, for instance, "is not to be found, either in Hall or Holinshed; and . . . it has greatly the air of fiction" (III: 154).

Lennox's point is not just to show that Shakespeare confounds
history with fiction. She also wants to demonstrate that Shakespeare's fiction is insufficiently novelistic: "That little fiction which
Shakespeare has introduced into [*Richard II*] is imagined with his
usual carelessness and inattention to probability" (III: 119). Shakespeare slips from "historical fact" to "fiction," but once there
foregoes probability for romance.

History is unlike the novel because it is factual. The novel is unlike
history because it is imaginative, or, as Lennox puts it, because it is
*fiction*.[18] Finally, the novel is better fiction than the romance because
it has probability. Much then depends upon the latter term. As
Douglas Patey has observed, probability was a singularly overloaded
category in enlightenment thought. In modern empirical language,
probability described the predictability of objects and events, as
opposed to the certain knowledge of demonstrable proof. In older
Aristotelian language, probability described the formal coherence of
poetry and drama, as opposed both to the factual discontinuity of
history and the mental abstraction of philosophy.[19] Lennox's use
compounds and alternates between the modern and classical
meaning. Predictability is the hinge for consistency of narrative and
character alike. This consistency is shaped by an overarching formal
unity distinct from historical fact. The claims made on behalf of the
novel are thus rather grand: it supplants epic poetry as the bearer of
an imaginative truth different in kind from historical truth.[20]

Probable narratives contain a predictable series of events. These
events are acted out by characters. Lennox's theory thus also
contains an elaborate theory of character, in particular the character
of women. As Margaret Doody has pointed out, *Shakespeare Illustrated*
frequently takes issue with the author's delineation of his heroines.
Doody argues that *The Female Quixote* and *Shakespeare Illustrated* share
a common project of rescuing the "romantic" female world from the
predations of masculine culture; just as Arabella's romances are
misunderstood and defeated by male Augustans, so too the romantic
source is misunderstood and defeated by Shakespeare. In *Shakespeare
Illustrated* as in *The Female Quixote*, Doody contends, Lennox looks
back to romance for "a common and large-scale world of literary
reference where women could be at home," and where the "private
experience" of every woman writer would be inscribed (299).
*Shakespeare Illustrated*, Doody concludes, exemplifies how "the
romance was of great importance because it allegorized every

woman's life for her" (299–300). Whatever one makes of Lennox's "Quixotic" deflation of the romance in *The Female Quixote* (the subject of Lennox criticism of the past fifteen years), it would be difficult to maintain that "romance" is the fulcrum of redemptive value in *Shakespeare Illustrated*. As we have seen, Shakespeare's "romantic" antiquity declares his inferiority to the paradoxically modern form of the sources. Lennox's work suggests that models of literary history and genre in the midcentury are not reducible to a simple binarism in which women are commensurate with "romance" and men with "Shakespeare."[21]

Doody is right to argue that Lennox's criticism turns on a notion of gendered character, but wrong to find in Lennox a model of romantic empowerment. Rather, *Shakespeare Illustrated* conceives of female characterization in comparatively austere terms. Lennox locates in the older sources a modern ideal of domesticity, a "character" version of the "propriety" she had initially constructed around narrative. In the discussion of *Measure for Measure*, for instance, Lennox credits Shakespeare for having Isabella refuse Claudio's request that she sleep with the Duke in order to save his life, but then criticizes Shakespeare for depicting Isabella as coarse and violent in her refusal, rather than (like Cinthio's Epitia) decorous and feminine:

the character of Isabella in the play seems to be an improvement upon that of Epitia in the novel; for Isabella absolutely refuses, and persists in her refusal, to give up her honour to save her brother's life; whereas Epitia, overcome by her own tendernous of nature, and affecting prayers of the unhappy youth, yields to what her soul abhors, to redeem him from a shameful death. (I: 33)

Despite Isabella's apparent piety, she "is a mere vixen in her virtue" (I: 33). Comparing Isabella's speech to Epitia, Lennox asks: "Is this the language of a modest, tender maid; one who had devoted herself to a religious life, and was remarkable for an exalted understanding, and unaffected piety in the earliest bloom of life?" (I: 33). Lennox then imagines how she might rewrite them both into a paragon of female propriety:

From her character . . . one might have expected mild expostulations, wise reasonings, and gentle rebukes: his desire of life, though purchased by methods she could not approve, was a natural frailty, which a sister might have pitied and excused, and have made use of her superior understanding to reason down his fears, recall nobler ideas to his mind, teach him what

was due to her honour and his own, and reconcile him to his own
approaching death, by arguments drawn from that religion and virtue of
which she made so high a profession; but that torrent of abusive language,
those course and unwomanly reflexions . . ., her exulting cruelty to dying
youth, are the manners of an affecting prude, outrageous in her seeming
virtue, not a pious, innocent, and tender maid. (i: 33–34)

This chastening combination of Epitia and Isabella (where the
former's femininity is retained along with the latter's virginity)
invokes a notion of probable female character as at once a formal
and social ideal. For this reason, Lennox is equally puzzled by
Isabella's inability to recant her lie about having given in to the
Duke: "Is this *natural?* Is it *probable* that Isabella would thus publicly
bring a false imputation of her honour, and, though innocent and
unstained, suffer the world to believe her violated?" (i: 34).

   Lennox's model of probable women repeats in microcosm her
generic metalepsis, this time by viewing the past through the lens of
a contemporary ideal of restraint and modesty.[22] She argues, for
example, that the various scenes of cross-dressing in Shakespeare's
plays evince a disregard not only for female propriety but for the
very gender boundaries that found novelistic modernity. In *Twelfth
Night*, Shakespeare "very much lessens the probability of the story"
by focusing on Viola's transvestism: "a very natural scheme this, for
a beautiful and virtuous young lady to throw off all at once the
modesty and reservedness of her sex, mix at once among men,
herself disguised like one: and, prest by no necessity, influenced by
no passion, expose herself to all the dangerous consequences of so
unworthy and shameful a situation" (i: 233–234). Lennox here
balances what Doody calls her "running argument in favor of
women" on a forbidding standard of behavior (Doody, "Shakespeare's Novels": 300). Olivia's desire for the disguised Viola lacks
"any of those emotions that bashfulness, delicacy, and a desire of
preserving the decorum of her sex and birth oblige" (Lennox,
*Shakespeare Illustrated*, i: 246). Not surprisingly, the source is better at
fixing gender in the appropriate body; "we find this incident
managed with much more decency in the novel" because the novel
tells restrained stories, with no excess of events, through chaste
characters, with no excess of desire (i: 244). A modern gender system
confronts an older "Shakespearean" system; the one consists in the
decorous binarism of male and female and the other the indecorous
violence of cross-dressing. The modern system of domestic propriety

dwells, paradoxically, in the anterior texts that Shakespeare confuses and "romanticizes." This metalepsis would explain even the moment of *Shakespeare Illustrated* where, as Doody rightly notices, the question does turn on Shakespeare's tendency to "humiliate his women," namely Lennox's account of the odd conclusion to *The Winter's Tale*, in which Hermione is magically transformed into a statue and then back into a human.[23] Lennox's difficulty with this scene is not simply that Shakespeare "humiliates" Hermione; it is that the story and the character are improbable. No one, in enlightened times, believes in magic; Hermione ought to have remained "a virtuous and affectionate wife" (II: 85). The attention to female characterization momentarily reinvents Shakespeare as unable to represent gender difference in order to advertise the way that the novel constructs female character and regulates female reading. That Lennox's feminism is conditioned by domestic ideology and does not, as Doody argues, appeal to a transhistorical model of empowerment should hardly lessen our appreciation of her position in the history of criticism. It is testimony to the importance and, as it were, novelty of her account that she derives from her notion of genre such a strong resistance to the eighteenth century's ideal of Shakespeare.

Women in the sources are described in the eighteenth century's typical language of feminine propriety, whereas Shakespeare's women arrive from the barbarous gloom of romance. Lennox further distinguishes the venerable modernity of the novel from the otiose antiquity of Shakespeare in the domain of social status. Novelistically proper and decorous behavior, she claims, is not only the province of "tender maids" but also and inseparably that of "quality." *Twelfth Night*'s cross-dressing "incident is handled with much more decency in the novel" than in the play, for example, because the former has such indecency performed by a lower class woman:

Catella acts the same part in the novel that Olivia does in the play; but Catella is a young gay libertine girl, whose birth was but mean, and education neglected; it was not therefore surprizing that she should so easily fall in love with a page, indecently court him, and resolve to marry him, such an inconsiderate conduct was agreeable to her *character*; but in the noble and virtuous Olivia, 'tis unnatural and absurd. (I: 247)

Lennox's reading of Olivia's pursuit of Viola in this passage is indicative of how she demands of Shakespeare that his characters act in ways "proper" to their social rank. If any part of *Shakespeare Illustrated* is anachronistic, as Lennox's biographer, Miriam Rossiter Small, and Doody both claim, we might suggest it is this insistence on the one-to-one correspondence between birth and worth, between "nobility" and "virtue."[24] Yet even this apparent anachronism is framed in new social and aesthetic terms. In a telling philological exchange with Thomas Rymer, Lennox reprimands the critic for mistaking Cinthio's Desdemona as a woman from the "middle rank" rather than one "of high birth":

Cinthio calls her Cittadina, which Mr Rymer translates a simple citizen; but the Italians by the phrase mean a woman of Quality. If they were, for example, to speak of a woman of the middle rank, in Rome, they would say, Una Romana; if a noble lady, Una Cittadina Romana: So in Venice they call a simple citizen Una Venitiana; but a woman of Quality, Una Cittadina Venitiana. (I: 132)

The novel's formal consistency depends on Desdemona's high birth since "there is less improbability in supposing a noble lady, educated in sentiments superior to the vulgar, should fall in love with a man merely for the qualities of his mind than that a mean citizen should be possessed of such exalted ideas, as to overlook the disparity of years and complexion, and be enamored of virtue in the person of a Moor" (I: 132). "Quality" is opposed not simply to a generalized "vulgar," but more pointedly to that new and equivocal class, "the middle rank."

Lennox similarly faults *Cymbeline* for shifting Boccaccio's setting in a tavern filled with middle class players to a court stocked with nobility. As with the discussion of *Othello*, social struggle occurs between "middle rank" and "quality": "Shakespeare makes the Lady in question, not the wife of the merchant, but the heiress of a great kingdom . . . The husband, who lays so indiscreet a wager, not a simple trader intoxicated with liquor, but a young noble" (I: 156). Boccaccio's novel represents the social order with probability. In contrast, Shakespeare confounds social status by letting heiresses and nobles act like traders and merchants. These social problems have formal consequences; they bring about "strange adventures . . . at the expense of probability" (I: 162). Reiterating that Shakespeare "has given the manners of a tradesman's wife, and two merchants intoxicated with liquor, to a great Princess, an English hero, and a noble Roman," Lennox adds that "to this injudicious change of the characters is owing all the absurdities of this part of Shakespeare's plot" (1: 156). As with the idea of gendered decorum, this commitment to status intends to formalize a social problem, to imagine an aesthetic semblance of a newly intricate social order by depicting it within the rigid matrix of probability.[25] Lennox's argument presumes, to borrow a phrase, that "genre is essentially a socio-symbolic message, or in other words, that form is immanently and intrinsically an ideology in its own right."[26] The novel is to be preferred to Shakespeare because it better represents gendered domesticity and social stability; its characters and stories give a more probable coherence to modern society.

The discrepancy of Lennox's literary history from the typical form of midcentury Shakespeare criticism did not go unnoticed by Johnson.[27] Writing in her name, he penned a dedication of the volume to Lord Orrery that sought to diminish the ensuing heterodoxy. Johnson begins by announcing Lennox's claims to antiquarian cultural capital: "I have no other pretense to the honour of a patronage, so illustrious as that of your Lordship, than the merit of attempting what has by some considerable neglect been hitherto omitted, though absolutely necessary to a perfect knowledge of the abilities of Shakespeare" (iii–iv). "I have diligently read the works of Shakespeare, and now presume to lay the results of my searches before your Lordship, before that judge whom Pliny himself would have wished for his assessor to hear a literary cause" (vi–vii). Johnson attempts to elevate the critic (as "diligent" reader of high-cultural texts) and Shakespeare (as the preferred text of the aristocracy). The nomination of *Shakespeare Illustrated* as "a literary cause" is not at all a misnomer, except that what "literary" signifies in the dedication is at some odds with its meaning in the rest of the work (vii).

Johnson is well aware that his understanding of the "literary" is not Lennox's. The bulk of his dedication is occupied with discounting the critical work to follow. He dismisses in advance the central terms of Lennox's criticism. "The truth is, a very small part of the reputation of this mighty genius depends upon the naked plot or story of his plays" (viii) and hence "it is not perhaps very necessary to inquire whether the vehicle of so much delight and instruction be a story probable, or unlikely, native or foreign" (xi). In place of these Lennoxian terms, Johnson prefers the categories of endurance and universality; Shakespeare's value derives from his lasting depiction of "human actions, passions, and habits" (viii). The preference for the general over the probable is, paradoxically, an historical argument. "He lived in an age when the books of Chivalry were yet popular, and when therefore the minds of his auditors were not accustomed to balance probabilities, or to examine nicely the proportion between causes and effects" (viii–ix). To straighten Lennox's metalepsis, Johnson claims that Shakespeare's sources in fact lead the author to write in ways contrary to the reading habits of the eighteenth century. *Romances*, not novels, are what lie behind and determine the formal structures of Shakespeare's plays; such "books of chivalry" explain Shakespeare's difference from the present, whose signal cultural form, the novel, "balance[s] probabilities." Shakespeare is to be credited for transcending the romantic source material and appealing to all humans at all times. Johnson and Lennox's literary histories are thus strikingly different. According to Johnson, "romances" or "books of chivalry" are either rewritten into the canon by Shakespeare or persist in literary history until they are revived by novelists in the eighteenth century. Shakespeare transfigures romance into literature while contemporary authors remake romance into the novel, a genre whose literary status is entirely unclear. Like Lennox, Johnson emphasizes the relationship between the source material and the novel but insists that it is one of continuity rather than identity. Narrative "probability" is an eighteenth-century invention, newly invented to manage literary culture.

Johnson's response to Lennox is part of his larger engagement with the novel as an emergent genre. His complex and ambivalent relation to the works of Fielding, Richardson, and Smollett is well known. Three years before his dedication to *Shakespeare Illustrated* he warned in the *Rambler* 4 that the curious

works of fiction with which the present generation seems . . . delighted . . . are written chiefly to the young, the ignorant and the idle, to whom they serve as lectures of conduct, and introductions into life. They are the entertainment of minds unfurnished with ideas, and therefore easily susceptible of impressions; not fixed by principles, and therefore easily following the current of fancy; not informed by experience, and consequently open to every false suggestion and partial account.[28]

Elsewhere Johnson will celebrate the taste of the "common reader" and position himself against cultural elitism, but the popularity of the novel only makes him uneasy.[29] Whereas the *Rambler* tries to solve the problem of the novel by stressing its exclusively didactic

vocation to "increase prudence without impairing virtue," the
dedication to Lennox's work pitches Shakespeare against the novel
(Johnson, *Rambler*, 4: 22). This "literary cause," he contends, is quite
a serious matter: "Some danger there is lest [Shakespeare's] admirers should think him injured . . . and clamour as at the diminution of the honour of that nation, which boasts herself the parent of
so great a poet" ("Preface": vii).

Saving Shakespeare and the national canon requires demoting the
novel on the very terms of Lennox's criticism. Still, Johnson's
account in the dedication is mediated by the novel form it intends to
bracket. The initial "danger" Johnson sees in *Shakespeare Illustrated*
has to do with its reversal of novel and Shakespeare in the domain of
narrative, "the naked plot or story" (vi). The engagement with
Lennox's account of character is of a different order. For Lennox,
Shakespeare's characters act "improbably" and "unbelievably";
Johnson asserts that Shakespeare deserves credit for having "exhibited many characters, in many changes of situation" (x). "These
characters are so copiously diversified, and some of them so justly
pursued, that his works may be considered a map of life, a faithful
miniature of human transactions, and he that has read Shakespeare
with attention, will perhaps find little new in the crouded world" (x).
Johnson here celebrates Shakespeare's delineation of character in
the manner of the conduct book, complete with attentive advice on
the "human transactions" that enable one to better get along in the
world.[30] The imaginary situation of reading Shakespeare, at this
point in Johnson's account, converges with that of reading novels as
he understands the practice in the *Rambler*, where he argues that
"common readers" are to "fix their eyes upon [a character] with
closer attention, and hope by observing his behaviour and success to
regulate their own practices, when they shall be engaged in the like
part" (23). A novel's characters must be undiluted, although probable, paragons for the "common mind": "I cannot discover why
there should not be exhibited the most perfect idea of virtue; of
virtue not angelical, nor above probability, for what we cannot credit
we shall never imitate, but the highest and purest that humanity can
reach" (23). The dedication's repetition of the *Rambler*'s understanding of how one ought to read a novel, in which Shakespeare's
characters are as regulative and imitable as a conduct book, allows
Johnson briefly to approximate Lennox's aesthetic. For nowhere is
the *Rambler*'s ideal of character more programmatically installed,

perhaps, than in the main body of *Shakespeare Illustrated* which finds
the "perfect idea of virtue" in Shakespeare's sources. Lennox is not
in disagreement with Johnson over how to read novels. (Her citation
of the *Rambler* at the close of *The Female Quixote* discusses just this
question.)[31] Rather, she diverges from Johnson over where to place
the novel in the canon and over the relative value of transcendence
and probability. Lennox applies Johnson's understanding of novelistic character to Shakespeare and finds him wanting, a move that
makes Johnson reconsider what in Shakespeare (or in high-canonical
literature in general) outstrips the novel.

Perhaps for this reason, Johnson changes his mind, virtually mid-
sentence, about the nature of Shakespeare's characterization: "It has
hitherto been unnoticed that his heroes are men, that the love and
hatred, the hopes and fears of his chief personages are such as are
common to other human beings, and not like those which later times
have exhibited, peculiar to phantoms that strut upon the stage"
("Preface": x). The characters in the world that Shakespeare paints
so accurately as to be a "faithful miniature" here achieve a state of
universality above what is merely useful for instruction in conduct.
They transcend, in other words, the gendered particularity upon
which Lennox had insisted. Shakespeare's male "personages" are
ultimately what distinguish his works from the novels "which later
times have exhibited" because, now returning to the narrative
argument, unlike novels "Shakespeare's excellence is not the fiction
of a tale, but the representation of life and his reputation is therefore
safe, till human nature shall be changed" (xi). This model will turn
out to be of some importance for Johnson's subsequent criticism.
That is, the question of depersonalized character crucial for his later
understanding of Shakespeare first takes shape as an argument
against gendered character, or rather a switching of emphasis from
an allegedly feminine probability to an allegedly masculine (that is,
abstract and neuter) transcendence.

Johnson's anxiety about Lennox's heterodoxy was not alone. Soon
enough the study gained a small notoriety for its "attack" on
Shakespeare and soon after that it was forgotten. The immediate
reception of the study, however, was of another order. *Shakespeare
Illustrated* received its first public notice from *The Gentleman's Magazine*
(1753) in a monthly catalog of new publications and an excerpt and
review a month later. The magazine's division of new publications
into eleven categories – divinity, morality, physic, policy, history,

antiquities, biography, poetry, entertainment, miscellaneous, and sermons – placed *Shakespeare Illustrated* under "entertainment," along with travel narratives, true histories, novels, ballads, and the like.[32] The classification of *Shakespeare Illustrated* as "entertainment" rests on the "entertaining novels" Lennox translates and condenses for the reader, the assumption being that one would go to Lennox's text not out of a scholarly or aesthetic interest in Shakespeare but for the lesser pleasure of reading novels.[33] As befits one of the first truly mass-produced periodicals, the "first *magazine*," in Carl Carlson's words, *The Gentleman's Magazine*'s classification scheme understands novels according to their status as light reading staked in opposition to the heavy weight of "poetry" or "antiquities."[34]

The choice of the category "entertainment," associated by Johnson's *Dictionary* with "lower-comedy," is telling.[35] The following month, the magazine printed Lennox's discussion of *Romeo and Juliet* in order to demonstrate the attractiveness of the play's source for their readers:

We have selected *Romeo and Juliet* for a specimen of what has been done by this writer to illustrate Shakespeare, because it is one of his most regular pieces, and at present more generally known than any other. But whoever would make a just estimate of his merit should see the whole work in which his resources are displayed, his faults detected, and many beauties of which he was supposed to be the inventor, restored to those from whom they were borrowed.[36]

Like Lennox, *The Gentleman's Magazine* prefers the novel to Shakespeare, applauding the critic's evaluative restoration of beauty to the source and noting that Shakespeare's most popular play will prove an even more entertaining novel. The "novel" of *Romeo and Juliet*, they go on to promise, is only one of many "entertaining" narratives set forth by Lennox's text. Unlike Lennox, the magazine makes a great deal of the popularity of the novel, a position that might be understood according to the magazine's presumptive audience and its self-declared proximity to the buying and selling of printed goods. The magazine's founder, Edmund Cave, was himself a middle-class printer-publisher and the subtitle for his periodical was "Trader's Monthly." From their position within the circuits of print culture (whose products they catalogue), *The Gentleman's Magazine* claimed to grasp the desire of the reading public for entertaining periodicals and novels. *The Gentleman's Magazine*'s opinion did not last; its interest for us lies in the translation of Lennox's metalepsis into a plea for mass culture, certainly one of the last occasions when a publication could, without hesitation, pose the apparently popular form of the novel against the works of the nation's canonical author.

## SHAKESPEARE'S LYRICS

Lennox was not the only critic with whom Johnson worked on Shakespeare in 1753 and whose writing addressed questions of genre, canonicity, and society. On March 8 of that year Johnson asked Joseph Warton to compose seven essays on Shakespeare's plays for the *Adventurer* serial he was writing along with John Hawkesworth. Johnson's letter opened:

Being desired by the Authors and proprietor of the adventurer, to look out for another hand, my thoughts necessarily fixed upon you, whose fund of literature will enable you to assist them with very little interruption of your studies.

   They desire you to engage to furnish one paper a month, at two guineas a paper, which you may very easily perform. We have considered that a paper should consist of pieces of imagination, pictures of life, and disquisitions of literature. The part which depends on the imagination is very well supplied as you will find when you read the papers, for descriptions of life there is now a treaty almost made with an authour and an authoress, and the province of criticism and literature they are very desirous to assign to the commentator on Virgil.[37]

The choice of Warton for the "province of criticism and literature" is suggestive for several reasons. For one, it is predicated on his credentials as an editor of Virgil, which authorizes his criticism with the aura of the Greco-Roman classics and with the sort of philological "commentary" practiced on these texts. While Warton's "fund of literature" is drawn from the ancients, the essays Warton eventually wrote were devoted to Homer *and* Shakespeare. Shakespeare now has the authority of the ancients and the critic has the quasi-professional status of the scholar. (It is not insignificant, in both these senses, that Warton's career move from deciphering ancient to vernacular texts is characteristic of his generation, beginning with Bentley, and followed by Theobald, Upton, and Joseph's younger brother Thomas Warton.) Warton's credentials derived from his editorial experience. The Virgil edition and then the *Adventurer* essays represented, however, an important and lasting change in Warton's writing. Before then, his reputation was as a poet. In fact, Warton's first publication was a fledgling attempt to reinvent the national lyric. He prefaced his *Odes on Several Subjects* (1746) with the claim that

the public has been so much accustom'd of late to didactic poetry alone, and essays on moral subjects, that any work where the imagination is much indulged, will perhaps not be relished or regarded. The author therefore of these pieces is in some pain lest certain austere critics should think them too fanciful and descriptive. But as he is convinced that the fashion of moralizing in verse has been carried to far, and as he looks upon invention and imagination to be the chief faculties of a poet, so he will be happy if the following Odes may be look'd upon as an attempt to bring back poetry into its right channel.[38]

Warton's critique of literary culture remains, at this point, an argument from within the community of practicing poets. He places his odes against what he understands to be poetry serving the worldly designs of the public and hopes by reviving fanciful imagination and evocative description to dethrone satire and restore the lyric.[39] "An Ode to Fancy," the first poem in Warton's series, culminates with an apostrophe to the slumbering Fancy, imploring her to return to England and anoint a poet fit to challenge the tyranny of modern, moral verse:

> O hear our prayer, O hither come
> From thy lamented Shakespeare's tomb,
> On which thou lov'st to sit at eve,
> Musing oe'r your darlings grave;
> O queen of numbers, once again
> Animate some chosen swain,
> Who fill'd with unexhausted fire,
> May boldly smite the sounding lyre,
> Who with some new, unequaled song,
> May rise above the rhyming throng,
> Oe'r all our list'ning passions reign,
> O'erwhelm our souls with joy and pain,
> With terror shake, with pity move,
> Rouze with revenge, or melt with love.          (125–138)

The concluding call for a reinvented sublime style, with its gesture toward Shakespeare, Fancy's favorite whom the poet demands she abandon in order to "animate" the self "chosen swain," encapsulates the terms of Warton's early project. He would elevate certain older poets in order to outline a new poetics. These poets would compose an English canon of unique vigor. (The ode concludes "O bid Britannia rival Greece.")[40] The relation to Shakespeare obeys a familiar dynamic. (Warton's now more widely read friend William Collins's "Ode to Fear" ends with precisely the same gesture.) Shakespeare is deigned the darling of Fancy so that Warton may position himself as that darling's heir. What distinguishes Warton's poetics, if not his actual poetry, is the position-taking against "didactic poetry," "moral poetry," "moralizing in verse," against, in short, social topicality. This distancing from topical reference and "moral" affect amounts to virtually an evacuation of content as such, in favor of an assembly of tropes whose distance from urbanity and politics Warton understands to be the signature of the lyric.[41]

The *Odes* were Warton's only sustained poetic project during his long career. After their publication, he turned to the writing of criticism. Speculations about vocational choice are at best suggestive, but looking at Warton's writing after the *Odes* we may get a sense of the imagined relation between criticism and canonical works. Shakespeare resides on the far side of a vast historical divide. Between the critic and the poet lies "the manifold alterations diffused in modern times over the face of nature, by the invention of arts and manufactures, by the extent of commerce, by the improvements in philosophy and mathematics, by the manner of fortifying and fighting, by the important discovery of both the Indies, and above all, by the total change of religion" (*Adventurer*, no. 63, 127). This description is part of a discussion of the enduring "charm" of Sophocles, Homer, and Shakespeare despite monumental change, despite commerce, imperialism, and secularization. In the marshaling of historical reasons for the cleft of ancient and modern, Warton shrouds Shakespeare in an antiquity of near antediluvian proportion. As we shall see, Warton's insistent antiquating of national literary monuments makes it difficult for him to imagine writing them anew. Writers are forbidden, by the fire-wall of historical time, to compose like their precursors. They may only write about their precursors' greatness in the modern form of the essay. The broadly historical dilemma, finally, has a particularly literary dimension: lyrical negativity is ill-supported by modern language and reading habits. Literature after the dominion of urbanity and satire is best served by the critic.

Warton begins his first essay on Shakespeare by claiming that "Of all the plays of Shakespeare, the Tempest is the most striking instance of his creative power."[42] The author "has there given the reins to his boundless imagination and has carried the romantic, the wonderful, and the wild to the most pleasing circumstances" (10). Warton embodies and then displaces the figure of the poet in Caliban, Ariel, and Prospero, respectively; each introduces the problem of poetry in relation to commerce and empire. The argument proceeds by means of a steady reduction and emptying out of the scene of poetry to the irreducible singularity of lyric. He begins by describing Shakespeare and Caliban in the same language of the "romantic," "wonderful," and "wild" (32, 33). While this similarity of description might suggest that, following contemporary primitivist discourse, Shakespeare is most like Caliban, innocent of the culturally vitiating effects of "modern times," Warton's connection of Shakespeare to Caliban soon gives way to one with the other-worldly Ariel, who is taken to figure the transcendent spirit of poetry itself. Ariel's song to Ferdinand on the occasion of his father's death is delivered in "aerial music . . . not fit for any but a spirit to utter," music "so truly *poetical* that one can scarce forebear exclaiming with Ferdinand: 'this is no mortal business, nor no sound / that the earth owns!'" (13). Warton displaces the momentarily primitivist association of Shakespeare and Caliban with something literally not of this earth. Ariel signifies that other worldly, not "mortal," sphere of literature. His song exemplifies how "the happy versatility of Shakespeare's genius enables him to excel in *lyric*" (13). Warton concludes by claiming that Shakespeare is ultimately most like Prospero, a magician, and literature itself like enchantment: "The poet is a more powerful magician than his own Prospero: we are transported into faery land; we are wrapped in a delirious dream, from which it is misery to be disturbed; all around is enchantment" (14). Imperialism turns into aesthetics, a flight back in time that is also a flight out of place. Shakespeare represents the aesthetic experience of inhabiting the literary world of transfigured and enchanted language, a "land" of tropes that both compensates for the "misery" of prosaic experience and distinguishes itself from public speech.

Shakespeare's distinctively literary language is reason for Warton's selection of *Lear* too, but here the lyric is counterpoised to the gendering of "modern times" and its cultural forms. His discussion begins by noting that

one of the most remarkable differences betwixt ancient and modern tragedy, arises from the prevailing custom of describing only those distresses that are occasioned by the passion of love; a passion which, from the universality of its dominion, may doubtless justly claim a large share in representations of human life; but which by totally engrossing the theatre, hath contributed to degrade that noble school of virtue into an academy of effeminacy. (113: 124)

Modern literature has been effeminized by authors who write "to gratify so considerable and important a part of the audience . . . the ladies and the beaux" (124–125). Since the predominance of senti- mentality or "the passion of love" stems from the reading habits of women and effeminate men, Shakespeare's historical distance from this market is an index of his virility: "Shakespeare has shown us, by his Hamlet, Macbeth, and Caesar, and above all by his Lear that very interesting tragedies may be written that are not founded on gallantry and love and that Boileau was mistaken when he affirmed: De l'amour la sensible peinture, / Est pour aller un cœuer la route la plus sûre / Those tender scenes that pictured love impart, / Ensure success, and best engage the heart." (125). To revive Shakespeare and the literary past is thus to distinguish the masculine from the feminine, the national from the foreign, and so to grasp an English classic.

The problem of literary history, the market and gender turns out to be resolved ultimately by the idea of literary language itself. *King Lear* is the quintessence of Shakespeare's masculine tragedy because of its lyrical strength, its capacity to convey emotion through the dense and transfigured language of "pure poetry." Warton's gen- dering of literary history in other words is inseparable from his argument on behalf of poetic language as literary language, as a form of speech distinct from a public discourse taken over by "the ladies and the beaux." He glosses Lear's exclamation on finding Kent in the stocks ("O me, my heart! my rising heart!") with the claim that "by [this] single line, inexpressible anguish of his mind, and the dreadful conflict of opposite passions with which it is agitated, are more *forcibly* expressed, than by the long and laboured speech, enumerating the causes of his anguish, that Rowe and other modern tragic writers would certainly have put into his mouth" (127). "Nature, Sophocles, and Shakespeare, represent the feelings of the heart in a different manner, by a broken hint, a short exclama- tion, a word or a look" (127).[43] As if to redouble the connection between his reading and his poetics, Warton concludes this gloss with six lines of his own verse:

They mingle not, 'mid deep-felt sighs and groans,
Descriptions gay, or quaint comparisons,
No flowery far-fetched thoughts their scenes admit;
Ill suits conceit with passion, woe with wit.
Here passion prompts each short, expressive speech;
Or silence paints what words can never reach.                    (127)

The distinction Warton draws here between Shakespeare and the
moderns, which in a remarkable stroke unites the former in a
trinity with nature and Sophocles, counterpoises the "expressive"
power of brevity, fragmentation, or even silence to the expatiatory
"speech" of prose and publicity, the enervating and sentimental
language of ladies and beaux. Warton emphasizes this point again in
a gloss on Lear's response to Kent, "Wilt break my heart," where he
writes

Much is contained in these four words; as if he had said "the kindness and
the gratitude of this servant exceed that of my own children. Though I
have given them a kingdom, yet have they basely discarded me, and
suffered a head so old and white as mine to be exposed to this terrible
tempest, while this fellow pities and would protect me from its rage. I
cannot bear this kindness from a perfect stranger it breaks my heart." All
this seems to be included in that short exclamation, which another writer,
less acquainted with nature would have displayed at large: such a
suppression of sentiments, plainly implied is judicious and affecting.
(no. 116: 144)

If the paraphrase is meant to denote the sheer volume of meaning
"contained" in four words of Shakespeare's poetry, Warton's delineation of this meaning might characterize what he takes to be the
problem of modern writing, its prosaic detailing of thoughts and
events. Warton parodically banalizes the unfolding of the lines "at
large" in order to devalue "long and labour'd speech" which here
stands in all of its prosiness against the preceding "four words."
Insofar as Shakespeare's poetry resides in his masculine and "judicious" "suppression of sentiments," modern drama and the novel
alike bespeak the enervated condition of sentiments unbound.
    The manner in which Warton invests Shakespeare finds an
allegorical double in his method. Warton is in fact among the most
detailed and adamant of midcentury critics about the protocols of
reading. He finishes the gloss on "wilt break my heart" by noting
that "the turns of passion in these few lines are so quick and so
various that I thought they needed to be minutely pointed out by a

kind of perpetual commentary" (145). This reading approximates what he takes to be the defining formal features of poetry, namely "short expressive" figures, detailedness, or what he summarily terms "particularity." Here Warton stakes his poetics in opposition to Johnson's notion of "generality" encountered above. As we shall see, Johnson depicts himself as attuned to the demands of the market, and like Dodd functionally integrates the idea of cultural consumption into his notion of the general or "universal." In contrast, Warton prefers the restricted category of the particular. A properly sociological difference between Warton and Johnson's criticism is integrated into method itself. Warton concludes his third essay on *Lear*, for example, with the declaration that "general criticism is on all subjects useless and unentertaining; but is more than commonly absurd with respect to Shakespeare, who must be accompanied step by step, and scene by scene, in his gradual developments of characters and passions, and whose finer features must be singly pointed out, if we would do complete justice to his genuine beauties" (148). This critical mimicry of the text, in which "perpetual commentary" is analogous to the "finer features" of poetry, is the introduction of "literary subjects" into the public Warton promised; it is the closest that a writer of essays may get to the historically impossible desire to be a poet. Warton imagines "particular" criticism to be the means by which he will "correct the taste of the present generation":

It would have been easy to have declared, "that the madness of Lear was very natural and pathetic," and the reader might then have escaped with what he may, perhaps, call a multitude of well-known quotations: but then it had been impossible to exhibit a perfect picture of the secret workings of Lear's mind, which vary in each succeeding passage, and which render an allegation of each particular sentiment absolutely necessary. (148)

The "allegation" of lyrical particulars combats the reading practice that would mine Shakespeare for generalized quotations and so transparently dispose the text as an object of conversation. Such generalizing of Shakespeare into an instrumental vehicle of "well-known quotations" is for Warton a specific example of the way in which "conversation has degraded learning." If one is to carve out a sphere of "literary subjects" in contradistinction to the subjects of public conversation, the "secret workings" of literature must be spun out of the text in minute detail. It is in this way that the project of the critic joins to that of the lyric writ large and criticism succeeds in accomplishing what modern poetry will always fail to do: redefine English literature as a canon of lyrics. It is in Warton's "disquisitions" rather than in his poetry, therefore, that "literature" comes to mean a transfigured and compressed form of language, situated in a negative and critical relation to the public. And it is in the very rejection of sociality and utility that Warton defines the social mission of the canon.

Because Warton's "disquisitions on literature" both look backward to Addison and forward to a new, lyrical understanding of Shakespeare, they are a suitable place to draw this chapter to a close. For critics of the early 1750s, the status of the vernacular canon remained unresolved. Dodd's rendition of the sublime attempted to reconcile a high-cultural Shakespeare with a nation of readers by imagining them in a sacred collectivity that would both elevate the text and overcome the social divisions of the audience. Unlike earlier models of genteel conversation, Dodd's community has no underlying social institution except the market. The instability of this formulation (to which Dodd testifies by ultimately abandoning his project) is answered by Lennox's heterodoxy. Lennox paradoxically elevates the novel as a genre and its public as a readership. While Lennox's literary history divides the novel from Shakespeare, it also provides the terms for Johnson's recasting of Shakespeare as high canonical. Johnson's Shakespeare assimilates as it critiques the didactic imperatives of Lennox's novel, suggesting that print and the public sphere are the conditions of Shakespearean transcendence. While Johnson moved toward a notion of transcendence bound up with reading, Warton saw the public as a linguistic problem and offered "literature" as a linguistic solution.

# CHAPTER 4

# The cultural logic of late feudalism: or, Spenser and the romance of scholarship, 1754–1762

In this chapter I discuss the critical formation that gave rise to the first fully canonical Spenser. Whereas Shakespeare was treated more or less continuously from the Restoration onward (although as I have attempted to show in shifting terms), Spenser was self-consciously revived during the 1750s and 60s. When Spenserians from this period began their projects they frequently invoked the lamentable forgetting of their poet, his ill-fitting in modern times. This man-euver entailed a varied reconsideration of language (archaism), genre (the romance), and history (feudalism), and was characteristi-cally used to elevate Spenser. The majority's refusal or inability to read *The Faerie Queene* signified the poem's valuable distance from modern culture.[1] The revival of Spenser has a relatively concrete register in the number and style of editions as well. After the 1679 two volume quarto edition of *Edmund Spenser: The Works of that Famous English Poet*, the first to contain the poet's "life," John Hughes's four volume duodecimo *Works of Spenser* (1715) remained the sole eighteenth-century edition of Spenser's poetry until Frank Birch's *Faerie Queene* in 1751. During the years that saw an intense debate over Shakespeare's status, Spenser remained relatively in the wings of critical culture. After the reprinting of Hughes's edition in 1750 and the appearance of Birch's a year later, however, a sharp turn in the treatment of Spenser occurred: two editions in 1758, one by John Upton, the other by Ralph Church, and two extended critical commentaries, Thomas Warton's *Observations on the Fairy Queen of Spenser* (volume one 1754; volume two 1762) and Richard Hurd's *Letters on Chivalry and Romance* (1762).[2] Once the revaluation of older vernacular texts according to aesthetic and historicist discourse had begun apace, Spenser's *Faerie Queene* could be viewed unapologeti-cally as the best example of the English romance. I shall argue, in fact, that it is in the treatment of Spenser that the idea of English antiquity is posed most explicitly as a series of problems: What makes the English past different from the present? Does antiquity include even Milton? Is literary history the same as social history?

The Spenser revival throws into relief the critical culture of the midcentury. Although problems of variants and authenticity were less pronounced than in Shakespeare's plays, Spenser's poem was still an important ground for historicist textual practice. Archaisms, for obvious reasons, provided ample material for philological scholars. And in this sense, as in others, the revival partakes of the larger recession of the paradigm of linguistic elegance. Beginning with Ben Jonson's summary declaration that Spenser "writ no language," the stark juxtaposition of Spenser's diction with the norms of common speech had vexed seventeenth- and early eighteenth-century critics.[3] By the time of Samuel Johnson's complaint that Spenser wrote "a mingled dialect which no human being ever could have spoken," however, the embarrassment of linguistic obscurity seemed rather antiquated itself.[4] It seemed to hearken back to the days of studied eloquence that Johnson elsewhere criticizes. Of equal concern to midcentury critics was the problem of *The Faerie Queene*'s genre, whether to assign it to the class of the epic – and so see its formal unity as particularly flawed or, as Spenser himself seemed to suggest, simply dispersed over twelve adventures under the unifying aegis of Arthur – or to assign it a version of the romance shorn of its relation to the novel and nostalgically revalued as an enchanted and sublime contrast to the secular and rational present.[5]

This chapter focuses on two major and two minor figures in the Spenser revival, Thomas Warton and Richard Hurd, and William Huggins and John Upton respectively. With Warton and Hurd, we witness the revisionary construction of Spenser as the epitome of the gothic romance. But this romantic reading was established through a series of generic and ideological encounters with other readings. Spenser's position derives from the working out, within the conflicted terms of midcentury criticism, of "difficulty" and "pedantry," at one moment, "the sublime" and "the beautiful" at another, and the "gothic" and "classic," at still another. These binarisms emerge in turn from rival interpretations of English social history. The midcentury's Spenser revival demonstrates, with notable clarity, the way in which the canon grew out of a wide-ranging discussion of England's imagined community and its history.

## THE PROFESSION OF SCHOLARSHIP

The gothic reading of *The Faerie Queene* was adumbrated by both John Hughes and Joseph Addison; Hughes wrote that "to compare [the unity of the poem] with the models of antiquity, would be like drawing a parallel between the Roman and the Gothic architecture,"[6] and, adopting Dryden's terminology, Addison's *Spectator* defended Spenser's "faery way of writing" as a pleasurable form of poetry. But it was not until the moment of Warton's *Observations* that gothicism combined with historicist scholarship and neo-Longinian aesthetics into a fully romantic and sublime Spenser.[7]

In 1759 an anonymous pamphlet complimented Thomas Warton's study. "Every reader of taste must congratulate the present age, on the spirit which has prevailed of reviving our OLD POETS."[8] The method of this revival has become a "fluctuating science":

Spenser, as he best deserves, has engaged the attention of ingenious critics. About five years since, Mr. Warton published a series of Observations on the Fairy Queen, in which he has thrown many new lights on a poem, before little regarded, and less understood. Not contented with the petty diligence of recovering lost syllables, nor acquiescing in the easy task of praising without reason, he has attentively surveyed with a learned hand the fashions which prevailed in the age of his poet. He has happily discovered the books which Spenser himself had read, and from whose obscure and obsolete sources he derived most of his principal fictions. By means of these materials, judiciously selected and conducted, he has been enabled to give the world a more new and original piece of criticism, than any before extant. (2)

Neatly encasing a half century of debate and discord, the "science of criticism" at once distinguishes itself from modernizing anachronism and musty scholasticism. The two share an immoderate interest in language, either its refinement to modern sensibility or its rootedness in England's past. Hughes's updating of the orthography, the public's lack of interest, and Bentley and Theobald's pedantry all exhibit a linguistic extravagance which Warton's science has overcome.

The sense in which criticism had arrived, in Warton's work, at a stable understanding of the national canon and how one might go about discussing it in a formal setting is similarly evinced by Samuel Johnson's response to the study in July, 1754.[9] Having received Warton's manuscript, he wrote:

I now pay you a very honest acknowledgment for the advancement of the literature of our native Country. You have shewn to all, who shall hereafter attempt the study of our ancient authors, the way to success; by directing them to the perusal of the books which these authors had read. Of this method, Hughes and men much greater than Hughes, seem never to have thought. The reason why the authors, which are yet read, of the sixteenth century are so little understood, is, that they are read alone; and no help is borrowed from those who lived with them or before them.[10]

Johnson's response captures several major categorical and conceptual developments: firstly the alignment of "literature" with the native tradition, and the notion that older authors are the epitome of that tradition; secondly, the recapitulation of the ancients and moderns division within English culture itself, so that the aura that had once accrued solely to Greco-Roman texts now applies to Elizabethan works as well; thirdly, the designation of a method of study peculiar to understanding the English ancients, namely the tracking down of sources, parallel usage, and the like; fourthly, the notion that critics from the early eighteenth century – such as Spenser's first editor, John Hughes – failed at such historical practice; and fifthly, the claim that the reading public for Elizabethan literature is vanishing, in need of the help of the scholar-critic, or reduced to the minority of the learned.

To what degree, then, did Warton's *Observations* entail such categorical maneuvers? Certainly Warton hangs much of the value of his study on the purity and consistency of method. "In reading the works of a poet who lived in an old age," he writes,

it is necessary that we should look back upon the customs and manners which prevailed in that age. We should endeavour to place ourselves in the writer's situation and circumstances. Hence we shall become better enabled to discover how his turn of thinking, and manner of composing, were influenced by familiar appearances and established objects, which are utterly different from those with which we are at present surrounded. For want of this caution, too many readers view the knights and damsels, the tournaments and enchantments of Spenser, with modern eyes; never considering that the encounters of chivalry subsisted in our author's age; that romances were then most eagerly and universally studied; and that consequently Spenser, from the fashion of the times, was induced to undertake a recital of chivalrous achievements, and to become, in short, a ROMANTIC poet.[11]

The notion that Spenser resides in "a remote age," "utterly different" from that of the reader, comprises the tendency to *periodize* Elizabethan texts, to place them in the dimness of a past whose lifeworld, in all meaningful senses, is unrecognizable to the common reader. Like Lewis Theobald before him, Warton adapted classical philology to the reading of English antiquity. His method included source study, etymology, variant readings, cross-referencing within the author's corpus and contextualizing within period production at large. While the ostensible goal of such historicist criticism was to place the reader in the past, in the period of the author, the effect of this placement was less to dissolve the distance between the reader and the text than to reinforce such distance as the condition of approaching great works. Like a work written in Latin or Greek, Spenser's poem demands that readers are educated. Learned reading allows one to appreciate the literary genre and historical period of the poem (the romance and feudalism), both of which are unfamiliar to readers steeped only in the epic and commerce.

The literary defense of Spenser is encased within an argument on behalf of his difficulty. Consider Warton's apology for the tedium of his method: "the lovers of Spenser, I hope, will not think I have been too tedious in a disquisition, which has contributed not only to illustrate many particular passages in their favorite poet, but to display the general cast and colour of his poem. Some there are, who still censure what I have collected on this subject, as both trifling and uninteresting: but such readers can have no taste for Spenser" (1: 65). Those who have no taste for Spenser are the uneducated, to be sure, but also readers who shrink from intellectual culture. Warton's reclaiming of the discourse of taste is, in this sense, a response to the familiar charge of pedantry. Not the polite exercise of genteel reading, taste is the ability to read difficult texts. In the postscript to the second volume, he defends Theobald against Pope's anti-intellectualism:

Experience has fatally proved, that the commentator whose critical inquiries are employed on Spenser, Jonson, and the rest of our elder poets, will in vain give specimens of his classical erudition, unless, at the same time, he brings to his work a mind intimately acquainted with those books, which though now forgotten, were yet in common use and high repute about the time in which these authors respectively wrote, and which they consequently must have read. While these are unknown, many allusions and many imitations will either remain obscure, or lose half their beauty and propriety . . . Pope laughs at Theobald for giving us, in his edition of Shakespeare, a sample of "all such reading as was never read". But these strange and ridiculous books which Theobald quoted, were unluckily the very books which Shakespeare himself had studied; the knowledge of which enabled that useful editor to explain so many difficult allusions and obsolete customs in his poet, which otherwise could never have been understood . . . If Shakespeare is worth reading, he is worth explaining; and the researches used for so valuable and elegant a purpose, merit the thanks of genius and candour, not the satire of prejudice and ignorance. (ii: 264–265)

The apology for Theobald repeats the notion that knowledge of the cultural past is necessary for a thorough understanding of English antiquity. It is a "labour which so essentially contributes to the service of true taste" (265). In contrast, Pope's hostility to scholarship is the enemy of literary knowledge, since it prevents the reader from transporting himself to the age of Shakespeare. *Classical* is hence a particularly overdetermined adjective, referring at once to the modern impulse to read Spenser in the tradition of the epic (and not in the tradition of the old romance), to the professional status of erudite critics whose methods have been tested on Greco-Roman texts but who need to learn the textual materials of Elizabethan England (the books that Spenser must have read), and to the aura of antiquity that Warton bestows on "our elder poets."

In each case, scholarship is a means to escape modern habits of reading. Warton restages Theobald's quarrel with Pope as an argument against public culture. The great enemy of Grub Street turns into its ultimate scion. This historical irony is nicely captured in the conclusion to Warton's discussion of Spenser's debt to Chaucer, worth quoting in its entirety:

I cannot dismiss this section without a wish, that this neglected author, whom Spenser proposed as the pattern of his style, and to whom he is indebted for many noble inventions, should be more universally studied. This is at least what one might expect in an age of research and curiosity. Chaucer is regarded rather as an old, than as a good, poet. We look upon his poems as venerable relics, not as beautiful compositions; as pieces better calculated to gratify the antiquarian than the critic. He abounds not only in the strokes of humour, which is commonly supposed to be his sole talent, but of pathos, and sublimity, not unworthy a more refined age. His old manners, his romantic arguments, his wildness of painting, his simplicity and antiquity of expression, transport us into some fairy region, and are all highly pleasing to the imagination. It is true that his uncouth and unfamiliar language disgusts and deters many readers: but the principal reason for his being so little known, and so seldom taken into hand, is the convenient opportunity of reading him with pleasure and facility in modern imitations. For when translation, and such imitations from Chaucer may be justly so called, at length become substituted as the means of attaining a knowledge of any difficult and antient author, the original not only begins to be neglected and excluded as less easy, but also to be despised as less ornamental and elegant. Thus the public taste becomes imperceptibly vitiated, while the genuine model is superseded, and gradually gives way to the establishment of a more specious, but false resemblance. Thus, too many readers, happy to find the readiest accommodation for their indolence and their illiteracy, think themselves sufficient masters of Homer from Pope's translation: and thus, by an indiscreet comparison, Pope's translation is commonly preferred to the Grecian text. (I: 197–198)

Here the recovery of older English literature crystallizes a series of oppositions inherited from Addison, Pope and elsewhere: original/ translation, difficulty/ease, ancient/modern, literate/illiterate. Warton's novelty is to suggest that in each case the first term's having given way to the second is the condition of degraded taste and indolent readers. Literacy is a scholarly facility with languages – not simply the ability to read, but the ability to read well. And reading well gives one access to canonical works. An argument that begins with the need to revive Chaucer for public consumption ends by listing the reasons why Chaucer, like Homer, is so difficult for modern readers. The aesthetic language of the passage has a curiously doubled function. Initially it describes how, properly read, Chaucer should appeal to modern taste. Soon enough, however, the aesthetic appreciation of Chaucer becomes indelibly attached to a language estranged from readers schooled on imitations. The effect is to push Chaucer along with Spenser further into the past. Chaucer, Homer, and Spenser share a common antiquity accessible only through expert knowledge.

The critique of the public's indolent pleasure with translations goes hand in hand with a turn to the cellular unit of the scholarly profession as the venue for reading. There is a pleasure in "research and curiosity," in library culture. "We feel a sort of malicious triumph in detecting the latent and obscure source, from whence an original author has drawn some celebrated description" (I: 54). The quarrel with Pope is a bid for the autonomy for scholars, free from the laugh of the public, the "prejudice and ignorance" of satire. When Warton claims that "if Shakespeare is worth reading, he is worth explaining," he argues for the legitimacy of scholarship as such. "Explanation" is the professional vocation of the scholar, in contradistinction to the evaluative practice of the old-style critic:

"That I have been deficient in encomiums on particular passages, did not proceed from a want of perceiving or acknowledging beauties; but from a persuasion, that nothing is more absurd or useless than the panegyrical comments of those, who criticize from the imagination rather than from the judgment, who exert their admiration instead of their reason, and discover more of enthusiasm than discernment" (II: 263). Evaluation splits from explanation. A division of labor between the public and the private sphere of readers recapitulates a division of knowledge between public and private modes of reading. Reading directed at the public may engage in all sorts of evaluative judgments about the relative refinement or pleasurable ease of a text. Reading directed at experts need only explain the inner workings of a text and its historico-literary context.

Warton's assertion of a professional prerogative had an institutional support. By the publication of the first edition of the *Observations* in 1754 he was already a university fellow. Two years later he was made Oxford's Professor of Poetry and served, like his father before him, two five year terms.[12] The 1762 edition of the *Observations* affixes to the title page that Warton is "Fellow of Trinity College, and Professor of Poetry in the University of Oxford." The professional claim broached by the title page as it were reverses Addison's inauguration of the public sphere of letters, bringing literature back from the "coffee houses and tea tables" and into the "closets and universities."[13] During these years, Warton occupied the position of *the* university critic (as he had in 1749 as the university poet, author of "Triumph of Isis" in response to William Masson's anti-Oxford satire, "Isis" [1748]). The *Observations* suggests that Warton's seat at Oxford is the place for the proper discussion of poetry, not only the Greek and Latin materials of traditional course work, but also "our ancients," who are valuable to such an extent that they warrant the attention of the professoriate. That Warton allegedly did not lecture on English while at Oxford – apparently he did not lecture much at all – does not detract from the importance of his lending the authority of the university to the discussion of national culture.[14] Warton's subjoining of his professional status to the Spenser volumes stakes a position within the community of practicing critics. At the same time, a serious discussion of Spenser by Oxford's Professor of Poetry documents the elevation of English texts to the height of the classics.

Warton's professional authority rests on an "intimate connection" with the books Spenser read. These books are of a distinctive stripe, however, and Warton's evocation of the cultural past is of a particular past. The twin project of reviving Spenser and revisiting his sources turns on a reconsideration of the romance as a literary genre and feudalism as an historical period. Warton begins the *Observations* with a defense of the "plan and conduct" of *The Faerie Queene*. He readily concedes that the poem does not obey the laws of epical form: it lacks unity of action, has no central hero, and thus fails to represent the sixteenth-century's revival of classical learning. After summarizing the case against Spenser in uncompromising terms – he has "remarkably failed" (10) in following the "method practiced by Homer and Virgil" (6) – Warton brings the historicist critique to bear on generic formalism as such. To judge Spenser on these terms is to hold him to strictures in which he had no interest or knowledge; it is to commit the double error of anachronism and ignorance. Underlying the poem is an entire "SPECIES" (II: 84) of texts, what he calls "the elder romance" or "books of chivalry," *Morte d'Arthur, Seven Knights of Christendom,* and the wider tradition of the "Provencial Bards" sprung from the Crusades. *The Faerie Queene* represents the last efflorescence of a genre that stretches back at least to the twelfth century and perhaps is woven in the immemorial fabric of Europe, in the "giants, necromancers, enchantments &c" of the deep past (I: 64).[15]

The attempt to pedigree the romance as a European and legitimate form for Spenser to have chosen for his poem leads to a momentous combination of historicist and aesthetic argument. Spenser's failure to write an epic ought to be understood in properly historical terms as the success at writing a romance.[16] Romance, in turn, bears with it a charm lost on its modern readers. The antiquity of the genre is interlaced with the vigor of its aesthetic: the imaginative force of the authorial mind, the agile thrust of the poetic image. A blandly historical thesis overlays itself with aesthetic brocade:

It is absurd to think of judging either Ariosto or Spenser by precepts which they did not attend to. We who live in the days of writing by rule, are apt to try every composition by those laws which we have been taught to think the sole criterion of excellence. Critical taste is universally diffused, and we require the same order and design which every modern performance is expected to have, in poems where they never were regarded or intended. Spenser, and the same may be said of Ariosto, did not live in an age of planning. His poetry is the careless exuberance of a warm imagination and strong sensibility. It was his business to engage the fancy, and to interest the attention by bold and striking images, in the formation and disposition of which little labour or art was applied. The various and marvelous were the chief sources of delight. Hence we find our author ransacking alike the regions of reality and romance, truth and fiction, to find the proper decorations and furniture for his fairy structure. Born in such an age, Spenser wrote rapidly from his own feelings, which at the same time were naturally noble. Exactness in his poem, would have been like the cornice which a painter introduced in the grotto of Calypso. Spenser's beauties are like the flowers in Paradise:

> ——————————— Which not nice Art
> In beds and curious knots, but Nature boon
> Pour'd forth profuse, on hill, and dale, and plain;
> Both where the morning sun first warmly smote
> The open field, or where the unpierc'd shade
> Inbrown'd the noon-tide bowers

If the Fairy Queen be destitute of that arrangement and oeconomy which epic severity requires, yet we scarcely regret the loss of these while their place is so amply supplied, by something which more powerfully attracts us: something, which engages the affections of the heart, rather than the cold approbation of the head. If there be any poem, whose graces please, because they are situated beyond the reach of art, and where the force and faculties of creative imagination delight, because they are unassisted and unrestrained by those of deliberate judgment, it is this. In reading Spenser, if the critic is not satisfied, yet the reader is transported. (1: 16)

Warton's attempt in the *Observations* to free Spenser from the reins of the epic turns on the rediscovery of the romance as the textual tradition subtending the poem; this is the argument spun out in great detail over the course of two volumes. Yet in this initial salvo the generic argument is deposed momentarily by the aesthetic one, in the guise, moreover, of an advertisement: to read Spenser in terms of the epic is not only anachronistic but is to miss the aesthetic pleasure of the romantic poem. This misreading is a paradoxical result of the dissemination of taste. Since refinement abounds among readers, the public has no appreciation for romantic and archaic forms that resist the dominant norms of "critical taste." Still, Warton's historicism turns out to be as anachronistic as the attempt to evaluate Spenser by the modern epic. What gets placed in the past is no longer "epic severity" but a new understanding of literature as "the force and faculties of creative imagination," an imagination that is not the receptive power of the mind or its ability to recreate images, as in Addison, but rather the ability *to create* marvelous things. The powerful attraction that readers have for the poem, the transport that one feels, distinguishes the literary text from the domain of science and philosophy; the latter attracts the head and judgment while literature attracts the "heart." As it aims to discriminate a sphere of high canonical fiction, Warton's secular insistence on the non-evaluative and rational vocation of historicist criticism wraps the sources in a normative understanding of the aesthetic: "romances . . . were the source from which young readers especially, in the age of fiction and fancy, nourished the SUBLIME" (1: 188). For all of the hermeneutical insistence on chronology, on the temporal relation of source to text, this bid to designate the lofty realm that the poem inhabits ends up explaining *The Faerie Queene* by referring to *Paradise Lost*.

The argument on behalf of the romance is thus also one for the aesthetic value of older literature, both of which are connected to Warton's scholarly understanding of *The Faerie Queene*'s generic hybridity. The investment in the romance (not to speak of "fiction"), however, is difficult, given the genre's relation in contemporary critical discourse to the novel. This problem is expressed in the seemingly displaced venue of adjudicating Spenser's debt to Ariosto. Warton goes to no great pains to mask his preference for the former's redaction of old romance. Spenser is not beholden to Ariosto; rather, the two are indebted to the "species" of "the old romances or books of chivalry"; and, Warton suggests, Spenser's copying is to be preferred to Ariosto's insofar as Spenser is more faithful to the sources. When Warton turns from describing Spenser's "imitation from old romances" in section two of the *Observations* to describing "Spenser's imitations of Ariosto" in section six, the difference between the two poets' romantic projects is laid bare:

But although Spenser studied Ariosto with such attention, insomuch that he was ambitious of rivaling the *Orlando Furioso* in a poem formed on a similar plan, yet the genius of each was entirely different. Spenser amidst all his absurdities, abounds with beautiful and sublime representations; while Ariosto's strokes of true poetry bear no proportion to his sallies of merely romantic imagination. He gives us the grotesque for the graceful, and extravagance for majesty. He frequently moves our laughter by the whimsical figures of a Callot, but seldom awakens our admiration by the just portraits of a Raphael. Ariosto's vein is essentially different from

Spenser; it is absolutely comic, and infinitely better suited to scenes of humour, than to serious and solemn description. He so characteristically excels in painting the familiar manners, that those detached pieces in the *Orlando* called Tales, are by far the most shining passages in the poem. (I: 225)

While Ariosto takes the romance in the modern direction of comedy, humor, and "familiar manners," Spenser retains the aura of the old romance, "revenging injuries, and doing justice to the distressed" (I: 17). The threshold between *The Faerie Queene* and *Orlando Furioso* is the sublime, as that category describes Spenser's retention and elevation of the old romance and, in its absence, Ariosto's transfiguration of the old romance into proto-novelistic "Tales."

In a telling footnote to the phrase "absolutely comic," Warton gives one sense in which Ariosto's comic fiction is to be distinguished from Spenser's sublimity:

I cannot forbear subjoining an anecdote, which highly displays Ariosto's early and strong disposition to drollery and humour. His father one day severely chiding him, Ariosto heard him with great attention, without urging a syllable in excuse of his fault. His brother, as soon as the father was departed, asked him, why he had made no defence or reply. Ariosto answered, that he was just at that instant writing a comedy, and that he was got to a scene, in which was introduced an old man chiding his son; and that the moment his father opened his mouth it came into his head, to examine him with attention, that he might paint after nature: that he was therefore entirely engrossed in watching the gestures, tone, and expressions of his father; and never had the least thought of making him an apology. (225)[17]

Ariosto's fiction is recounted here as a mimesis of "familiar manners" in quite a literal sense, that is, as the manners of a family. Ariosto's lowness is revealed by his style and his subject. He is uncritically mimetic and fails to elevate the setting from the domestic scene of family romance.

Warton's reading of Ariosto places the Italian squarely in the critical discourse of the novel, as a writer of conduct books. He quotes the following description of Ariosto's style by Gianvincenzo Gravino:

"Ariosto could not have attained his end, nor could his readers have reaped that instruction which poetry aims at, if this poem had described not only great actions in general, but, in some places, those that are mean and low. So that by this conduct, every passion, and every species of behaviour, was imitated. Whence, the reader might perceive what he should avoid or embrace in the common practice of civil life, according to the beauty or deformity of each object so described. This mixture of various persons, introduced with art, not only resembles the productions of nature, which are never simple, but always compounded, but is by no means unsuitable to the common course of heroic actions, which are still carried on by operations of inferior instruments and agents." (226–227)[18]

Gravino's judgment is utilized by Warton not so much to explain the mixed style of *Orlando Furioso*, as to describe how Ariosto writes in a distinctively lower mode than Spenser, and in two interdependent senses: first, in the mimesis of "mean and low" characters; and second, in the refraction of these characters onto genre itself. In both senses, Warton casts Ariosto's text, through the mediating criticism of Gravino, in the guise of a middle-brow conduct book. The *Orlando* affords "instruction" in the "common practice of civil life." The labor of the aesthetic is to sublimate social "mixedness" and the culture of conduct, "to separate high from low, fair from deformed; to compound rather than to copy nature, and to present those exalted combinations, which never existed together, amid the general and necessary defects of real life" (1: 228). Spenserian sublimity in this passage is understood in characteristic fashion as loftiness, but of a particular stripe. Ariosto's novels shape the terms in which canonical works fly above and negate the everyday world of family life.

Spenser represents the end of one romantic line and Ariosto the beginning of another. Even as Spenser sublimates "real life," this sublimation has determinate underpinnings. Spenserian transcendence is born from older social institutions. The exaltations one experiences in reading *The Faerie Queene* are of a particular historical origin: the feudal past, whose "chivalry" nourishes and promotes literature.

Chivalry is commonly looked upon as a barbarous sport, or extravagant amusement, of the dark ages. It had however no small influence on the manners, policies, and constitutions of antient times, and served many public and important purposes. It was the school of fortitude, honour and affability. Its exercises, like the Grecian games, habituated the youth to fatigue and enterprise, and inspired the noblest sentiments of heroism. It taught gallantry and civility to a savage and ignorant people, and humanised the native ferocity of the northern nations. It conduced to refine the manners of the combatants, exciting an emulation in the devices and accoutrements, the splendour and parade, of their tilts and tournaments:

while its magnificent festivals, thronged with noble dames and courteous knights, produced the first efforts of wit and fancy. (II 267).

Chivalry represents the historical meridian between the savage age of cultural "barbarism" and the contemporary, prosaic "age of reason and refinement" (II: 268). Between savagery and over-refinement, then, lies the apogee of cultural development. Looking back at "antient chivalry" Warton finds all that is presumably missing in modern culture: undifferentiated heroism across gender, literature, and social rank. Importantly for Spenser's reputation, Warton's historical periodization includes Elizabethan England at the outer border of the chivalric age. *The Faerie Queene*'s place in the generic tradition of the old romance is at one with its historical position in late feudalism, when social relations had yet to fall into atomized and privatized modernity.

Warton's historical and generic defense of Spenser acknowledges, however, that the waning of feudalism in the sixteenth century is immanent in the form of the poem. Spenser's appeal derives from his conscious evocation of an age at its conclusion. The use of allegory in particular signals the desire to hold on to the historical spirit one is inhabiting while acknowledging its incipient loss. In this sense, Warton argues, *The Faerie Queene* partook in the larger political project of the Tudor court. Spenser's allegorical system, he argues, reflects the court's deliberate reinvestment in the romance and chivalry. Spenser became "an ALLEGORICAL poet" because the "public shews and spectacles" put on by Elizabeth suggested to him the aesthetic possibility of "emblematic types" (II: 89). These pageants represented the court's revival of its own romantic past, a return to chivalry through the supplementary device of emblems. As the Elizabethans stood at the close of the feudal epoch, such emblems were the only means to grasp chivalry itself. The aesthetic achievement of the poem, Warton argues, has much to do with Spenser's need to route the representation of feudal relations through allegorical figures, which, as they carry the burden of historical recovery, are invested with the full-scale "imaginary" power of the sublime. Allegory, that is, indicates for Warton the abstraction and symbolization of feudal life as it is no longer merely lived but rather self-consciously evoked. The sublimity of the allegorical figures by this token amounts to an aesthetic embellishing of the feudal past, which, because of its relative abeyance in late Tudor culture, must be imaginatively rewritten by Spenser.

Since Spenser's historical situation, both within the Elizabethan court and at the close of the feudal epoch, underlies the figural and aesthetic dimension to the poem, Warton may then make the claim for the *interpretive* priority of his own method. The argument for the genesis of Spenser's allegorical practice, and for the court's interest in pageants, turns accordingly on the historicist focus on political context and manuscript evidence. A clue to the dual problem of allegory and Spenser's relation to the old romance, for instance, is found in "an antient book entitled, A LETTER, wherein part of the entertainment untoo the queens majesty at Killinworth-castle in Warwicksheer in the soomers progress 1575, is signified" (I: 28). "Killingworth-castle," Warton writes in a footnote, "was early made the theatre of romantic-gallantries; and was the place where tilts and tournaments, after a long disuse, were re-established in their original splendor by Roger Earl of Mortimer, in the reign of Edward I" (I: 28). The re-establishment of the romance, however, was filtered through the quasi-absolutist desires of the court; the book recounts the dramatization of an episode from *Morte d'Arthur*, in which the "lady of the lake" meets Queen Elizabeth on a floating island to surrender "her lake and power therein; with promise of repair to the court" (I: 29). By Warton's estimation, allegory is the "meter and matter" of the Elizabethan monarchy as it invokes the cultural past to unify the nobility around its image (I: 29). The genre of the romance (like feudalism) is thus at once contemporary to Spenser and in the deep past. This point is crucial for Warton's understanding of the fate of the romance across literary historical periods, and of the difference between mass-cultural and high-cultural variants of the genre. The rootedness of the old romance in court culture distinguishes it from the modern romance.

Warton's historicist recovery of the political intrigues beneath Spenser's allegory once more differentiates *The Faerie Queene* from *Orlando Furioso*:

I do not deny that Spenser was, in great measure, tempted by the *Orlando Furioso*, to write an allegorical poem. Yet it must still be acknowledged, that Spenser's peculiar mode of allegorising seems to have been dictated by those spectacles, rather than by the fictions of Ariosto. In fact, Ariosto's species of allegory does not so properly consist in impersonating the virtues, vices, and affectations of the mind, as in the adumbration of a moral doctrine . . . [Spenser] proves himself a much more ingenious allegorist, where his imagination bodies forth unsubstantial things, turns them to shape, and marks out the nature, powers and effects, of that which is ideal and abstracted, by visible and external symbols. (II: 91)

Again the contrast between Spenser and Ariosto falls on the difference between two levels of writing, and again Ariosto provides a foil to the literary achievement of "ideal and abstracted symbols," this time through the novelistic and modern insistence on "moral doctrine." The nature of Spenser's transcendence of Ariostian allegory, however, is bound up with Spenser's courtliness and his proximity to the literary project of late feudalism. "We may call the Orlando a moral poem; but can we call the Fairy Queen, upon the whole, a moral poem? Is it not equally an historical or political poem? For though it be, according to it's author's words, an allegory or darke conceit, yet that which is couched or understood under this allegory is the history, and intrigues of Queen Elizabeth's courtiers" (II: 91). The alternative to morality is the literary domain of idealized and abstracted symbols, but these turn out to be grounded in a specific political context. To the degree that allegory is the means for the court to hold on to its romantic past – and to suture that past to the designs of the present – it also designates a social topos and, more distantly, its correlative mode of literary production. We may call this mode, following Pierre Bourdieu, "restricted cultural production," since the condition of courtliness, as supposedly unitary and unreproducible, as "the theatre of romantic-gallantries," strikes an alternative to "the large scale production" bodied forth by print. Warton places the courtly "theatre" at the origins of the writing of *The Faerie Queene*. The scene of printing and distribution is confined and, at moments, obscured from view.

Warton's interest in the historical underpinnings of allegory is double: he wants to decode the figural level of *The Faerie Queene* to the literality of the court (insofar as that designates Spenser's place in the field of restricted literary production) and to describe how allegory is the last expression of the old romance in England. Both maneuvers are realized in Warton's understanding of the history of allegory as a mode. That "allegorical poetry, through many gradations, at last received its ultimate consummation in the Fairy Queen" signals an overall decline in literary achievement after Spenser (II: 112). "After the Fairy Queen," Warton writes, "allegory began to decline," and with it went the heroic romance as well (II: 110). Warton's restatement of the now familiar narrative of literary history as degeneration, as it points specifically to the decline in popularity of allegory and romance, describes a wholesale shift in the location of literary culture. After Spenser's "consummation" of allegory,

a poetry succeeded, in which imagination gave way to correctness, sublimity of description to delicacy of sentiment, and majestic imagery to conceit and epigram. Poets began now to be more attentive to words, than to things and objects. The nicer beauties of happy expression were preferred to the daring strokes of great conception. Satire, that bane of the sublime, was imported from France. The muses were debauched at court, and polite life and familiar manners, became their only themes. The simple dignity of Milton was either entirely neglected, or mistaken for bombast and insipidity, by the refined readers of a dissolute age, whose taste and morals were equally vitiated. (II: 111–112)

Warton's account focuses both on the particular situation of the Restoration court and the cultural politics of the 1750s. The importation of satire and the cult of "versification" during Charles II's reign persisted into the next century, Warton suggests, in disguised form as the literature of "polite life and familiar manners." His concluding paradox – in which a "dissolute age" is at one with "refined readers" – may thus be explained with reference to the mode of literary production Warton criticizes, in which the "feudal" age of restricted production has given way to the "refinement" of the market, and the aesthetic power of sublime verse to the enervations of delicate "sentiment." Correlative with this institutional narrative is the epistemological narrative of secularization and rationalization. As literary production moves from the court to the market it is necessarily depleted of the very "magic and enchantment" which, as we have seen, Warton casts as the preconditions for "true poetry." Warton's critique of "modern taste," either its predilection for the literature of "familiar manners" or its wholesale disregard for older and better forms, reinvents the feudal past as an antidote to the commercial present, and so pays attention to the still enchanted lifeworld of the sixteenth century and the still courtly milieu of literary production. Warton's understanding of literary history is connected to his position as a critic in a relatively concrete sense: while the court has been rendered obsolete by the market, it maintains a shadow existence in the contemporary university where disinterested scholars recover and revalue older forms.

### GENTILITY UNDER DURESS

Warton's position-taking within the cultural field, particularly as it was embodied in the dismissal of Ariosto, did not go unnoticed. William Huggins, a translator of *Orlando Furioso*, responded to the first volume of the *Observations* with the pamphlet *The Observer Observ'd: or Some Remarks on a Curious Tract, intitled, Observations on the Faerie Queene of Spencer. By Thomas Warton, A.M. &c.* (1756).[19] Huggins's rejoinder to Warton was slightly more than a defense of a poem that he had just translated. A landed gentleman and occasional critic, Huggins addressed, rather, the social institution of scholarship as such.[20] "It has frequently given me disagreeable concern in companies," Huggins opens his pamphlet,

> where each is well capacitated to judge for themselves, to find a general alarm, at some one's beginning to make remarks on any production set before him; attended with an united cry, *O, this Gentleman is a Critic!* Taking that title in as evil a sense, as smugglers, or other delinquents against the law, would an informer: when really the term means no more than, that he is one of themselves; provided that they did but divest themselves of that unsuitable modesty, or, rather more frequently, that thoughtless indolence, which renders people either afraid to utter their sentiments, or too incurious, for want of practice, to form any.[21]

Huggins is taken aback that criticism has become a pejorative category, a retreat from the community rather than its ultimate expression. It is in this sense that we may understand the analogy to smuggling. If the reading public is a community built on trust, to "inform" on it would amount to a particular sort of treachery, an assertion of the private individual's authority over the public. The choice of this simile to describe the situation of the reading public, however, might indicate the degree to which Huggins is self-consciously evoking a critical moment (that of Addison) he knows to have passed, and which he accordingly figures in terms of a closely knit conspiracy. Huggins "observes" in Warton a transformation within critical culture during the midcentury, its breaking away from the norms of the early eighteenth century's public sphere toward the historicist aesthetics of the literary past, away from the market toward restricted culture. On Huggins's account, the critic should be merely another reader or consumer, whose particular "remarks" on "the production set before him" are part of the ongoing constitution of public taste. Criticism of this sort is a socially *positive* act: "But sure an honest, fair disquisitor, who writes or speaks from an innocent delight he has in the investigation of truth, as well as to elucidate circumstances not so apparent to all inspectors, ought to be *deem'd a friend to society*: Such is the true candid critic!" (4). From Huggins's hindsight such gentility can only look like a palliative contrast to the critical quarrels of his day, and to the hubris of scholars like Warton who assert their private and professional will over and against the public. But one might underscore the historical continuity between Warton and Huggins as well by pointing to their shared concern that the cultural market has eroded the basis of public consensus. This concern becomes rather pronounced over the course of the pamphlet but is implicit already in Huggins's nostalgia for a genteel taste he sees to be under attack from vulgar pedantry.

Like Addison and Pope before him, Huggins defines the critic against the scholar. The intellectual critic qua "pedant" here returns, in the manner of *The Dunciad*, as that most peculiar contradiction of the eighteenth-century print market, the unified Grub Street hack/textual scholar. Following his celebration of the "true candid critic," Huggins describes a new breed of bad critics:

But when that glorious character is debased, and a person, instead of a judge becomes an accuser, exchanging the lenity of the former, for the too usual virulence of the later, with the view of pulling down another's merit to set up his own, the severest resentment cannot counterbalance the demerit of so unpardonable a depravation of those talents, which are so flagrantly misused. (4)

The particular point has to do with the treatment of Ariosto, but Huggins is making a larger statement about the institutional and methodological position of Wartonian criticism. "In this last light," Huggins continues, "appears an author, one Mr. Thomas Warton, so manifestly, that he seems to decline the ceremony of disguise; as if he conceived the merit of his success depended on the barefacedness of his attacks" (4). Warton's arrogant elevation of the "critic" to a position outside of the reading public is, according to Huggins, indicated on the very title page of the *Observations* by the simple printing of the author's own name. Huggins's anonymity, by contrast, is of a piece with his aristocratic disdain for professional criticism. To print one's name is to assert the position of the critic as an autonomous professional identity, to drop the dignified cloak of the aristocratic amateur. Huggins's quarrel with Warton in this sense registers what we have described as the historical disjunction of criticism as a vocation from criticism as an avocation. While Warton's transgression of the stately anonymity of conventional criticism amounts to the end of the reading public as the *beau monde* from which critics can be drawn at will, it also signifies the overtaking of judgment by a coterie of professional writers, who speak a vocational language and have self-serving interests.

Since Warton's proper name is the marker of his pedantry and parochial, interested knowledge, it is no surprise that the baiting of his name leads directly to the baiting of the space from which he writes, the university:

I was sorry to see a person dignified with a degree, as also a fellowship in one of our universities, had degraded his pen so much; and tho' the *lucri bonus odor*, which seems, by his extracts and quotations to swell his performance, to be his main point, may not be without its charms, yet one would have thought, his pursuit therein should not have been so vehement, as to drop, by the way, all regard to reputation, or even discretion. (4)

Huggins's momentary obeisance to the university feigns a surprise that Oxford has produced such a pariah. Warton's indiscreet hubris, from the printing of his proper name on the title page of his book to the "poisonous acrimony" of his readings, Huggins wants to suggest, originates from the university's cloistered relation to the public just as much as it does from his position as a professional critic selling his wares on the cultural market. Oxford is indeed a reborn court, as Warton imagined, but in the negative sense of its being of no use to "society," while the courtliness of writing as an anonymous pastime poised indiscreetly against the heteronomy of the print market is, in contrast, the very signature of "genuine criticism." Later on in the pamphlet Huggins compares his own critical status to Warton's – "if the Universities teach not that doctrine [of reputation and discretion], I shall no more lament my not having had the honour of a university education" (46) – in order to again suggest that critics ought to practice within "companies" and not in the restricted circuits of the academy.[22] The "learned Collegian" represents for Huggins a two-fold transformation of critical culture: the retreat of criticism to the university and the infiltration of Grub Street into the socially refined sphere of judgment (49).

Warton's criticism is swelled with "the *lucri bonus odor*" which, depending on how one translates "*lucri*," means either "the sweet smell of gain" or the "the sweet smell of money." In either case, Huggins equates historicist criticism with the pursuit of profit: the personal reputation gained at the expense of the reputation of poets like Ariosto, or the money gained by the sale of books of criticism. The semantic instability of "*lucri*" in Huggins's accusation is particularly suggestive. It allows Huggins to accuse Warton of privatized egotism ("poor Spenser! – wretched Ariosto!" Huggins exclaims, "And oh! most mighty Warton!" [18]), *and* to repeat the Popean alignment of scholars with Grub Street and mass culture. Huggins understands profit as both reputation and money, cultural and commercial capital. Both are lamentable consequences of professional criticism and the book trade. In a marginal comment to his copy of Warton's *Observations*, Huggins describes Warton's aside that he was "obliged to the admirable author of the Rambler" for the idea that Ariosto "deals largely in identical cadences" as a "confession of a novice, condescension of a puff" and then adds "But this mt help sell a book, full of trumpery to make it salable."[23] In the pamphlet, Huggins figures the smell of money perhaps not surprisingly as the smell of feces. Burlesquing the scholar's revival of the romance, for example, he writes,

Let us pass the Chronicler of Seven Champions, Morte Arthur, St. Tristan, The Blatant Beast, The Questyn Beast, which is afterwards more particularly described with a bedroll of quotations, no less delectable than erudite, most appositely collected, to give not only a dignity, but also a magnitude, to this important tome; that purchasers may be well supply'd, for their disbursement of pence, either in their meditative fumigations or at the Cloacinian Offertory. (Huggins, *The Observer Observ'd*, 18)

Warton's methodical and pretentious readings are so many "fumigations." His "important tome" ought to be read while defecating and then used as toilet paper. The stink of the "Cloacinian offertory" (the toilet) is the *eucri bonus odor* wafting from the scene of purchasing (the disbursement of pence). Thus when Warton takes on *Orlando Furioso* "he empties his sewer in Ariosto's face" (35). While Huggins's scatology may be a relatively conventional response to commerce – the linking of money to excrement is, one might say, as old as commodity exchange itself – I would stress how, in keeping with Huggins's recourse to the Augustan model of the public, the "sewer" of the market is used to offset the purity of "genuine criticism."[24] Huggins's scatological rendition of the commercial culture in fact makes reference to book II of *The Dunciad*, where "Cloacina," the "goddess of the common sewers," presides over the race of the booksellers as they "scour and stink" to the "brown dishonours" of victory (*Dunciad*: II, 83–120). The bodily purity of the now departed public sphere is set against the "degraded" odor of triumphant historicism. Images of the lower body and defecation place Huggins's text within the constellation of high-Augustan satire, in particular the space of critical and aesthetic purity carved out by his idols Pope and Addison, and demote Warton to the dirty space of economic exchange: "Fain would I hurry out of this heap of rubbish," Huggins laments, "but am fallen again, worse into the mire" (*Observer Observ'd*: 34).

Huggins's resentment may thus be said to have as its ultimate foundation the commodification of criticism itself, the inescapability of the *lucri bonus odor* that underlies the deformation of critical culture which Warton exemplifies, and so impels the longing for that heyday when, as Huggins understands it, critics were drawn from the refined "company" of readers. The deleterious effect of "purchasing" writ large, that is, mediates Warton's professional desire for "the merit of his success," not just because Warton wants to make money from the sale of his book, but also because Warton's self-promotion is placed against the public of purchasers in the first place. His academic hubris is paradoxically coextensive with his position in mass culture: for as much as his pride is defined by disavowing the reading public, this disavowal also signals the challenge to the public by the forces of commerce and literacy. In Huggins's doubled and ambiguous use of *lucri*, the profit of reputation is inextricably bound up with the profit of money: "his vein of pride and stile of indecency sullies his paper so much, that it must disgust every candid reader" (9).

The paradox of Huggins's position may be captured in Bourdieuian terms as such: the disgust at the heteronomy of the market is directed as well at the autonomy of scholarship (figured as pride, pedantry and so forth). The idealized space of "genuine criticism" in turn emerges as the double negation of scholarly autonomy and commercial heteronomy by collapsing the two poles into versions of the same "disgusting" practice. Huggins's choice to take up the mantle of the critic is thus represented as the reluctant act of a cultivated amateur, who, free from the reigns of both the university and exchange value, stepped into public conversation only at the last minute to right the aesthetic wrongs committed against Ariosto:

it may not be improper to mention, not only my own consciousness of inability to treat on these matters, in a manner suitable to appear in public, (little thinking of enlisting myself at the press,) made me delay even setting pen to paper, in hopes some of those persons before mentioned [the editors of the *Monthly Review*] would have thought the observer's detestable performance worthy of reply: which should not now be attended with mine, such as it is, but that, first, That Poem [*Orlando Furioso*] has afforded me such delight, in both languages, that I could not patiently admit it to be so grossly maligned: and secondly, I have an abhorrence to see dead authors stripp'd of their fame and merit, to adorn the *Corinthian* countenance, or supply the empty pocket of any one, who has effrontery enough, right or wrong, to coin and utter whatever he can pass current for his own advantage. (14)

What seems like a rather conventional disclaiming of authority in these lines, I would suggest, is a rather complex position-taking, dialectically opposing itself to the "Corinthian countenance" engendered by the universities and the "empty pocket" engendered by the market. Huggins's "inability" to speak in a vulgar, technical idiom about critical matters, and his disinclination to "appear in public" or sully himself "at the press," are neither an attempt to disown criticism as such nor a modest deferral to the scholarly class; rather, they are the highly arched gestures of a gentleman of taste, whose critical position arrives by means of the above double negation at "genuine" or "candid criticism."

Huggins's resentment operates at many levels of his engagement with Warton's text, but focuses particularly on the signature markings of historicist *method*, insofar as it is method more than anything else that designates Warton's institutional position. His disgust begins with the opening pages of the *Observations* where Warton "sets out most pompously with 'the works of Homer and Aristotle begun to be restored in Italy – Gothic ignorance – *provençal bards' – then slap at Ariosto . . .'" (3). Finding the spelling of "Provencal" a particularly telling example of the critic's pomposity, Huggins devotes a lengthy footnote to the social conditions that led Warton both to forget the cedilla and drop the i:

Having been unavoidably compell'd, in the course of this tract, to accuse the *Observer* of want of knowledge of too many subjects, which he, with great ease and freedom, passes his judgment upon; over which deficiency, he seems desirous to cast a certain veil, used on such occasions, namely *pedantry*, either to raise an admiration of his science, in such of the vulgar, as should approach him, or to keep others at a suitable distance, it is necessary here to be brief; for were these matters of dignity sufficient to merit investigations, they must take up too much place in this work; – but one instance must suffice–It is remarkable that the *Observer* entertains us, no less than three times, at the entrance of his magnificent structure of Criticism, with the word, *provencal*, in order doubtless to give an hallowed impression in the gazing multitude; not unlike the effect produced in our Courts of Justice, by the sonorous, trinal exclamation of *O Yes*; – The Sense of which the *Elevated Cryer* is as well acquainted with, as his gaping croud beneath him: the veracity of which assertion will scarce be doubted by my Reader, unconversant with the French Language, when informed that the nonsense only arises from false spelling or pronunciation: The true being *Oyez* – Hear ye, i.e. Be silent there. To avoid the application already pretty visible, the word should be *Provencial*, from *Provence*, in France . . . The Word may possibly be used with or without the i, as by the Observer; but without the cedilla or what the French call the cedille, mark'd thus ç, it is absolutely absurd and inexcusable. (9–10)

According to Huggins's digression on the adjectival form of Provence, Warton's professional and restricted knowledge amounts to a remystifying of cultural products by the "veil" of an academic clergy. This cultural mystification has become a kind of secularized obscurantism (a half-hearted attempt to return cultural authority to the Church via its center of learning in Oxford) and so now is simply "pedantry," the old enemy of the disinterested and general discourse of the public sphere. Taken together, Warton's distance from the public, his presumptive "magnificence" and his "veil" of knowledge, provide a foil for what Huggins understands to be the norms of critical culture and rational conversation. Warton's desire for "admiration," the obscurity of his terms and methods, and the cloistered site of his practice all mark the emergence of criticism as a vocation, a professional identity with a particular language and authority apart from the "company" of readers. Huggins senses Warton's identification with the older forms and institutions of restricted culture (the Court, the Church, and the Romance), and casts this nostalgia as the abnegation of the reading public. Hence he aligns the general tenor of Warton's method with two institutions whose authority derives simply from tradition as such: the Church, whose "magnificent structures" and "hallowed" aura are recapitulated by the recondite language of the *Observations*, and the Law, whose sonorous obscurantism rings over the gaping crowd much as the critic's textual maneuverings soar over the reading mob.

The analogy among Wartonian criticism, the Church, and the

Law, derives in no small degree from Warton's musty obsession with linguistic oldness and textual tradition. Huggins suspects the methodological investment in the past for the past's sake, in particular the historicist fetish of the "original" over and against the translation. Warton's anti-Popean defense of "explanation" over "translation" is "a voluminous farrago of pedantry and impertinence!"

Observe, Master Observer. Altho' I have read Homer and Virgil too, thorough, perhaps more than once, in the Original, yet I am not without elegant entertainment, let me peruse when I will their two translations: the one of Mr. Pope and the other by Dr. Trapp. When I speak of books, a sort of, natural (it may be unhappy) frankness ever calls forth my opinion, which I wish may not be judg'd as guilty of arrogance, in approving the latter, as it would be of impertinence, either to praise or dispraise the former: But, tho' I have many pens to encounter, which may, I conceive, be in general considered under two sorts, either the sportive (to avoid a worse epithet) or the admissive of tradition for a guide, I cannot forbear expressing my surprise, that a translation, perform'd by a person, who has evinc'd himself so strict an admirer of Virgil, as well as so exquisite a critic upon him, and with such exactness has perform'd his work so as not to overlook, or neglect the closest investigation of each doubtful point, – consequently the spirit kept up and the whole dignity of our language for that purpose assembled, in a very glorious manner, by choice of the soft or sonorous, sweet or harsh, as the circumstances require, so as to captivate the most delicate ear: I say – That such a production should, on fair examination and upright sentence, find one judge to condemn, is indeed exceedingly astonishing. But I must lay all digression to this prohibiter of translation: Let him read Chaucer unmolested, if he can, which we may have just reason to suspect to be a puff, by what he has already shewn in regard to Ariosto. (27–28)

The quarrel with Warton at this point has to do with the overall question of periodization and the valuing of the past. Warton's interest in maintaining the distance of the past, the difference of *its* language from the polite conversation of the present, is here overturned as so much pedantry. But the accusation of pedantry is also put in the service of describing a normative understanding of literature and critical conversation. Warton's historicist privileging of the difficulty of older texts is countered by Huggins's aestheticist recourse to "elegant entertainment." This reversal may be said to be a shrinking away from Warton's emphasis on the sublime as well; in both cases, the modifier "elegant" is crucial, since it elevates "entertainment" from its place as simply, in Johnson's words, "lower comedy"[25] – the theater, the novel, and so forth – to the rather more lofty position described by Addison in the *Spectator* essays or Pope in the *Essay on Criticism* (the two main reference points in Huggins's description of "genuine criticism"). If literature is to be a pleasing diversion, criticism should be an open conversation among equals, whose "natural frankness" does not descend to the "impertinence" and "arrogance" of professional writers. Finally, just as Warton's critique of textual and linguistic modernization turned on a new estimation of the linguistic capital of Chaucer and Spenser's diction, Huggins's response contains its own version of such capital, namely, the "dignity of our language" in its *present* incarnation as "soft or sonorous, sweet or harsh, as the circumstances require" for the "delicate ear." Warton and Huggins represent two positions within a larger discussion of literary language. In this passage, it is the polite language of the public sphere which, having overcome the barbarous roughness of the past to establish "delicate" norms of social intercourse through the mediating institutions of print and conversation, is now threatened by the emergence of a new barbarism: the professional dialect of historicist critics.

Against historicist method, Huggins places "open and communicative" and "publick spirited" criticism. But the rhetoric of his pamphlet ironically converges with the very "poisonous acrimony" for which he derides Warton. One way of understanding this irony is to suggest that Huggins's inability to raise himself to the stately equipoise of Addison (except in his anonymity) is a fully historical development and not simply a personal failing. The critical profession and the cultural market thwart Huggins's gentility. The charge that Warton does not write in the proper manner of the cultivated amateur may thus be grasped as merely another position-taking within a determinate structure of positions, albeit one that gestures toward a recently departed orthodoxy. "Genuine criticism" is a threatened and increasingly diminished space. Following his admonition to be "public spirited," Huggins writes, "perhaps it may be said the intuition of sound judges needs no such hints. – How few they may be, perhaps the fingers of one hand may numerate; but to such I would make an appeal" (54–55). The winnowing of the "sound judges" to whom Huggins would make his case registers the larger transformation of literary culture he decries just as much as the emergence of Wartonian scholar/hacks. And, although Huggins hopes for "sound judges" as his audience, he seems to sense that his own prose is infected by the commodity system and the professionalization of criticism. Huggins's sense of the windowless closure of Grub Street on his writing, and the inaccessibility of the classical reading public he desires, leads at the end of the pamphlet to a certain pathos, a pathos that is registered as a regret that he had to stoop to such rhetorical impoliteness in the first place. "The raw head and bloody bones hurt the credit of a critic" he concludes; thus, one ought to "let all the condemned wretches get off merrily" (55). The juxtaposition here of a scene of dismemberment with a scene of happiness is instructive, as if the merriment of critical conciliation is meant to compensate for the degradation of critical battle to which Huggins has been party as much as Warton. Huggins is, however, rather unable to manage this compensation on his own, since the scene of such merriment – the classical public sphere in which readers are also critics and both have polite, gentlemanly taste – is historically unavailable. He accordingly marshals a sequence of particularly telling citations to do the work for him. "Call out a reprieve, and, after our dance, end with some verses, which may reduce all our irascible muscles now, and, if well attended to, alkalize the bile of any future observers, who may be too precipitate.

> At every trifle, scorn to take offense;
> That, always shews great pride or little sense.
>   Mr. Pope's *Essay on Criticism*

> You then whose judgment the right course would steer,
> Know you well each *Ancient's* proper character;
> His fable, subject, scope in ev'ry page,
> Religion, Country, genius of his age:
> Without all these at once before your eyes,
> Cavil you may, but never criticize.
>   *ibid.*                                      (55–56)

As the pamphlet closes, Huggins suggests that "genuine criticism" may have been entirely overcome, present only as a cultural memory of the moment of the *Essay on Criticism*. That the tonic for critical bile turns out to be Huggins's very model of critical practice is perhaps no surprise, but it is interesting to reflect how in this case Pope is bodied forth as a paragon of stately restraint, an image of a better time when criticism followed the ancients and resisted the "trifles" of "pride." (Pope's Dennis here becomes Huggins's Warton, as the citation erases the passage of time and the shifting of institutions.)

The memory of Pope no longer has the equanimity of a settled doxa, however, and is now a critical position and an ideology in its own right.

## CLASSICISM UNDER DURESS

Our understanding of the critical controversy surrounding Warton's revival of Spenser – and, by extension, the romance and feudalism – may be complicated by introducing a third interlocutor whose position, while certainly disavowing Huggins's public sphere rationalism, does not quite correspond to Warton's scholarly romanticism either. The reading of Spenser as an *epic* poet of a distinctive but still classical variety was elaborated most fully by John Upton in his two volume quarto edition of *The Faerie Queene* in 1758. Upton's earlier insistence, in *Critical Observations on Shakespeare* (1746, 48), that Shakespeare not be held to modern criteria of formal judgment is oddly complemented by his argument ten years later that Spenser's "epic" followed classical rules, and that these rules constitute literary achievement:

The Fairy Queen . . . seems to have been hitherto very little understood; notwithstanding that [Spenser] has opened, in a great measure, his design and plan in a letter to his honoured friend Sir W. R. How readily has every one acquiesced in Dryden's opinion? That the action of this poem is not one . . . that there is no uniformity of design; and that he aims at the accomplishment of no action. It might have been expected that Hughes, who printed Spenser's works, should not have joined so freely in the same censure: and yet he tells us that the several books appear rather like so many several poems, than one entire fable: each of them having its peculiar knight, and being independent of the rest.

In every poem there ought to be simplicity and unity; and in the epic poem the unity of the action should never be violated by introducing any ill-joined or heterogeneous parts. This essential rule Spenser seems to me strictly to have followed: for what story can well be shorter, or more simple, than the subject of his poem? – A British Prince sees in a vision the Fairy Queen: he falls in love, and goes in search after this unknown fair; and at length finds her – This fable has a beginning, a middle, and an end. The beginning is, the British Prince saw in a vision the Fairy Queen, and fell in love with her; the middle, his search after her, with the adventures that he underwent: the end his finding whom he sought.[26]

These are unexpected statements from a critic who had argued so vehemently for the historical specificity of Shakespeare against the imposition of modern rules. Here the argument is made again on behalf of older writers, but with the claim being that they embody the very categories that they are claimed to lack, as if to say that Shakespeare did in fact write as politely as Pope had wanted him to. Whereas Warton divided the romance from the epic and revalued Spenser on the former's terms, Upton claims that *The Faerie Queene* is an English classic, hence its formal contours in the most basic sense are akin to those of antiquity. The antiquity of Shakespeare's text here becomes the antiquity of Spenser's genre.

Yet in reducing *The Faerie Queene* to its bare plot, Upton's formalist revival of Spenser does in fact share an affinity with his earlier revival of Shakespeare: an English classic has been overlooked or abused, and this betokens the poverty of contemporary culture and its habits of reading. Having drawn the analogy of Spenser to the classics at the level of genre, and responded to the abuse of the moderns, Upton can return to the topics that characterize for him the status of high-cultural texts and the vocation of the editor, to the philological handling of a "difficult" text and its "obscurities." In his 1751 bid for subscribers, "A Letter Concerning a New Edition of Spenser's Fairy Queene," Upton writes that "an editor of Spenser should be a master of Spenser's learning: for otherwise how could he know his allusion to various beauties."[27] The method Upton advertises in the letter and practices in the edition is similar to the method for which Johnson applauded Warton. As such, Upton's edition is the first to treat Spenser as a classic, and of all the period's Spenser editions, the most elaborate in its annotation and glossary. As he had in his Shakespeare work, Upton embraces the scholarly role of an editor with "mastery" and "learning." The problem of Spenserian archaism is resolved by philology. Spenser adumbrates distantly the critic's own practice; his rescuing of old words forms literary language, and this language distances the obscure text from its modern reader. Older poetry resides uneasily in the modern idiom. Spenser is a uniquely scholarly poet (with Cambridge credentials), and his poem is singularly learned, demanding that readers are "tolerably taught" (*Letter*, 32). "Spenser began in his most early writings to affect the old English dialect; and though rebuked by his beloved Sidney, yet he knew from no bad authorities, that the common idiom should be often changed for borrowed and foreign terms; and that a kind of veneration is given to antiquity even in phrases and expressions. He had not only Homer for his example, but likewise the courtly Virgil" ("Preface": xxxiii). The "veneration" for older words is lost on modernizing critics who "generally follow the spelling of the times" (xxxix).

For as much as he sees the epic genre of *The Faerie Queene* to be timeless, Upton insists that the oldness of its language is an indissoluble element of the reading experience: "the reader will be pleased to remember that the spelling is not the editor's, but the poet's: nor will he be surprised to see it so different from his own time, if he is at all acquainted with our old English writers" (xli). In glossing and annotating a text that nonetheless retains its aura of oldness – and in particular by paying attention to the history of the language – Upton imagines that he is significantly revising the 1715 edition: "Mr. Hughes has likewise printed a Glossary, explaining as he says the old and obscure words in Spenser's works. But as he transcribed the glossaries mentioned above [E. K.'s glossary to *The Shepheard's Calender* and the glossary to the 1679 *Faerie Queene*]: so what is applicable to the Pastorals, is not always applicable to the Fairy Queen: for words often differ very much though spelt the same . . . His explanations likewise are in many instances not only misleading, but *unscholarlike*" (xlii). Hughes is faulted not so much for the sort of intrusive errors Theobald found in Pope, but rather for failing at his avowed task of philology. Upton imagines that the two editors inhabit the same professional community stretched over time; he looks back to Hughes and sees a version of a scholar like himself, whose failure demonstrates how editorial procedure had not yet achieved regularity or precision.

Upton shares Warton's sense of scholarly prerogative. Yet there remains something distinctive about the former's seemingly anachronistic insistence on the epical purity of *The Faerie Queene*, not just the lengths to which it will go to conform the plot of the poem to the unities, but more strikingly the extent to which it reverses Warton's emphasis on the romance. This generic reversal did not go unnoticed by Warton. In one of the few comments Warton made in response to Upton's edition when he added a second volume and re-issued the *Observations on the Fairy Queen* in 1762, he derided Upton for his inattention to the romantic precursors to the poem, and to the romance as a category. Arguing against an instance of Upton's annotation, Warton writes:

Mr. Upton observes, that we have here an instance of Spenser's learning, and that he makes his knights swear by their swords, agreeably to such a custom practiced among the goths and huns, and related by Jornandes, and Ammianus Marcellinus. But I am inclined to believe, that our author drew this circumstance from books that he was probably much more acquainted with, old romances. (*Observations*: II, 84)

Warton then footnotes this observation:

Mr. Upton [Letter to G. West pag. 17. 19] while he is probably speaking of Spenser's imitations from the romance writers by specifying only such romance writers as Heliadorus and Sidney did not appear, at that time, to have had any notion of the *species* of romances in which Spenser was principally conversant, and which he chiefly copied: I mean the romances of the dark ages, founded on Saracen superstitions, and filled with giants, dwarfs, damsels and enchanters. (II: 84)

Upton and Warton's quarrel takes place within the community of scholars, hence the figure of a learned Spenser strung between critics who vie for the most accurate resurrection of source material. To the degree that Warton and Upton share the same interest in reviving Spenser's works and the same notion of scholarly and elite culture, however, the debate over genre signifies a curious intercalation within the theory of high-culture. According to Upton, one must at least pay heed to the rankings of genre if one is to make an argument on behalf of the linguistic and historical distance of a text; hence in the Shakespeare book he compares at length Shakespeare and Sophocles, while in the Spenser edition he draws together Spenser and Homer. In contrast, Warton is interested in reconstituting the rankings of genre themselves, in submitting them to the historicist critique, and then in revaluing the romance.

The opposition of Upton's classicism and Warton's romanticism signals a transition in the understanding of high cultural genres, and in particular a struggle over the long-standing supremacy of the epic. Yet the persistence of classical genre categories in Upton's thought is as much a question of politics and the conceptualization of history as it is a museum piece of eighteenth-century critical culture. Whereas Warton situated the romance within a realm of pre-modernity, Upton views the epic as a salutary antidote to the domination of the modern, French romance. For Warton, literary history charts a descent from the high culture of the Elizabethan court, and its penchant for allegory, to the rationalized politeness of satire and the modern novel. To the degree that Upton narrates a literary history, by contrast, it places the epic in the position Warton carved out for the romance, as the apogee of value against which the modern romance pales. In the *Critical Observations*, Upton's argument against "modern and French refinement" conflates the popular romance with the dangers of French absolutism. Invoking the Longinian notion of the "mutual connection between civil liberty and polite literature," Upton asks, "what taste must it show to fly to the crude productions of an enslaved nation? Yet, this is our reigning taste" (28).[28] The romance is political tyranny displaced onto the domain of the literary, and the source of the present corruption of taste. Upton's preference for the classical genres, in turn, is one for a certain republican ethos, which he places in the past as a contrast to the tyranny of continental politics and its shadow form in the romance.[29] The romance, in its turn, maintains its familiarly negative position as, on the one hand, dangerous and foreign, and, on the other, unstable and feminine. Upton's account of Spenser's epic is as much a rendering of high culture as anti-romance as it is an anachronistic neo-classicism.

### THE RE-ENCHANTMENT OF THE WORLD

The romantic and nostalgic reading of Spenser survived Upton's and Huggins's critiques to emerge in altered form in Richard Hurd's *Letters on Chivalry and Romance* (1762). "Of Dr. Hurd, Bishop of Worcester," wrote Boswell, "Johnson said to a friend, 'Hurd Sir is one of a set of men who account for everything systematically; for instance, it has been a fashion to wear scarlet breeches; these men would tell you that according to causes and effects, no other wear could at that time have been chosen.'"[30] According to Johnson, Hurd's criticism is systematic because it seeks to ground texts in a kind of inevitable determinism; in this case, the view that "no other" genre but the romance could have dominated the feudal age. In the *Dictionary*, Johnson defines "system" as "a scheme which reduces many things to a regular dependence or cooperation," and "systematical" as "written or formed with regular subordination of one part to another" (1186). Hurd's system mimics the finely articulated hierarchy of feudal society. The reciprocal dependence of the various ranks and levels of the feudal system is the political counterpoint to a certain double "reduction," of the literary text to its historical setting and the aesthetic to its instantiation in the sublime. Hurd's system would reduce politics, genre, and aesthetics to a constellation of homologues, which Johnson argues is a "subordination" of the autonomous specificity of each part to the overweening authority of the whole. In his 1765 edition of Shakespeare, Johnson disavows this critical system in favor of a tactical and tendential surrender of authority to the "reader." For Hurd, however, feudal systematicity is the very condition of a robust culture. In this sense, Hurd is characteristically conservative, and indeed his investment in the Elizabethan moment has an ideological pedigree stretching back to Bolingbroke.[31] Yet Hurd's conservative literary history – replete with a notion of organic hierarchy and immemorial tradition – imparts stability to the sixteenth century in order to understand the instability of the eighteenth century.[32] Understood from this perspective, Johnson and Hurd share some fundamental presuppositions.[33] While Johnson's resistance to Hurd's systematic approach to the past indicates his own commitment to separating the aesthetic from the political, Hurd's emphatic reconnection presumes their prior disjunction by degraded modernity.

Hurd began to concoct his literary historical system in the third of his *Moral and Political Dialogues* (1759), "On the Age of Queen Elizabeth." This dialogue was substantiated and extended by *Letters on Chivalry and Romance* (1762), which "illustrate some passages in the third dialogue" and focus particularly on Spenser.[34] The dialogue takes as its *mise-en-scène* Arbuthnot, Digby, and Addison visiting the ruins of the Earl of Leicester's castle in 1711. While at the castle the travelers meditate on the relative merits and problems of the Elizabethan period. Among the interlocutors, "Arbuthnot" is the unequivocal Tory champion of the Elizabethans, "Addison" his Whig and modern adversary, and "Digby" mostly a spectator who occasionally intervenes on "Arbuthnot's" behalf.[35] The ruins are a particularly telling site, since Hurd reminds the reader that Leicester stood for the persistence, during Elizabeth's reign, of the old nobility supposedly subordinated after the War of the Roses. This distant remnant of precapitalist society is then the subject of awe and dread by its merely Augustan beholders:

What chanced to take their attention most, was the monument of the great Earl of Leicester. It recorded his titles at full length, and was besides, richly decorated with sculpture, displaying the various ensigns and trophies of his greatness. The pride of this minister had never appeared to them so conspicuous, as in the legends and ornaments of his tombstone: which had not only outlived his family, but seemed to assure itself of immortality, by taking refuge, as it were, at the foot of the altar. (*Dialogues*: 38)

Valorizing England's past and its fundamental social class, the monument at the same time criticizes the present and celebrates an "immortal" aristocratic greatness. In Hurd's conservative idiom, the aristocracy are both rooted in old institutions and sublimated in perennial tradition. As they continue to survey the ruins, this version of the past opens up into a series of problems. Debating Leicester's aura leads "Addison" and "Arbuthnot" to ask: how does one explain the historical basis of the aesthetic? Is there a systematic relation between the social formation that gave rise to Leicester and its paramount literary forms?

During the first encounter with the ruins, the three are "struck . . . with admiration" and "kept silent." "Arbuthnot" then muses, "'why [is it] that the mind, even while it laments, finds so great a pleasure in visiting these scenes of desolation. Is it' continued he, 'from the pure love of antiquity, and the amusing train of reflexions into which such remains of ancient magnificence naturally lead us?'" (20–41). Before he can answer this question (and abandon the "pure love of antiquity" for a highly politicized understanding of the past), he is interrupted by "Addison," who gives at least what Hurd understands to be the modern's hostility to Elizabethan barbarity:

I know not, returned Mr. Addison, what pain it may give you to contemplate these triumphs of time and fortune. For my part, I am not sensible of the mixt sensation you speak of. I feel a pleasure indeed; but it is sincere, and, as I conceive, may be easily accounted for as nothing more than a fiction of the imagination, which makes me think I am taking a revenge on the once prosperous and overshadowing height, *praeumbrans fastigium*, as somebody expresses it, of inordinate Greatness. It is certain, continued he, this theatre of a great statesman's pride, the delight of many of our princes, and which boasts of having given entertainment to one of them in a manner so splendid, as to claim a remembrance, even in the annals of our country, would now, in its present state, administer ample matter for much insulting reflection. (41)

It would be wrong to say at this point that "Addison," as a modern, fails to appreciate historical distance, since it is precisely the passage of historical time over which he here rejoices. But the pleasure "Addison" feels upon beholding the ruins stems from the present's triumph over the past as the latter is reawakened only to be vanquished once more by modern institutions and taste. The pleasure of progress, of putting to rest the demons of one's cultural past, is worked up into an entire "fiction of the imagination" allowing the Whiggish modern a fanciful "insulting reflection" on the "inordinate" power of his aristocratic predecessor. "Addison's" deflation of the old nobility, as it is cast in aesthetic terms, might be viewed as a deflation of the sublime, which then adumbrates in its place a nicely modern and restrained beautiful (hence for example the pejorative focus on "greatness").

"Addison's" beautiful amounts to a tolerant aesthetic of mixed forms, whether political or literary. The politics of this overturning of the sublime is established in greater detail as "Addison" criticizes the supposed achievements of the feudal system:

Where, one might ask, are the tilts and tournaments, the princely shows and sports, which were once so proudly celebrated within these walls? Where are the pageants, the studied devices and emblems of curious invention, that set the court at a gaze, and even transported the high soul of our Elizabeth? Where now, pursued he, (pointing to that which was formerly a canal, but at present is only a meadow with a small rivulet running through it) where is the floating island, the blaze of torches that eclipsed the day, the lady of the lake, the silken nymphs her attendants, with all the other fantastic exhibitions surpassing even the whimsies of the wildest romance? What now is become of the revelry of feasting? of the minstrelsy, that took the ear so delightfully as it babbled along the valley, or floated on the surface of this lake? See there the smokeless kitchens, stretching to a length that might give room for the sacrifice of a hecatomb; the vaulted hall, which mirth and jollity have set so often in an uproar; the rooms of state, and the presence-chamber: what are they now but void and tenantless ruins, clasping with ivy, open to wind and weather, and representing to the eye nothing but the ribs and carcase, as it were, of their former state? And see, said he, that proud gate-way, once the mansion of a surly porter who, partaking of the pride of his lord, made the crowds wait, and refused admittance, perhaps, to nobles whom fear or interest drew to these walls, to pay their homage to their master: see it now the residence of a poor tenant, who turns the key but to let himself out to his day labour, to admit him to a short meal, and secure his nightly slumbers. Yet in this humble state, it hath had the fortune to outlive the glory of the rest, and hath even drawn to itself the whole of that little note and credit which time hath continued to this once pompous building. For, while the castle itself is crumbled into shapeless ruins, and is prophaned, as we there see, by the vilest uses, this outwork of greatness is left entire, sheltered and closed in from bird and beast, and even affords some decent room in which the human face divine is not ashamed to shew itself. (41–43)

The achievements of the Elizabethans are here cast as so many antiquated mannerisms of a dead culture. What has survived them, interestingly enough, is the small residence of a tenant, a proto-capitalist rentier who suffered under the feudal integument but whose rebirth as the capitalist farmer is demonstrated by the survival intact of his residence, an "outwork," in "Addison's" modernist eyes, against both the tyranny of feudal barons and the vulgarity of the common (this last figured here in the form of the porter whom Hurd describes in a footnote: "tall of person, big of limbs, stark of countenance [with] a rough speech full of passion of meter" [42]). Whereas "Arbuthnot" finds the intricately spun unity of the aristocracy and the commoners to be a venerable feature of premodernity, "Addison" finds feudal unity to be the condition of a tyrannical sublime which he would replace with a beautiful mixture of public and private life. The ruins accordingly cause "Addison" to reflect on political and economic change, and, crucially, to note these in two distinct registers:

It brings to mind the fraud, the rapine, the insolence, of the potent minister, who vainly thought to immortalize his ill-gotten glory by this proud monument. Nay, further, it wakens an indignation against the prosperous tyranny of those wretched times, and creates a generous pleasure in reflecting on the happiness we enjoy under a juster and more equal government. Believe me, I never see the remains of the past ages which arose on the ruins of public freedom and private property, but congratulate with myself on living at a time, when the meanest subject is as free and independent as those royal minions; and when his property, whatever it may be, is as secure from oppression, as that of the first minister (26).

From the vantage of the modern division of knowledge, which maintains that the political and the economic occupy two incommensurable domains, the past is "wretched" because "government" tyrannically holds sway over both. The pleasure "Addison" has in reflecting on historical change is that the public has disentangled itself from the private, or to be more specific, that the "public freedom and private property" suppressed by feudalism have developed in his day to the auspicious, beautiful form of commercial capitalism and the constitutional State.

When Hurd turns to "Arburthnot's" response one is struck first with how much he has the two travelers agree over the fundamental difference between the Elizabethan past and the Augustan present even as they dispute the meaning of this difference: "I never contemplate the monuments of that time, without a silent admiration of the virtues that adorned it. Heroes and sages crowd in upon my memory. Nay, the very people were of a different character above what we are acquainted with in our days. I could almost fancy, the soil itself wore another face, and, as you poets imagine in some occasions, that our ancestors lived under a brighter sun and happier climate than we can now boast of " (46). Hurd's sense of periodicity runs across the two opposing views of the past. When "Arbuthnot's" endowment of the Elizabethan age is quickly answered by "Addison's" opposing sense of the past – "what can these objects call to mind but the memory of barbarous manners and a despotic government?" (47) – we receive a different gloss to what is in broad form a similar understanding of the distance of the past. Where "Addison's" memory is of feudal despotism, however, "Arbuthnot's" is of feudal organicity. "Arburthnot's" response to "Addison's" query, and to his hostile reading of Leicester's feast, is perhaps the most evocative instance of feudal nostalgia in all of Hurd's work:

> You gave an invidious turn to this circumstance, when you chose to consider it only in the light of wasteful expense and prodigality . . . Can it deserve this censure, that the lord of this princely castle threw open his doors and spread his table for the reception of his friends, his followers, and even for the royal entertainment of his sovereign? Is any expense more proper than that which tends to conciliate friendships, spread the interests of society, and knit mankind together by a generous communication in these advantages of wealth and fortune? The arts of a refined sequestered luxury were then unknown. The same bell that called the great man to his table, invited the neighborhood all around, and proclaimed a holiday to the whole country. Who does not feel the decorum and understand the benefits of this magnificence? The pre-eminence of rank and fortune was nobly sustained: the subordination of society preserved: and yet the envy, that is so apt to attend the great, happily avoided. Hence the weight and influence of the old nobility, who engaged the love, as well as commanded the veneration of the people. In the mean time, rural industry flourished: private luxury was discouraged: and in both ways that frugal simplicity of life, our country's grace and ornament in those days, was preserved and promoted. (49–50)

What begins in this passage simply as a defense of aristocratic expenditure against the strictures of bourgeois rectitude becomes an elegy for the organic society and collective experience before the atomized and privatized present. The "Feudal system" was a sanctified hierarchy free from bourgeois "envy" and the public-private distinction alike. The defense of luxury turns on the historical fact that luxury was not yet at that time "refined or sequestered," was not as Hurd calls it a "private luxury," but rather spread over the whole of society. "Public freedom," "Arbuthnot" exclaims, "throve best when it wound itself around the stock of the ancient nobility" (50).

It scarcely matters at this point whether or not Hurd accurately captures the feudal mode of production as the "extra-economic" (or political) extraction of surplus value.[36] But it does seem important that his nostalgia retrieves a "feudalism" that is in all essential respects a compensatory response to the "private property and public freedom" of commercial capitalism. In the past, all social classes were entwined in a finely striated hierarchy and the comfortable simplicity of agrarian production was preserved. If this vision were not so evidently setting the stage for chivalry, one might say that its genre was pastoral, a precapitalist idyll. "The times of Elizabeth may pass for golden, notwithstanding what a fondness for this age of baser metal may incline us to represent it" (74). Once we accept that Elizabethan "feudalism" was the golden age before the iron age of bourgeois emulation and privatized individualism, it becomes easier to imagine that "subordination" was in fact the positive condition of collective life. And once we grant that the great enemy of "public freedom" is "private property" it becomes possible to see how the problems of one's own age can be resolved by an entirely different and *older* mode of production. At moments such as these in the *Dialogue* Hurd's sympathy seems most clearly to lie with "Arbuthnot" (a supposition born out in the *Letters*). But what is perhaps of equal interest, finally, is that "Addison's" capitalist modernism and "Arbuthnot's" feudal nostalgia existed as such clear alternatives and mutual antitheses in Hurd's mind, that out of the preceding decades of debate over the meaning of historical change and periodization such a sharp and "systematic" opposition had crystallized.

The *Dialogue*'s subsequent consideration of literary questions is set against the backdrop of a fundamental historical dispute. As Johnson had complained, Hurd finds Elizabethan feudalism and chivalry (which he does not distinguish until the *Letters*) to bear an intrinsic relation to its literature. As the Tudor Court softened the "fierceness" and "ferocity" of the "darker ages," it allowed for a certain literary flowering (59). Like Warton, "Arbuthnot" places the Elizabethan/Jacobean age at the crest of literary history, between barbarism and enlightenment. Although Hurd only sketches a literary historical narrative in the *Dialogue*, he is nonetheless emphatic about the singularity and specificity of his favorite period. "Arbuthnot's" literary line neatly follows the fate of feudalism and chivalry as discrete social institutions, which body forth the equally discrete and untranscendable moment of Spenser and Shakespeare. "And now that the poets have fallen my way, let me further observe . . . the manifest superiority of this class of writers in Elizabeth's reign, and that of her successor, over all that have succeeded them . . . We find in the phraseology and mode of thinking of that time and that time only, the essence of the truest and sublimist poetry" (70–71). "Addison" replies in kind with a defense of contemporary literature and an ahistorical view of the past, in which "such prodigies as Shakespeare and Spenser would do great things in any age, and under every disadvantage" (71).[37] "Arbuthnot's" response sharply distinguishes Elizabethan language as literary language ("pure, strong and perspicuous without affectation . . . the high figurative manner . . . so peculiarly [fit] for the uses of the poet [not yet] controlled by the prosaic genius of philosophy and logic" [72]) and nostalgically invests that language as the masculine precursor to contemporary, delicate and effeminate speech. "The tastes of the age, the state of letters, the genius of the English tongue, was such as gave a manliness to their composition of all sorts . . . which we would do well to emulate and not deride" (73).

Hurd's *Letters on Chivalry and Romance* take off from the *Dialogue*'s attempt to connect the achievement of Elizabethan literature to its social ground. "Nothing in human nature, my dear friend, is without its reasons," Hurd begins the first letter: "The modes and fashions of different times may appear, at first sight, fantastic and unaccountable. But they, who look nearly into them, discover some latent cause of their production" (*Letters*: 79). This line of thinking is evidently what Johnson meant by Hurd's tendency to explain the systemic inevitability of all phenomena. Asking the question "from what causes [was] the institution of chivalry derived?" obliges Hurd to separate out and systematically connect "chivalry" and "feudalism." In the *Letters* the two are no longer identical, but rather mediated; "Chivalry, properly so called, and under the idea 'of a distinct military order, conferred in the way of investiture, and accompanied with the solemnity of an oath and other ceremonies, as described in the old historians and romancers' . . . seems to have sprung immediately out of the FEUDAL CONSTITUTION" (83). The description of chivalry Hurd quotes is his own from the *Dialogue*. But his position in the *Letters* is complicated by the suggestion of a genetic relation between chivalry and its foundational substrate. In order to account for *The Faerie Queene*, one must first understand the romance, and thus chivalry, and so, finally, feudalism. The systematic analysis of the *Letters* takes the reader to the origin of feudalism itself:

The first and most sensible effect of this constitution, which brought about so mighty a change in the policies of Europe, was the erection of a prodigious number of petty tyrannies. For, though the great barons were closely tied to the service of their Prince by the conditions of their tenure, yet the power which was given them by it over their own numerous vassals was so great, that, in effect, they all set up for themselves; affected an independence; and were, in truth a sort of absolute SOVEREIGNS, at least with regard to one another. Hence their mutual aims and interest often interfering, the feudal chiefs were in frequent enmity with each other; the several combinations of feudal tenants were so many separate armies under their head or chief: and their castles were so many fortresses, as well as palaces, of these puny princes. (83)

Since they were always fighting, knights had to demonstrate allegiances to their lords; and "this condition of the times, I suppose, gave rise to that military institution which we know by the name of chivalry" (84). One need hardly stress that this frankly medieval scene hardly describes Elizabethan England, its gradual and uneven (and ultimately failed) development of an absolutist monarchy.[38] Still, the problem of periodizing feudalism, and Spenser's situation in it particularly, continually vexes the *Letters*. "The Faery Queen," Hurd writes, "derives its METHOD, as well as the other characters of its composition, from the established modes and ideas of chivalry," from "the real practice, in the days of pure and antient chivalry" (119). This practice spans the end of the Crusades to the close of the sixteenth century. According to the relatively strict logic of Hurd's "system," Spenser *must* write under feudal conditions (however attenuated they may be), for "the Gothic manners of chivalry, as springing out of the feudal system, were as singular as that system itself; So that, when that political constitution vanished out of Europe, the manners that belonged to it, were no longer seen or understood" (119). Spenser's poem could only have been written in a feudal society. Yet like Warton, Hurd also wants to argue that Spenser is *belated*, that he writes between the dusk of chivalry and the morning of disenchantment, and for that reason needs allegories, is misunderstood by prosaic readers, and the like. The compulsion to wrap Spenser in a fantasy of premodernity (in the manner of "Arbuthnot's" invocation of Leicester's feast) eddies against the pathos of Spenser's ill-fitting in his own, proto-modern times.

The desire to read Spenser as a feudal poet is perhaps most clearly legible in one of Hurd's occasional readings of *The Faerie Queene*. Explaining why the poem abounds with "knights-errant encoun-tering Giants, and quelling Savages," Hurd explains the social allegory as the following: "These Giants were oppressive feudal Lords, and every Lord was to be met with, like the Giant, in his strong hold, or castle. Their dependents of a lower form, who imitated the violence of their superiors, and had not their castles, but their lurking places, were the Savages of Romance. The greater Lord was called a Giant, for his power; the less, a Savage, for his brutality" (96). The stubbornly feudal code of this allegorical system, Hurd goes on to suggest, is best demonstrated by an episode in book v of *The Faerie Queene*:

All this is shadowed out in the gothic tales, and sometimes expressed in plain words. The objects of the knight's vengeance go indeed by the various names of Giants, Paynims, Saracens and Savages. But of what family they all are, is clearly seen from the Poet's description:

> What mister wight, quoth he, and how far hence
> Is he, that doth to travellers such harms
> He is, said he, a man of great defence,
> Expert in battle, and in deeds of arms;
> And more embolden'd by the wicked charms
> With which his daughter doth him still support;
> Having *great Lordships got and goodly farms*
> *Thro' strong oppressions of his pow'r extort*;
> By which, he still them holds and keeps with strong effort;

> And daily he his wrong encreaseth more:
> For never wight he lets to pass that way
> Over his bridge, albee he rich or poor,
> But he him makes his passage-penny pay:
> Else he doth hold him back or beat away.
> Thereto he hath a *Groom of Evil Guise*
> Whose scalp is bare that bondage doth bewray,
> Which polls and pills the poor in piteous wise,

But he himself upon the rich doth tyrannize.
(Spenser, Bv C2 [stanzas 5 and 6]) – (emphasis in Hurd's original)

"Here we have the great oppressive Baron very graphically set forth," Hurd concludes, "And the *Groom of evil guise* is as plainly the Baron's vassal" (96–97). The allegory encodes the structure and nomenclature of a perennially feudal mode of dominion, down even to the unity of politics and economy in the integral term vassal. Oppression carries the doubled and as yet undivided combination of liege-loyalty and land rent extracted from vassals who, in turn, "tyrannize" peasant labor.

To get a sense of Hurd's nostalgic rewriting of the Spenserian past we need only take a brief look at the episode in *The Faerie Queene* to which Hurd is here referring. The social situation of canto II of book V is a great deal more complex than immemorial feudalism, and is in fact particularly rich on the difficult subject of feudal and *absolutist* politics. The lines Hurd cites to exemplify the allegorical relation between mythic giants and feudal barons describe how Artegall and Talos are waylaid on their journey to Florimel by a Saracen and his daughter, who, from their control of a bridge, demand usurious duties of unfortunate travelers. Artegall and Talos confront first the Saracen's "villaine," whose demand for "passage money. . . according to the custom of the law" brings him a swift death.[39] Enraged over the death of his servant and the violation of the honors and duties "customary" for his station, the Saracen attacks Artegall and also meets a bloody end. Their battle, as Spenser depicts it, is doubtless a sociopolitical allegory, but not so much of the control of feudal society by an ancient aristocracy as of the defeat of a recalcitrant nobility by an emboldened monarchy. The allegory is drawn less from the stability of feudalism than its terminal crisis, as sociopolitical power fleetingly centralized itself around the royal court and its deputies. Seen from this perspective, Artegall's bludgeoning and beheading of the Saracen is preeminently a political message:

> His corps was carried downe along the Lee,
> Whose waters with his filthy bloud it staynecl:
> But his blasphemous head, that all might see,
> He pitcht upon a pole on high ordayned;
> Where many years it afterwards remayned,
> To be a mirrour to all mighty men,
> In whose right hands great power is contayned,

> That none of them the feeble ouerren,
> But alwaies doe their powre within iust compasse pen. (stanza 19)

Lest this reigning in of baronial rule be taken in a democratic direction, however, the "just compasse" in which men ought to "pen" their power is further elaborated through the mediating figure of the leveler Giant whom Artegall and Talos encounter immediately after they cross the bridge. This Giant holds the "vulgar" or "commoners" in thrall with his account of the ultimate equality and equivalence of all things. While the Saracen sought to maintain tyrannical power, the Giant's "surquedrie" (arrogance) would flatten social hierarchy *tout-court*. Holding a "balance in his hand" in which "all the world he would weigh equalie," the Giant turns out merely to embody a negative version of precisely the same "surquedrie" we are shown in the rapacious Saracen. Against the overarching might of the medieval baronial class *and* the leveler desire that "all things would reduce unto equality" (v.2.32 line 9), therefore, Spenser places Artegall's eminently monarchical, "heauenly iustice" (v.2.36 line 1):

> They liue, they die, like as he doth ordaine,
> Ne euer any asketh reason why.
> The hils doe not the lowly dales disdaine;
> The dales do not the lofty hills enuy.
> He maketh Kings to sit in souerainty;
> He maketh subiects to their powre obay;
> He pulleth downe, he setteth vp on hy;
> He giues to this, from that he takes away.
> For all we haue is his: what he list doe, he may. (stanza 41)

With this vision of a divinely ordained monarchy we may perhaps get a fuller sense of what the Saracen's head portends as it is lodged on a pike and mirrors the world, namely, the subjugation of the old baronial class, not by proto-bourgeois levelers,[40] but by the absolutist Gloriana (through her minion Artegall). It is against the backdrop of this transitional context, then, that we may see how Hurd elides the specificity of Tudor absolutism. Spenser's early modernity is repressed, as the dangerous carrier of the very modernity Hurd dreads, the final negation of Spenser's organic society.

The nostalgic account of Spenserian feudalism (or if one prefers, precapitalist village culture, *Gemeinschaft*, and so on) is further developed in Hurd's account of how what we might call feudal consciousness affects both the reading and the value of the poem. The categories Hurd most often uses to evoke the cognitive lifeworld of premodern society are "gothic" and "enchanted." These describe an entire mode of belief: the magical endowment of the world and its nocturnal inhabitants, from Giants and Wizards to Elves and Faeries. Midway through the *Letters*, Hurd engages in a brief thought experiment – what would Homer have felt had he been born into feudal rather than antique times? – and answers that "he certainly would have preferred . . . the improved gallantries of feudal times; and the superior solemnity of their superstitions"(108). The term superstition suggests the modern disenchantment of older belief systems as benighted mysticism, antiquated exotica and so forth. For Hurd, however, superstition refers to the omnipresence of religion in premodern life. "The superstition of the times in which Chivalry arose was so great that no institution of a public nature could have found credit in the world, that was not consecrated by the Churchmen, and closely interwoven with religion" (91). Since social life is no longer "interwoven" with religion, the daily practices of demotic belief appear to us as superstition and romance when they were in fact an indissoluble part of the feudal system. "Religion" hence means slightly more than domesticated, Anglican Christianity:

Popular tales of Elves and Faeries were even fitter to take the credulous mind, and charm it into a willing admiration of the *specious miracles*, which wayward fancy delights in, than those of the old traditionary rabble of pagan divinities. And then, for the more solemn fancies of witchcraft and incantation, the horrors of the Gothic were above measure striking and terrible. The mummeries of the pagan priests were childish, but the Gothic Enchanters shook and alarmed all nature. (110)

This vision of popular belief or what Hurd here calls "the credulous mind" – complete with its defense of vernacular paganism over its classic precursor, its combination of rustic tradition and demonic terror – might seem like "superstition" in a rather conventional sense. Hurd's reading is anachronistic in a deeper sense, however, not so much charging the past with a quaintly premodern animism as inventing the past as an aestheticized and *re*-enchanted contrast both to secular modernity and classical antiquity:

We are upon enchanted ground, my friend; and you are to think yourself well used that I detain you no longer in this fearful circle. The glympse you have had of it, will help your imagination to conceive the rest. And without more words you will readily apprehend that the fancies of our modern bards are not only more gallant, but, on a change of the scene, more sublime, more terrible, more alarming, than those of the classic fablers. In a word, you will find that the manners they paint, and the superstitions they adopt are the more poetical for being gothic. (114)

The baleful magic and dread that runs through the older world is the condition of the sublime and of poetry itself. This account is no simple primitivism. It is, rather, another expression of Hurd's systematic theory, which understands the feudal system to extend from social organization, through modes of collective belief, to aesthetic and literary forms. Before reason and taste erased the lines of the circle, one experienced no difference between aesthetics and politics, literature and superstition, or the religion that "interwove" them all. The difference and distance of this lifeworld does not go unnoticed. Hurd's unavoidably secular reading leads both to the anachronistic, aesthetic rendering of the past – the separating out of the sublime from miracles and manners alike – and, ultimately, to the pathos of the critic as an embattled reader of enchanted texts. The nostalgia for the enchanted world of feudal England in this passage is only amplified by the awareness that the critic stands outside the "fearful circle" of belief. All that stands within the circle, from this belated position, is sublime.

As he plucks the sublime from the larger context of "feudal manners and superstition," Hurd gives the aesthetic reason for his preference for *English* premodernity over and against Greco-Roman antiquity and Augustan refinement alike. Hurd's sense of period-ization in this highly charged passage is thus rather complex. He aims to distinguish the English gothic at once from the classical and the contemporary (which turn out, not surprisingly, to amount to the same thing). Suspended between the classical age and modernity, the gothic period of English history is endowed with an entire surplus of meaning and belief and filled with what from hindsight may be grasped as a tradition of national classics. "Nothing shews the difference of the two systems under consideration more plainly than the effect they really had on the two greatest of our poets; at least the two which an English reader is most fond to compare with Homer, I mean Spenser and Milton . . . [who] both appear when most inflamed to have been more particularly rapt with the Gothic fables of chivalry" (114). Hurd then quickly completes the trinity: "I say nothing of Shakespeare, because the sublimity (the divinity, let it be, if nothing else will serve) of his genius kept no certain rout . . . Yet one thing is clear, that even he is greater when he uses the Gothic manners and machinery, than when he employs classical: which brings us again to the same point, that the former have by their nature and genius, the advantage of the latter in producing the sublime" (117). The case of Milton at this point in the *Letters* is significant. The effort to define the canon as rooted in an imme-morial past pushes Milton into what seems an almost deliberately invented national antiquity. (Warton makes a similar move in the comparison of Spenser's poem to Milton's paradise.) No longer a poet of the late seventeenth century, and certainly not of the revolution, Milton is a gothic author like his canonical brethren.[41] Spenser's position is of course unique because of his self-conscious romanticism. But at this point Hurd is concerned to bring together Spenser, Shakespeare, and Milton who were fortunate enough to live in enchanted times and so write with a sublimity exceeding even the Greco-Roman poets.

The Augustan use of the term "gothic" to reject antique culture and idiom comes full circle. Responding to Shaftesbury's abuse of the "gothic" in the *Characteristicks*, Hurd writes, "Our noble critic himself condescended to take this trite theme: And it is not to be told with what alacrity and self-complacency he flourishes upon it . . . The Gothic manner, as he calls it, is the favourite object of his raillery"; but, Hurd continues, "this ingenious nobleman is, himself, one of the gallant votaries he sometimes makes himself so merry with. He is perfectly enamoured of his noble antients, and will fight with any who contends, not that his Lordship's mistress is not fair, but that his own is fair also" (132). Hurd's exposure of Shaftesburian anti-romance as another version of the romance signals a trans-position within the critical discussion of English literature, in which low-cultural gothicism and high-cultural classicism switch places. By the time of Hurd's *Letters*, Shaftesbury's aristocratic affiliation with tasteful norms and polite society has, as it were, fled the present moment and affixed itself to the past.[42] Shaftesburian classicism by the midcentury is insufficiently aristocratic. Hurd's revision of Shaftesbury retains the social affiliation while flipping its generic equivalent. As he dresses the ancients up in the regalia of the domestic nobility, Hurd suggests, Shaftesbury's aesthetic properly belongs with the very gothic it derides. Hurd's point is not just that the vernacular gothic is a good home for Shaftesburian aristocrats, who find their desires and exploits richly described within its romances; it is also that the social class of gothic characters can be seen to represent the class of the gothic as high-canonical literature. When Hurd reiterates Warton's generic position-taking and writes that "[Spenser's] purpose was not to write a classic poem. He chose to adorn a gothic story," (127) therefore, he makes what is for him the highest claim for the English canon.

Just as Spenserian feudalism was a nostalgic fantasy of social stability, so the gothicizing of Elizabethan England is, by Hurd's own admission, a drastic simplification of the "religious" context. Hurd's discussion of the feudal social formation attempted to elide instability. But epistemological instability turns out to be quite instrumental for Spenser's relation to "belief." In the closing section of the *Letters*, Hurd makes much of the fact that Spenser wrote during the waning of enchantment, as reason and science stood in the wings of literary culture. Indeed, Spenser's lateness is the condition of a certain aesthetic. "Spenser and Tasso came too late, and it was impossible for them to paint truly and perfectly what was no longer seen or believed" (108). Like Warton, Hurd argues that Spenser's lateness moved him to write allegorically, not because allegory evoked a passing age of chivalry, as Warton had suggested, however, but rather because it legitimized Spenser's "faeries" by pretending that they encoded a deeper, moral meaning. "The age would no longer bear the naked letter of these amusing stories; and the poet was so sensible of the misfortune, that . . . he gave an air of mystery to his subject, and pretended that his stories of knights and giants were but the cover to an abundance of profound wisdom. In short to keep the eyes of the profane from prying too nearly into his subject he threw about it the mist of allegory: he moralized his song: and the virtues and vices lay his under his warriors and enchanters" (150–151). By making the literal story seem to suggest deeper things, Spenser confounds the "profane" who skeptically resist the "sacred" stories of "the land of faery" (150). According to Hurd's inverse hermeneutic – in which the nominally deeper meaning turns out to figure or body forth the literal narrative – allegory is something like a last redoubt of the enchanted world during the morning of reason.

According to this reversal of the allegorical code, Spenser's poem remains within the "fearful circle" even as its readers are enlightened. Spenser's success in rendering literary his transitional moment is managed by the pretense of allegorical depth, but perhaps more strongly, Hurd suggests, by the production of interest among the skeptics in the literal story itself. "When reason was but dawning, as we may say, and just about to gain the ascendant over the portentous spectres of the imagination," the world remained split between what Hurd calls the "popular belief and that of the reader" (136). "The fictions of poetry," he contends, "do, in some degree at least, require the first (they would otherwise, deservedly pass for dreams indeed): But when the poet has this advantage on his side, and his fancies have, or may be supposed to have, a countenance from the current superstitions of the age in which he writes, he dispenses with the last, and gives his reader leave to be as sceptical and as incredulous, as he pleases" (136). This division between demotic, pre-literate belief and sophisticated, skeptical literacy complicates Spenser's position within the narrative of disenchantment by placing a social division between the world from which he drew his "fiction" and the audience for whom that "fiction" was intended. *The Faerie Queene* maintains a vital relation to "popular belief," and so may freely refer to, alternatively, "a legend, a tale, a tradition, a rumour, a superstition"; but the poem appeals to the "sceptical" and (one assumes) elite reader, who, separated from plebeian superstition as he may be, is still able to enjoy being "made to conceive (he minds not by what magic) the existence of such things as his reason tells him did not, and were never likely to, exist" (136). *The Faerie Queene* is, as it were, always-already high culture, in the case of its originary moment in the sixteenth century, the property of a minority divorced by literacy and reason from the majority.

This aesthetic relation to the superseded life-forms of the lower classes may seem by now a relatively typical example of the critical tendency to cast high-cultural literature as secularized magic, immune from philosophical reason and historical fact alike. But what is new and puzzling in the above passage is the way in which the division between the "credulous" and the "incredulous," the illiterate and the literate, requires the existence of "popular belief." As soon as this belief is erased by the implacable process of disenchantment, the poem loses its appeal. The division Hurd imagines between high culture and popular culture in the sixteenth century thus has built within its structure its own imminent upheaval, since the very skepticism that produces pleasure in enchantment can only continue to erode superstition writ large. Eventually "popular belief" succumbs to the same secularization as readerly "incredulity." Such is indeed the condition under which Hurd imagines himself to write. As feudalism gave way to capitalism, the institutions and modes of consciousness it "systematically" secreted inevitably faded:

The Gothic manners of Chivalry, as springing out of the feudal system, were as singular as that system itself: So that, when that political constitution vanished out of Europe, the manners, that belonged to it, were no longer seen or understood. There was no example of any such manners remaining on the face of the Earth: And as they never did subsist but once, and are never likely to subsist again, people would be led of course to think and speak of them, as romantic, and unnatural. The consequence of which was a total contempt and rejection of them. (148)

Given the historical finality of this development, Hurd is moved next to ask, how does one read Spenser in fully disenchanted times, how does one rebuild the ruins of high culture? "The success of these fictions will not be great, when they have no longer any footing in the popular belief"; and, he continues, "the reason is this, that readers do not usually do, as they ought, put themselves in the circumstances of the poet, or rather of those, of whom the poet writes" (143). The "circumstances" of those "of whom the poet writes" amount to precisely the sort of "popular belief" that earlier readers had been able (skeptically) to access. The problem of secularization – the erosion of the very "popular belief" in which skeptical readers plant their feet – is thus displaced onto the problem of criticism; disenchanted readers, it turns out, fail to be properly historicist critics. From this perspective, Hurd may then argue with some ease that history itself has placed Spenser's text with a minority of contemporary readers – not the "sceptical" literati of Spenser's own day, but their lineal descendants: the scholarly community, who have the knowledge and training to read enchanted material. *The Faerie Queene* is by historical necessity unpopular and arcane, the "belief" it presupposes reachable only by means of scholarship. Hurd's systematic literary history thus becomes one of the period's grandest articulations of the vanishing of an audience for older literature: "The *Faery Queen*, one of the noblest productions of modern poetry, is fallen into so general a neglect, that all the zeal of its commentators is esteemed officious and impertinent, and will never restore it to those honours it has, once for all, lost" (149). In this rather instrumental lament, however, the waning of audience is the condition for Spenser's singularly *critical* revival:

Poor Spenser then

> – 'in whose gentle spright
> The pure well-head of Poesie did dwell'

must, for ought I can see, be left to the admiration of a few lettered or
curious men: while the many are sworn together to give no quarter to the
marvelous, or, which may seem still harder to the moral of his song. (150)

Spenser's oblique relation to his eighteenth-century public ensures
his "honours" as they are now returned to him by the champions of
a vanquished past.

What if not Spenser pleases the modern public? Hurd left one
clue about his thinking on this matter near the end of his career in
the *Dissertation on the Idea of Universal Poetry* (1766). In that study, Hurd
asked, "what are we to think of those *novels* or *romances*, as they are
called, that is, fables constructed on some private and familiar
subject, which have been so current, of late, through all Europe?"
His answer was tart:

As they propose pleasure for their end, and prosecute it, besides, in the way
of *fiction*, though without metrical numbers, and generally, indeed, in harsh
and rugged prose, one easily sees what their pretensions are, and under
what idea they are ambitious to be received . . . yet as they are wholly
destitute of measured sounds (to say nothing of their numberless defects)
they can, at most, be considered but as hasty, imperfect, and abortive
poems.[43]

Canonical works are written in verse, non-canonical in prose. The
defects of the modern romance are "numberless" but chief among
them is that it is without "numbers." Or so it would seem. The
dominion of poetry is indeed "universal." Its place at the pinnacle of
culture is so secure that even lower forms are, ultimately, to be
evaluated in its idiom. The prose of the modern romance means it's
but a horrid poem. Hurd's difficulty with the emergent novel here is
not, as René Wellek argued, a revision of his earlier defense of the
romance.[44] Rather, Hurd distinguishes between the relative cultural
status of two forms of the romance, the Spenserian and the
novelistic. The "pretensions" of the novel are to usurp the space
occupied by the older romance, which stands in greater relief when
contrasted to its fallen descendent.

The division between high-cultural poetry and low-cultural prose,
Spenser and the novel, is in fact already worked out in the *Letters*.
The epistemological defense of "poetic fiction" as the literary

secretion of the premodern mind had built within it, as it were, a preformed distinction between the older romance and its later mass-cultural elaboration. Hence while Hurd's neo-Aristotelian defense of the old romance turns on its generic difference from both history and philosophy – "So little account does this wicked poetry make of philosophical or historical truth. All she allows us to look for, is *poetical truth*; a very slender thing indeed, and which the poet's eye, when rolling in its finest frenzy can but just lay hold of" (*Letters*: 137–138) – this difference is quickly described as that between the possible and the probable, imagination and experience. Poetical truth is "something much beyond the actual bounds and only within the conceived possibility of nature" (138). The enchanted poetry of the imagination is here formally distinct from and superior to the disenchanted prose of phenomenal experience and empirical reality. "A poet, they say, must follow Nature; and by Nature we are to suppose can only be meant the known and experienced course of affairs in the world," when in fact, "the poet has a world of his own, where experience has less to do, than consistent imagination" (138). "He has, besides," Hurd continues,

a supernatural world to range in. He has Gods, and Faeries, and Witches at his command: and,
    – O! who can tell
The hidden pow'r of herbes, and might of magic spell?
Thus in the poet's world, all is marvelous and extraordinary; yet not unnatural in one sense, as it agrees to the conceptions that are readily entertained of these magical and wonder-working Natures. (138)

To gauge the relation of poetry and prose in this formulation, we might recall that for Lennox the natural was synonymous with the probable and both were contained in the novel; "is this natural?" Lennox asked of Shakespeare, "is this probable?" Hurd's epistemological defense of Spenser distinguishes his poetry from modern prose and satiric verse alike. But the recourse here to imagination and enchantment is not simply "preromantic."[45] Hurd makes such claims only for *older* poetry; likewise, the fulsome description of "the poet" above refers only to writers prior to the historical instance of disenchantment. Unlike Joseph Warton in the preface to the *Odes*, then, Hurd is rather adamant that "imaginative" poetry is historically impossible. "I would advise no modern poet to revive these faery tales in an epic poem. But still this is nothing to the case in hand, where we are considering the merit of epic poems written under other circumstances" (143).

The argument that "some ages are not fit to write poems in" at once condemns the present to a windowless rationalism and elevates the past to an iridescent literariness (143). Hurd's nostalgia longs both for the particularly *literary* past and the "feudal" institutions to which it is indissolubly bound. Conversely, Hurd's hostility to the present takes aim both at the novel and polite verse and at that larger social condition he calls "disenchanted" (154). Literary history is a privileged narrative for representing the condition of modernity after the loss of the feudal world.

At length the magic of the old romances was perfectly dissolved. They began with reflecting an image indeed of the feudal manners . . . The next step was to have recourse to *allegories*. Under this disguise they walked the world a while: the excellence of the moral and the ingenuity of the contrivance making some amends, and being accepted as a sort of apology, for the absurdity of the literal story.

Under this form the tales of faery kept their ground, and even made their fortune at court; where they became, for two or three reigns, the ordinary entertainment of princes. But reason, in the end, (assisted however by party, and religious prejudices) drove them off the scene, and would endure these *lying wonders*, neither in their own proper shape, nor as masked in figures.

Henceforth, the taste of wit and poetry took a new turn: And *fancy*, that had wanted it so long in the world of fiction, was now constrained, against her will, to ally herself with strict truth, if she would gain an entrance into reasonable company.

What we have gotten by this revolution, you will say, is a great deal of good sense. What we have lost, is a world of fine fabling; the illusion of which is so grateful to the *charmed spirit*; that, in spite of philosophy and fashion, *Faery* Spenser still ranks highest among the poets; I mean with all who either come of that house, or have any kindness for it.

> *Earth-born* critics, my friend, may blaspheme,
> 'But all the Gods are ravish'd with delight
> Of his celestial song, and music's wondrous might.'     (153–155)

Hurd's counter-enlightenment presents a comprehensive history of literature and social relations. Once magic and belief flee the modern world they take with them "fancy" and "fiction" and leave in their place the desolation of "strict truth." The inevitable super-session of "feudal manners" by what "Addison" pithily terms "private property and public freedom" entails the equally insuper-able waning of the aura, as the twin forces of rationality and commodity exchange root out the last vestiges of the premodern world and dissolve its various animisms. As soon as the aura is buried, however, it is also disinterred and endowed with the nostalgic half-life of the aesthetic. The aesthetic in such formulations amounts to what Benjamin would later call the "profane cult of beauty," a secular attempt to reinvent the sacred world by substituting in its place a number of new categories: here, the sublime and the gothic, but also fancy, fiction, wonder and literature itself. These categories emerge in Hurd, as elsewhere, through a necessarily belated and maudlin attempt to experience "what we have lost," both the "fine fabling" of poets like Spenser and their organic, feudal world. Disenchantment is one with re-enchantment as the past shines with the "charmed spirit" drained from modernity. Re-enchanting the past provides of course a refuge for disgruntled moderns, whose anomie may at least be temporarily relieved through reading and aesthetic experience. But it also redefines the cultural field of the present, at once devaluing cultural products written after what Hurd calls "the great revolution in modern taste," and also constituting a domain of restricted culture within the vernacular (108). The gothicism of the gothic – its "nobility" – means not only that Spenser "ranks highest" but that this very ranking is preserved by a literary elect, the "few lettered and curious men."

With Hurd's vertiginous nostalgia we arrive at the end of our analysis of the midcentury Spenser revival. To the degree that the four critics maintain distinct positions, they also comprise a larger movement to elevate Spenser within a revised understanding of English culture and literary history. The points of affiliation between Warton and Hurd are clear enough, and it would not be wrong in the present context to suggest that Hurd completes at the level of "systematic" abstraction the project of Warton's *Observations*. But the feudal or romantic rendering of *The Faerie Queene* encounters along the way of its nostalgic articulation two "classical" critiques, the first from Huggins's memory of gentility and the second from Upton's epic anti-romanticism. Seen from this perspective, Hurd's system answers to the former with an implacable history the public's dissolution and to the latter with the reintegration of genre into the institutions of social life. Johnson's reading of Hurd is in this sense quite correct. The systematic determinacy of the *Letters* derives from the patterns of conflict and mediation in midcentury criticism.

# PART THREE

CHAPTER 5

# Shakespeare's nation: the literary profession and "the shades of ages"

I found no difficulty in getting admittance to Monsieur Le
Count B****. The set of Shakespears was laid upon the table,
and he was tumbling them over. I walk'd up close to the table,
and giving first such a look at the books as to make him
conceive I knew what they were – I told him I had come
without any one to present me, knowing I should meet with a
friend in his apartment who, I trusted, would do it for me – it is
my countryman the great Shakespear, said I, pointing to his
works – *et ayez la bonté, mon cher ami*, apostrophizing his spirit,
added I, *de me faire cet honneur la.*

Laurence Sterne

The preceding chapters have argued that the midcentury rethinking
of English literary history happens in response to change in the
institutions of cultural life, from the trade in books and the growth of
criticism, to consumer culture and the novel. The last chapter
argued that these developments were understood by mid-eighteenth-
century critics within a comprehensive sense of historical change.
Modernity spawns tradition: whether Dodd's sublime overcoming of
a differentiated audience, for example, or Hurd's feudal fantasy of
an older and better world. One might imagine that Hurd's literary
history would be an appropriate place to draw to a close, since its
claim for the value of older works is so evocative, and since one can
hardly picture a more complete and thoroughgoing elevation of the
past, whose literary preeminence is assured by a "systematic"
historical narrative. Yet to end on Hurd, as tempting as it may be for
the argument advanced in these pages, would privilege an argument
that generates in its turn a substantial critique. In this chapter, I
follow the formation of the English canon into the 1760s, returning
to the treatment of Shakespeare and looking in particular at
Johnson's 1765 *Works*, William Kenrick's response to Johnson, and

Elizabeth Montagu's *Essay on the Genius of Shakespeare* (1769). During these years, criticism's shift from progressive nationalism to retrospective gothicism makes another turn. This moment marks an end to my study of canon formation in the eighteenth century. Like all turning points, it is neither final nor consensual; in fact, it is marked by one of the more acrimonious debates in eighteenth-century criticism. The debate has the virtue for us, however, of bringing out the positions that comprised the midcentury understanding of the canon at a pivotal instance of its formation.

## I

Johnson's career, like that of many others, began with a calculated position-taking in relation to his predecessors. Whereas criticism had once sought to be the expression of sociable refinement, he suggested, it ought now to withdraw, slightly, from the public sphere. *Rambler* no. 23, for example, examines just how different his project is from that of the *Spectator*. The essay's conceit is that the Rambler's distance from publicity and refinement has, paradoxically, caused a stir in the public itself:

My readers having, from the performances of my predecessors, established an idea of unconnected essays . . . were impatient of the least deviation from their system . . . Some were angry that the Rambler did not, like the Spectator, introduce himself to the acquaintance of the public by an account of his own birth and studies, and enumeration of his adventures, and description of his physiognomy. Others soon began to remark that he was a solemn, serious, dictatorial writer, without sprightliness or gaiety, and called out with vehemence for mirth and humour. Another admonished him to have a special eye upon the various clubs of this great city, and informed him that much of the Spectator's vivacity was laid out upon such assemblies. He has been censured for not imitating the politeness of his predecessors, having hitherto neglected to take the ladies under his protection, and give them rules for the just opposition of colours and the proper dimensions of ruffles and pinners.[1]

The public warily responds to a form of criticism that seems to come at an unusually oblique angle to its essential concerns and essential sociability. The *Rambler*'s suspicion of its public is not meant to signal a retreat from publication; as Johnson mentions over and again, his essays were produced for a market of readers, whose demands shaped his "weekly labour" (127). Rather, it is the curiously anti-public publicity, the professed refusal to curb style or content to meet the expectations of one's audience, that places Johnson in the thick of midcentury criticism. The calculated involution, moral posturing, and periodic bravura that formed his critical personality were each shaped by the shifting perception of commodity culture. (We can perhaps quickly grasp how each of these stylistic habits would function in this context: the Latinate heaviness of the language wrenched the prose from the "sprightly" sociolect of coffee-house parlance, even as the periodic balancing sought to add, in its place, Johnson's own brand of order; this order was then completed at the level of content by an exacting piety.)[2] In any case, the posturing here takes what was even by then a familiar form: the demands of the public are experienced as a cloying, "female" presence, the solution to which is a rejection of the polite mode for that of a "serious, solemn dictator." It is in the mode of the dictator, then, that Johnson pronounces a summary end to the narrative of refinement: "taste and grace, purity and delicacy, manners and unities, sounds which, having been once uttered by those that understood them, have been since re-echoed without meaning, and kept up to the disturbance of the world, by a constant repercussion from one coxcomb to another" (127).

Over the course of the 1750s, however, Johnson's thinking about the role of criticism in relation both to the literary past and to its public transforms importantly. In the parodic figure of "Dick Minim" in *Idler* no. 60 (1759), for instance, he brings together the narrative of polite refinement and that of gothic descent into a single critical error. The paper begins with the prototypical scene of literary history as modernization:

Of all the great authors he now began to display the characters, laying down as an universal position that all had beauties and defects. His opinion was that Shakespeare, committing himself wholly to the impulse of nature, wanted that correctness which learning would have given him; and that Jonson, trusting to learning, did not sufficiently cast his eye on nature. He blamed the stanza of Spenser, and could not bear the hexameters of Sidney. Denham and Waller he held the first reformers of English numbers, and thought that if Waller could have obtained the strength of Denham, or Denham the sweetness of Waller, there had been nothing wanting to complete a poet.[3]

The caricatured rehearsal of the stock terms and moves of critical culture registers a certain crystallization of refinement after its dominance as a model for understanding the past and the past's relation to the present has already expired. Modern refinement is itself antique. But, as Johnson continues, the parody also subsumes the antithetical position of midcentury historicism. In the second paper, Minim

> often wishes for some standard of taste, for some tribunal, to which merit may appeal from caprice, prejudice, and malignity. He has formed a plan for an academy of criticism . . . When he is placed in the chair of criticism, he declares loudly for the noble simplicity of our ancestors, in opposition to the petty refinements, and ornamental luxuriance. Sometimes he is sunk in despair, and perceives false delicacy daily gaining ground, and sometimes brightens his countenance with a gleam of hope, and predicts the revival of the true sublime. He then fulminates his loudest censures against the monkish barbarity of rhyme; wonders how beings that pretend to reason can be pleased with one line always ending like another; tells how unjustly and unnaturally sense is sacrificed to sound; how often the best thoughts are mangled by the necessity of confining or extending them to the dimension of a couplet; and rejoices that genius has, in our days, shaken off the shackles which had encumbered it so long. (II: *Idler*, no. 61, 190–191)

That Minim could move from the refinement of numbers to the "sublime" refusal of "petty refinements and ornamental luxuriance" demonstrates less a similarity between these two positions than their emergence as clear opposites: refinement and gothicism. The professional trick of Johnson's exasperated accounting of criticism's favorite terms – refinement and recession, politeness and the sublime – is to make it appear as if he were somehow outside of the institution he mocks.

Johnson's double critique did not leave him without an account of public culture and literary history. In fact, he rejected gothicism and refinement because of their inability to provide such an account. As is well known, Johnson's remarks on literary works were often shaped by an overarching agon between the general and the particular, the grand and the small, the exemplary and the singular, the species and the individual.[4] As a theory of canonicity, the preference for general forms turns on their transcendence of temporally or geographically confined tastes. Johnson often conceives of particularity as a type of blockage, an impediment to transcendence.[5] Consider the discussion of melancholia in *Rambler* no. 47 (1750):

> it too often happens that sorrow, thus lawfully entering, gains such a firm possession of the mind that it is not afterward to be ejected; the mournful

ideas, first violently impressed, and afterward willingly received, so much engross the attention as to predominate in every thought, to darken gaiety, and perplex ratiocination. An habitual sadness seizes upon the soul, and the faculties are chained to a single object, which can never be contemplated but with hopeless uneasiness. (III: no. 47, 255)

The mind's engrossment in a singular object of loss obstructs the generalizing balm of "social duties, and the common avocations of life" (255). The "antidote against sorrow" is, in turn, the annulment and transcendence of the particular by the mind's "enlarging the variety of objects" (257). This mini-dialectic is important for our understanding of Johnson and the canon because it stages the relation among reading, sublimity, and transcendence and because this relation, in turn, poses the question of nostalgia (a common mode, as we have seen, of approaching older texts during the period): "Sorrow is properly that state of the mind in which our desires are fixed upon the past, without looking forward to the future, an incessant wish that something were otherwise than it has been, a tormenting and harassing want of some enjoyment or possession which we have lost, and which no endeavours can possibly regain" (254). Through the insuperable fixation on the singular, sorrow brings together an account of objects and an account of time; the past is a repository of particulars into which the self dissolves via windless spirals of retrospection. This psychological argument articulates an important problem for Johnson's understanding of literary history. Nostalgia for a lost moment of literary achievement is henceforth an insufficient principle for understanding the relation between the past and present. The sublime, the particular, and the obscure are likewise insufficient markers of canonical achievement. Nostalgia expresses a curious attachment to objects that have fallen out of usage, modes of expression that fail to please recurring generations of readers.

This concern underlay many of Johnson's seemingly idiosyncratic judgments in the years leading up to the edition of Shakespeare. Several times in the *Rambler* series, for instance, he takes skeptical notice of the Spenser revival as a peculiar instance of literary nostalgia. "The imitation of Spenser," he observes in *Rambler* no. 121, "by the influence of some men of learning and genius, seems likely to gain upon the age" (IV: 285). What is disturbing about this influence is that Spenser's language represents nothing so much as the failure to be abstract. "His style was in his own time allowed to be vicious, so darkened with old words and peculiarities of phrase, and so remote from common usage, that Jonson boldly pronounces him 'to have written no language'" (285). In another *Rambler*, Johnson calls Spenser's linguistic eccentricity a "mingled dialect which no human being ever could have spoken" (III: no. 37, 202–203). The point in either case is that the language fails to be used continuously enough for it to be recognizable to readers. The assertion is not simply that Spenserian diction has no use; it is rather that the use is too narrow, fixed to the particular moment of its production, of singular "mingling." There is no common repetition of Spenser's dialect by modern audiences. "A studied barbarism," his idiom can only be reproduced by his epigones, never reconsumed by his readers (III: no. 37, 202). And so Spenserianism is just nostalgia, a relation to the past shorn of any vital connection to the present: "the style of Spenser might by long labour be justly copied; but life is surely given us for higher purposes than to gather what our ancestors have wisely thrown away, and to learn what is of no value but because it has been forgotten" (IV: *Rambler*, no. 121, 287).

The final reference to value in this passage is telling. The name for culture's currency here is memory, the accretion of particular uses into a general medium of recollection. In contrast to Spenser and Spenserians, twin figures of nostalgia, Johnson begins to establish a version of the past secured by consumption. The same *Rambler* discussion that rejects Spenser's "studied barbarism" serves up an antithetical image of general value: "poetry cannot dwell upon the minuter distinctions by which one species differs from another without departing from that simplicity of grandeur which fills the imagination; nor dissect the latent qualities of things, without losing its general power of gratifying every mind by recalling its conceptions" (III: no. 37, 204). Now, the difficulty of analyzing this sort of frequent pronouncement lies in the very generality that is its theme. Virtually devoid of positive content, poetry amounts to a sort of ineffable approximation of "every mind." Yet it is the very sparseness of this definition that contains Johnson's early theory of canonicity. Poetry is the name for the abstraction of particularity into the lowest common denominator of the universal. The only way of evaluating poetry, then, is in terms of the memorial perpetuity of response, the praise of readers across the expanse of time and location. And the only way that Johnson can arrive at this denominator is by continuously emptying poetry of concretion. "The business of a poet," exclaims Imlac famously in *Rasselas* (1759), "is to examine not the individual but the species, to remark general properties and large appearances: he does not number the streaks of the tulip, or describe the different shades in the verdure of the forest. He is to exhibit in his portraits of nature such prominent and striking features as recall the original to every mind." What causes Rasselas to respond "enough! Thou hast convinced me that no human being can ever be a poet" might be described as the radical emptiness of Imlac's description.[6] One can never "be a poet" because that identity is assigned by the retrospective glance of cultural memory. In passages such as these, Johnson strains to describe the pervasively negative process of a nation's collective recollection. Memory voids the past of specificity and holds on to what persists into the present.

In the years leading up to the Shakespeare edition, Johnson began to develop this idea of literature as a separate order of discourse into an idea of the canon as the means of ranking that discourse. The preface to *A Dictionary of the English Language* (1755), for example, contains an important, if curiously incomplete, discussion of the national literary tradition. Describing the impracticable plan of including the full passage in which a given word appears in the citation, Johnson says he "was forced to depart from my scheme of including all that was pleasing or useful in English literature."[7] By "English literature" Johnson does and does not mean a canon of high-cultural writing. The account of the various discourses he planned to include is instructive: "I therefore extracted from chemists complete processes; from divines striking exhortations; and from poets beautiful descriptions" (318). "Literature" in this formulation is not yet "literary" in the modern sense. It is still the catholic category of all good writing. Nevertheless, Johnson claims that a canon of such writing will be the lasting monument of his dictionary. "The chief glory of every people arises from its authors: whether I shall add any thing by my own writings to the reputation of English literature must be left to time . . . but I shall not think my employment useless or ignoble, if by my assistance foreign nations, and distant ages, gain access to the propagators of knowledge and the teachers of truth" (327). Literature covers all good writing, but within that category a pantheon of authors expresses the "chief glory" of the nation. One half of the canonical equation develops ahead of the other. The temporal brackets of the canon, moreover, are portentous. "English literature" amounts to a scant eighty years of the history of vernacular writing: "So far have I been from any care to grace my pages with modern decorations that I have studiously endeavoured to collect examples and authorities from the writers before the Restoration, whose works I regard as *the well of English undefilde,* as the pure sources of genuine diction" (319). Canonical English necessarily comes to us from the past. Modern English writers are excluded. But Johnson's backward looking glance only extends so far. Where Spenser was happy to find "the wells of English undefyled" in "Dan Chaucer," Johnson will go no further than the 1580s: "as every language has a time of rudeness antecedent to perfection, as well as of false refinement and declension, I have been cautious lest my zeal for antiquity might drive me into times too remote, and crowd my book with words now no longer understood. I have fixed Sidney's work for the boundary beyond which I make few excursions. From the authors which rose in the time of Elizabeth, a speech might be formed adequate to all the purposes of use and elegance" (319). The ease in which Johnson phrases the idea of English antiquity reveals the degree to which the establishment of England's past on the model of the classical age had by then settled. Yet antiquity carried with it the threat of philological nostalgia and particularity. The solution, in this case, was a quick demarcation of boundaries, a literalizing of the compromise between refinement and gothicism. Stretching from 1580 to 1660, English literature is dramatically shorn at either end.

The idea of a canonical order of writing and the idea of a separate domain of the literary come together in the edition of Shakespeare. The *Preface* is notable for the volatile stridency of its opening pages. Above all other English authors, Johnson begins, Shakespeare deserves the accolades of antiquity:

That praises are without reason lavished on the dead, and that the honours due only to excellence are paid to antiquity, is a complaint likely to be always continued by those, who, being able to add nothing to truth, hope for eminence from the heresies of paradox; or those, who, being forced by disappointment upon consolatory expedients, are willing to hope from posterity what the present age refuses and flatter themselves that the regard which is yet denied by envy, will be at last bestowed by time.

Antiquity, like every other quality that attracts the notice of mankind, has undoubtedly votaries that reverence it, not from reason, but from prejudice. Some seem to admire indiscriminately whatever has been long preserved, without considering that time has sometimes co-operated with chance; all perhaps are more willing to honour past than present excellence; and the mind contemplates genius through the shades of age, as the eye surveys the sun through artificial opacity. The great contention of criticism is to find the faults of the moderns, and the beauties of the ancients. While an author is yet living we estimate his powers by his worst performance, and when he is dead we rate them by his best.[8]

The consideration of the honors one pays to older cultural works in this passage is suggestively fraught. The magisterial opening paragraph – an eighty-seven word long sentence – sets the tone and terms for the neater and more clipped periods that follow. The immensity of the sentence's hypotaxis displays Johnson's characteristic effort to restrain, through style itself, the problems with which he is concerned, in this case the dilemma of past and present, restricted and public culture. As it follows on the syntactic upheaval of the opening paragraph, the balanced listing of the reasons the past may radiate an undeserved aura has a certain calming effect. But what is ushered in during these smaller units is a pronounced sense of Shakespeare's distance from the eighteenth-century reader. As one looks backward to older works, one must gaze through "the shades of age."

This attempt to work around the aura of the past takes from it a crucial term: Shakespeare like Homer resides in "Antiquity." Placing Shakespeare in antiquity leads to what will become a singularly influential test of canonicity, the test of time:

To works, however, of which the excellence is not absolute and definite, but gradual and comparative; to works not raised upon principles demonstrative and scientifick, but appealing wholly to observation and experience, no other test can be applied than length of duration and continuance of esteem. What mankind have long possessed they have often examined and compared, and if they persist to value the possession, it is because frequent comparisons have confirmed opinion in its favour. As among the works of nature no man can properly call a river deep or a mountain high, without the knowledge of many mountains and many rivers; so in the productions of genius, nothing can be stiled excellent till it has been compared with other works of the same kind. Demonstration immediately displays its power, and has nothing to hope or fear from the flux of years; but works tentative and experimental must be estimated by their proportion to the general and collective ability of man, as it is discovered in a long succession of endeavours. Of the first building that was raised, it might be with certainty determined that it was round or square, but whether it was spacious or lofty must have been referred to time. The Pythagorean scale of numbers was at once discovered to be perfect; but the poems of Homer we yet know not to transcend the common limits of human intelligence, but by remarking, that nation after nation, and century after century, has been able to do little more than transpose his incidents, new name his characters, and paraphrase his sentiments. (60)

There is an inevitable gap, Johnson suggests, between the writing of a text and its ascendancy to high-cultural permanence. This gap is literary historical time itself, which must pass in order for the verdict of generations and ages to hold.[9] As subsequent readers, immersed in different lifeworlds, with new-found passions and distinct interests, repeat the preference of their ancestors, they confirm earlier opinions of a writer's greatness; they etch in stone the judgment of earlier periods. Literary works require a different mode of valuation from works of science or philosophy, whose proof may be demonstrated within their historical period. Consequently, Johnson follows Hume in finding that the only reliable standard one can apply to the order of literary knowledge is derived from endurance, since this standard does not presume a set of intrinsic qualities in works themselves but rather follows on the response of readers over time, what Johnson calls elsewhere the "suffrage of futurity."[10]

The test of time brings together an account of canonicity and an account of literature, both how works are valued and what makes them valuable. As history moves at its inexorable pace, it cleaves a fault line between the aesthetic ("works tentative and experimental") and the empirical (works "demonstative and scientifick"), and throws forth the occasional "genius" whose literary achievement shines through the shades of ages. How do literary texts differ from non-literary texts? Johnson's tentative answer begins by invoking the opposition of the probable to the demonstrative, or so it seems. The famous defense of Shakespeare's neglect of the "three unities" imagines that the pleasure of reading is distinct from the gathering of facts:

Imitations produce pain and pleasure, not because they are mistaken for realities, but because they bring realities to mind. When the imagination is recreated by a painted landscape, the trees are not supposed capable to give us shade, or the fountains coolness; but we consider, how we should be pleased with such fountains playing beside us, and such woods waving over us (78).

When we read "the action is not supposed to be real" (79). Yet the argument against the unities claims that probable as well as demonstrative knowledge is insufficient, or unnecessary, for the rational pleasure we find in objects we know to have been fabricated. (Hence the famous example, "We are agitated in reading the history of Henry the Fifth, yet no man takes his book for the field of Agincourt" [78–79].) Johnson's pragmatic argument against the unities – we are not fooled; we coolly enjoy the bringing to mind of literature – projects and defends a distinct aesthetic: "It is false that any representation is mistaken for reality; that any dramatic fable in its materiality was ever credible, or for a single moment, was ever credited" (76). Shakespeare is "read without any other reason than the desire of pleasure" (61). Incredulity and pleasure unite in "fiction"; it is neither requisite that we believe the action to be real, nor that we could imagine the probability of ourselves believing. Rather, we need only desire to read or view a series of lines, whose composite beauty yields a certain pleasure: "the truth is, that the spectators are always in their senses, and know, from the first act to the last, that the stage is only a stage, and that the players are only players. They come to hear a certain number of lines recited with just gesture and elegant modulation" (77). At the very instance in which Johnson seems "to lose faith in art" (as both William Kenrick in the eighteenth century and René Wellek in the twentieth century will accuse him), he also shores up "art" as one part of a larger division of knowledge and labor: we go to a play or read a book in order to have a certain experience, the experience of the aesthetic, just as we go to a shop in order to purchase a certain product.[11] Both are equally rational acts of consumption. And, as a necessary, if oblique, corollary to this account, both objects are also products of social labor, items made or fabricated according to rational technique. "It will be asked," Johnson writes, "how the drama moves, if it is not credited," to which he responds, "it is credited, whenever it moves, as a just picture of a real original," that is, as something skillfully made (78).

This attempt to work around probability and demonstration revises his earlier position, in the introduction to *Shakespeare Illustrated*, that "Shakespeare's excellence is not the fiction of the tale but the representation of life" (x). Twelve years later, the apology for Shakespeare's violation of the unities invokes the reader's "consciousness of fiction" ("Preface": 78). Between Lennox and Johnson lies the notion of Spenserian or gothic fiction as premodern enchantment. In the gothic reading, one may claim that Shakespeare writes fiction while still maintaining that probability is too infected with demonstrative and "scientifick" forms. According to Lennox, by contrast, fiction is only valuable to the degree that it predicts and conforms to social behavior and its gendered forms, to the degree that it is a novel. Johnson's rejection of the unities repeats his rejection of Lennox's model by suggesting that Shakespeare's appeal lies beyond credibility. The earlier argument against novelization – it matters not if Shakespeare's plays have the probable structure we desire of novels; they are of a different species – is simply refashioned on behalf of Shakespeare's pleasurable difference from science and the "real." Yet Johnson distinguishes his position from the gothic reading also, and does so by invoking Lennox's critique of "enchantment": "Shakespeare approximates the remote, and familiarizes the wonderful . . . he who has mazed his imagination, in following the phantoms which other writers raise up before him, may here be cured of his delirious ecstasies, by reading human sentiments in human language" (65). The problem that Johnson's aesthetic argument sets for itself is to describe the pleasure in fabricated objects, a pleasure that abjures belief in fictional actions and images. His critique of enchantment at once raises the stakes of this problem and procures its tendential solution. Our incredulous delight in fiction cannot come from spectral wonderment any more than it can from novelistic manners; both exhibit the baleful charm of the particular. Pleasure in fiction can only come from the approximation of something called "humanity," the general condition of which Shakespeare evinces in his appeal to readers across time. As we shall see, Shakespeare is the ticket to perennial humanity. The human is the sign and image of *general* value.

Johnson's humanism is, however, both enabled and threatened by its grounding in an edition. The general humanity of Shakespeare resides in a particular object. How is one to act responsibly as an editor without falling into the argot of scholarship? Much of the terminology and apparatus of philological criticism passes into the 1765 *Works*.[12] It is from classical philology, after all, that Johnson derives the notion that Shakespeare's works arrive at the eighteenth century from "antiquity." Like the historicists, Johnson separates editorial practice from aesthetic judgment. In the *Proposal for Printing, by Subscription, the Dramatick Works of William Shakespeare* (1756), he maligns Pope and Warburton for their insertion of evaluative markings into the text:

I have never observed that mankind was much delighted or improved by their asterisks, commas, or double commas; of which the only effect is, that they preclude the pleasure of judging for ourselves, teach the young and ignorant to decide without principles; defeat curiosity and discernment, by leaving them less to discover; and at last show the opinion of the critick, without the reasons of which it was founded, and without affording any light by which it may be examined. (*Proposal:* 57)

The division of authority between the editor and reader grants to the former a sort of professional task to manage the philological problems (which, in the case of Shakespeare, are especially pronounced due to the lack of manuscripts and existence of multiple variants) and to the latter the entire province of aesthetic consumption. Johnson further describes this division in language taken almost verbatim from Theobald: "The editor, though he may less delight his own vanity, will probably please his reader more by supposing him equally able with himself to judge of beauties and faults, which require no previous acquisition of remote knowledge" (57). Where Theobald's disavowal of judgment emphasized the technical expertise of the editor, however, Johnson's emphasized the reader's pleasure. Hence nine years later in the *Preface* he writes:

The poetical beauties or defects I have not been very diligent to observe. Some plays have more, and some fewer judicial observations, not in proportion to their difference of merit, but because I gave this part of my design to chance and to caprice. The reader, I believe, is seldom pleased to find his opinion anticipated; it is natural to delight more in what we find or make, than in what we receive. (104)

Johnson's disinclination to pronounce upon the beauties and faults of the plays may seem to belie the typical sense of his critical authority (a sense well developed by the publication of the 1765 edition, as we shall see) and to eddy against the erection of standards and tradition around Shakespeare and Spenser during the mid-century.[13] Yet the attention to the reader's "pleasure of judgment" simply enlarges the domain of the aesthetic surrendered by historicism. Considered from this perspective, Johnson's theoretical recourse to the reader is of a piece with his understanding of literary tradition and aesthetic autonomy, and on two interlinked counts. The lax attitude toward judgment actually brings in a newer and more stringent form of judgment implicit in philological method. At the same time, the pleasure that the reader finds in objects that are "not supposed to be real" measures, however dimly, Shakespeare's perseverance across the span of literary history.

Johnson's philological task is to protect the reader from the danger of particularities, in this case the ruck of historical and philological detail.[14] He concludes the *Preface* with an apology for the tedium of the notes: "Particular passages are cleared by notes, but the general effect of the work is weakened. The mind is refrigerated by interruption; the thoughts are diverted from the principal subject; the reader is weary, he suspects not why; and at last throws away the book" (111). Annotation threatens to block the pleasurable experience of the majority of readers, and so to oppose precisely what makes Shakespeare valuable, his august generality. "Nothing can please many, and please long but just representations of general nature. Particular manners can be known to few, and therefore few only can judge how nearly they are copied" (61). Gothic arcana and historical detail alike "refrigerate" the commonality, who lack the expert knowledge of Hurd's "few curious and learned men." Particularity like Spenserianism fails the test of time.

Later on in the edition, Johnson develops these matters of editorial procedure into the familiar opposition of sublime and beautiful. Consider his well-known reading of *Lear*.[15] Edgar's lines upon gazing over the cliffs at Dover prompt this reflection:

> He that looks from a precipice finds himself assailed by one great and dreadful image of irresistible destruction. But this overwhelming idea is dissipated and enfeebled from the instant that the mind can restore itself to the observation of particulars, and diffuse its attention to distinct objects. The enumeration of the choughs and crows, the samphire-man and the fishers, counteracts the great effect of the prospect, as it peoples the desert of intermediate vacuity, and stops the mind in the rapidity of its descent through emptiness and horror. (695)

The note faults Shakespeare for dropping the sublime description he begins. While Johnson appears to be within Burke's model, whose terms form the standard against which Shakespeare pales, particularity turns out to be precisely what blocks sublimity. The enumeration of colloquial detritus *enfeebles* the effect of the scene. Johnson recapitulates, at the level of judgment, his understanding of editing, where the reader wants the "pleasure of judgment" but is chilled by philology. Both sides of the argument exhibit a cultivated weariness of the sublime, in its customary articulation, the eremitic character of which proves a difficult foundation for canonically enduring "general nature."[16]

To what degree, then, does Johnson fall back on the older discourse of the beautiful? Consider the summation of *Hamlet*:

> We must allow to the tragedy of *Hamlet* the praise of variety. The incidents are so numerous, that the argument of the play would make a long tale. The scenes are interchangeably diversified with merriment and solemnity; with merriment that includes judicious and instructive observations, and solemnity, not strained by poetical violence above the natural sentiment of man. New characters appear from time to time in continual succession, exhibiting various forms of life and particular modes of conversation. (1011)

Unlike the samphire men or fishers, *Hamlet*'s "particular modes" continuously give way to each other within a composite structure. The play illustrates "unity in variety," the aesthetic principle handed down by Hutcheson, Hogarth and others.[17] *Hamlet* survives the ages because it is a projection and image of the natural and because, what amounts to the same thing, "all pleasure consists in variety" (67). This recourse to sociable "variety" would seem to locate Johnson closer to Addison than to Burke, to imagine the text, once more, as an analogue to the harmonious order of a civil society into which the reader nicely fits.[18] Yet, the beauty which Johnson finds in Shakespeare exhibits an instrumental tension between sociality and pastness: social because general, general because old. If beauty customarily produces an imaginative intimacy with an intricate and ramified social order, and if "variety" describes the harmonious composition of that order, Johnson must be said at once to confirm and oppose the customary account. While reading joins one to a community of fellow Shakespeare lovers, that community comes to the present from the past. The fit between the singular reader and the manifold of readers falls backward in time.

Shakespeare is the icon of a national community moving across the arch of historical time. We are allied in the pleasure we share in reading Shakespeare, and, of equal importance, we are like past ages of readers who are also like us. The symmetrical coupling of taste proves Shakespeare's canonical value.

> As his personages act upon principles arising from genuine passion, very little modified by particular forms, their pleasures and vexations are communicable to all times and to all places; they are natural, and therefore durable; the adventitious peculiarities of personal habits, are only superficial dyes, without any remains of former lustre; but the discriminations of

true passion are the colours of nature; they pervade the whole mass, and can only perish with the body that exhibits them. The accidental compositions of heterogeneous modes are dissolved by the chance which combined them; but the uniform simplicity of primitive qualities neither admits increase, nor suffers decay. The sand heaped by one flood is scattered by another, but the rock always continues in its place. The stream of time, which is continually washing the dissolute fabricks of other poets, passes without injury by the adamant of Shakespeare. (70)

Midway through this dramatic passage the metaphor switches from repetition – the ritual genuflection successive generations make to the reputation of Shakespeare – to oceanic change. Literary history erodes all but the most elemental forms. The point of the memorable image is that literary works require a certain deferral before they become canonical. One can only see the obdurate immutability of Shakespeare's texts through the shades of ages. It is only after the fact that one can be sure that Shakespeare is not part of the sand and dross kicked up by history. Shakespeare's adamantine solidity stems from his imitation of the customary forms of human life. Readers find in him a projection of "common humanity" raised to a higher order of aesthetic law (62). Having the accolades of successive generations, Shakespeare earns the title of English classic: "The poet of whose works I have undertaken the revision may now begin to assume the dignity of an ancient, and claim the privilege of established fame and prescriptive veneration. He has long outlived his century, the term commonly fixed as the test of literary merit" (61). Johnson adduces Shakespeare's classical status from the simple fact of his survival, but survival contains a new literary standard; it demonstrates the accretion of generations of acts of reading and viewing, whose quantity achieves, by the mid-eighteenth century, a new quality, the quality of "the human."

It is on these terms, then, that we might understand the way in which the hypothetical reader of Johnson's Shakespeare enjoys hermeneutical and aesthetic pride of place. "The reader" will choose among textual variants, and, since the edition is a variorum, the reader will decide which editor's approach to follow. The reader is the subject of aesthetic pleasure, whether in forming judgments or experiencing beauty. Above all, the collective order of readers is the agent and framework of literary endurance. This is no doubt why Johnson's criticism is so often identified with English cultural nationalism, a nationalism rooted in the sense that reading older cultural artifacts joins one to a community reaching back into an immemorial past.[19] Readers are common not in their social status, but in their lack of particular traits (of class, region, gender, and so on).[20] We are alike in our identification with Shakespeare's characters; "Shakespeare has no heroes; his scenes are occupied only by men, who act and speak as the reader thinks that he should himself have spoken or acted on the same occasion" (64). Widespread reading depersonalizes individual tastes into the general medium of literature. Literature abstracts consumption into a perennial identification with masculine character raised to aesthetic law. The canon, in turn, rests on the stability of historical repetition, on one reader reading like a generation of readers, on the sliding of reading into the adamantine density of England's past.

How might Johnson be situated within the larger emergence of the English canon? The tendential suturing of antiquity to consumption illustrates a tacit shift in the understanding of the cultural market. Many of the critics we have encountered viewed the reading public as the origin of literary descent. In this account, the exclusivity of a public centered on the court produced a robust national literature, while the potentially boundless public founded on the market produced the enervated literature of politeness and the novel. Here the aesthetics of the particular bore a strict analogy to the particularity of the cultural field. As long as writers wrote for a small audience, their works were in the literary language of the concrete. As soon as authors wrote "to satisfy the ladies and the beaux," their language descended to the expatiatory prose of the market. The effect of this literary history was to imagine the past in almost mythical terms. Johnson is fully in this tradition when he declares Shakespeare to be "an ancient." For as much as his literary history seeks to revise the abiding model of his contemporaries and (as he puts it famously in the *Life of Gray*) to "rejoice in concurring with the common reader," it also articulates their model at an even higher order of emphasis. No longer antithetical to cultural achievement, the reader is the arbiter of imperishable fame. Popularity joins to value with the sobering ballast of historical time. Shorn of gothic particularity and vouchsafed by generations of readers, high canonical works arrive to us from the deathless past. The return to reading as the condition of national canon formation entails, however, a rethinking of what reading accomplishes. Reading is now understood according to an analogy between culture and the economy. Just as economic consumption leads to the abstraction of exchange value, cultural consumption leads to the abstraction of aesthetic value. The one defines the value of a commodity in terms of its exchange, its convertibility into the medium of money; the other defines the value of a text in terms of its survival, its convertibility into the medium of literature. Both systems abstract from the particular uses of a given artifact and canonize lasting forms of generality.

## II

Shakespeare withstands time and shines through the "shades of ages" because he grasps at what appeals to the generality of readers. The canon binds together antiquity, reading, and history. This binding in turn obliges a certain aesthetic, a "consciousness of fiction" that abjures the empirical and the fantastical alike. Johnson's larger designs were not lost on the first major respondent to his edition. In two separate articles in the *Monthly Review* and then again in a longer pamphlet, William Kenrick delivered an extensive rejoinder to Johnson's aesthetic and his critical position-taking. A frequent contributor to the *Monthly*, Kenrick wrote from the institution of the periodical press at an important moment of its transformation.[21] He wrote neither as Addison's polite Spectator, whose essays were to be enjoyed at leisure by the *beau-monde* of coffee-house *cognoscenti*, nor as Joseph Warton's authoritative Adventurer, whose taste dictated the norms of an untrained public. Kenrick's cultural identity stemmed, rather, from the new and unstable position of professional journalist. For the first time in Shakespeare criticism, the words "professional" and "journalist" are invoked, as accusation and defense alike.

One gets a sense of the novelty of Kenrick's position in Boswell's description of the journalist's quarrel with Johnson:

Shakespeare was virulently attacked by Mr. William Kenrick, who . . . wrote for the booksellers in a great variety of branches . . . I remember one evening, when some of his works were mentioned, Dr. Goldsmith said, he had never heard of them; upon which Dr. Johnson observed, "Sir, he is one of the many who made themselves *publick* without being *known*." (*Life of Johnson*: 301–302)

The literary labor that Boswell describes is that of a writer for whom "publick" means the anonymity of the market, for whom the profession of writing is distinctively non-charismatic. As we shall see, Kenrick's sense of his unknown labor greatly informs his response to Johnson, who is taken to task for abandoning his professional duties in favor of the lax pleasure of a government pension. This engagement entails an important reversal of the earlier understanding of professional and anonymous criticism, in which anonymity provided a stately contrast to professional self-assertion. For Kenrick, Johnson's charisma only marks him a dilettante, while his own anonymity (maintained in the *Monthly*, then abandoned in the pamphlet) marks the quintessence of dutiful labor. Kenrick's caustically anti-Johnsonian pamphlet touched quite a nerve, prompting a response from James Barclay, the *Critical Review*, and his own organ the *Monthly Review*, among others. The varied stances in this public debate all assumed a certain Shakespearean orthodoxy. Each accused the other of heresy.

In considering Kenrick's treatment of Johnson's edition in the *Monthly Review*, one might begin with the periodical's subtitle: *A Literary Journal*. The *Monthly* exhibits not just the professionalization of criticism, but the reciprocal narrowing of its object to literature.[22] A dutiful servant to the literary, Kenrick begins the review by noting how ill-served Shakespeare (who "least requires and most deserves, a comment, of all the writers of his age produced"[23]) has been by modern criticism, including Johnson.

Among so many eager scholiasts that have employed themselves in elucidating his writings, hardly one of them hath been of aid in any degree worthy of him. They all seem to have mistaken the route, in which only they could do honour to themselves, or be useful to the reader. Engaged in the piddling task of adjusting quibbles, and restoring conundrums, they have neglected the illustrating of characters, sentiments and situations . . . From the present editor, it is true, we hoped for better things. But what shall we say? When he himself confesses, that, as to "the poetical beauties or defects of his author, he hath not been very diligent to observe them: have given up the post to diligence and caprice." (286)

Johnson continues the lamentable tradition of philological solipsism. True criticism consists in the honorable and useful track of elucidating beauty. Kenrick here adopts the familiar opposition to historicist method. He reclaims the aesthetic mode of reading for the periodical press and surrenders philology to the scholiasts. His disappointment is that Johnson the critic has given way to Johnson the lexicographer, that antiquarianism has usurped literature: "we were encouraged to hope that Shakespeare would no longer be treated like an obsolete writer: whose works were of no other use than to employ the sagacity of antiquarians and philologers. But perhaps our editor found the task of commenting on Shakespeare as a poet, much more difficult than he had conceived it to be" (286). Kenrick's chiding of Johnson for having abandoned the aesthetic vocation turns out to be well within the designs of a "literary journal." Reading for beauty is reading for poetry, while reading for quibbles is reading for something else (obsolescence, antiquarianism, and the like). Here Kenrick dismisses the notion that philology is a technical skill and reclaims the discourse of expertise for periodical criticism. Literary journalism implies an adept and professional rigor.

Kenrick's critique begins by accusing the charismatic pensioner of not being literary enough. The *Monthly* takes issue, for instance, with Johnson's claim that Shakespeare was morally diffuse by arguing for the relative autonomy of literature from the ethical domain that properly belongs to philosophy, for literature's specific way of conveying morality by other means. Kenrick begins the argument by quoting Johnson's verdict that "[Shakespeare] sacrificed virtue to convenience, and is so much more careful to please than to instruct, that he seems to write without any moral purpose. From his writings a system of social duty may be selected, for he that thinks sensibly must think morally; but his precepts and axioms drop casually from him; he makes no just distribution of good or evil" (291). What Johnson misrecognizes here, Kenrick contends, is an important separation within the division of knowledge: Shakespeare "did not conceive himself bound, as a *poet*, to write like a *philosopher*" (291). Poetry's lack of a "just distribution" or axiomatic system is what defines its difference from philosophy and what gives form to its morality. "If it be admitted, as our Editor actually admits," Kenrick asks,

that a system of social duty may be selected from his writings, and that his precepts and axioms were virtuous; we may justly ask, whether they are less so for dropping casually from him? Must a writer be charged with making a sacrifice of virtue, because he does not professedly inculcate it? Is every writer *ex professio* a parson or a moral philosopher? It is doubtless always the *moralist's* duty, to strive at least, to make the world better; but we should think it no inconsiderable merit in a *comic poet*, to be able to divert and amuse the world without making it worse; especially if he should drop such virtuous precepts and axioms, as would serve to make a system of social duty. (291)

The question assumes not just that Shakespeare was actually a decent person, that his plays had the poetic justice so important for Rymer's generation, but also that the "casual" form of this morality constitutes the difference between literature and other forms of discourse (in particular, here, theology and philosophy).[24] Kenrick identifies the literary, in this passage, as an aesthetics of casual dropping. Johnson glimpses how such dropping can be aesthetically systematized but he fails to see how this prevents the dissolving of literature into morality, the writer into "the parson or moral philosopher."

For as much as Kenrick accuses Johnson of abandoning the casual rigors of literature for the easy precepts of morality, their exchange was not so much a disagreement between an exponent and opponent of the relative autonomy of literature as a collision between two versions of that autonomy. Johnson, after all, had his own notion of the literary, as we have seen, and Kenrick was well aware of this notion. The longest and most significant part of the review engages the very section of the *Preface* in which Johnson dramatically asserts the difference of literature from other orders of discourse: the critique of the three unities. Here Johnson "shews himself to be as indifferent a pleader for Shakespeare as he hath proved *against* him" (293). The review moves from the ethical to the epistemological register; the opposite of literature derives not just from moral axioms but from the faculty of the understanding, what Johnson calls "consciousness." The problem of the mind's relation to literature's fictionality, its not being, strictly speaking, "real," had beguiled aesthetic discourse as far back as Addison's account of the imagination as a mediating faculty between the understanding and its material object. Johnson's answer – that there is a specific pleasure in beholding objects that one knows to be fabricated – is, thus, a development with a long pedigree; the pleasure that the imagination procures from the object reflects back on that object as its intrinsic fictionality. Kenrick protests that this account places too much emphasis on rational reflection, on the understanding's *conscious* incredulity.

Johnson is right to suggest that we need not believe the action to be real; but, Kenrick quickly adds, we need not disbelieve either.

Belief is ultimately beside the point. Another faculty and pleasure intervenes before the act of rational cogitation takes place: "A spectator, properly affected by a dramatic presentation, makes no reflection about the fiction or reality of it. The spectator is unquestionably deceived; but the deception goes no farther than the passions; it affects our sensibility but not our understanding: and is by no means so powerful a delusion as to effect our belief" (299). Johnson over-embellishes the role of cognition in the reading of literature or the viewing of plays and, conversely, diminishes the role of affect, passion, and sensibility. There is too much consciousness in his "consciousness of fiction." In the place of consciousness, Kenrick places sensibility, in place of reason, passion, and in place of judgment, affect: "That the judgment never mistook any dramatic representation we readily admit; but that our senses frequently do, is certain, from the affect it hath on our passions" (299).

This is, for Kenrick, no minor item. Johnson's embellishment of consciousness initiates a serious misunderstanding of the way in which literature operates. The point is not whether one believes the action to be real but whether one is induced to feel by the action. On the stealthy wings of the passions, literature flies beneath the understanding. Kenrick thus responds to Johnson's statement that "the delight of tragedy proceeds from our consciousness of fiction; if we thought murders and reasons real they would please no more" ("Preface": 78) by asserting that

it may be safely affirmed, that we neither fancy the players nor ourselves unhappy: our imagination hath nothing to do with the immediate impressions whether of joy or sorrow; we are in this case merely passive, our organs are in unison with those of the players on the stage, and the conclusions of grief or laughter are purely involuntary. As to the delight we experience from tragedy, it no more proceeds directly from consciousness of fiction, than the pleasure we reap from Comedy; but in the *physical* consequence of having the transient sense of pain or danger excited in us by sympathy, instead of actually or durably feeling it ourselves, hence that diminution of pain, which gives rise to the pleasing sensation, to which the ingenious author of the enquiry into the origin of our ideas of the Sublime and the Beautiful, gives the name *delight*. (*Monthly*: 301)

The invocation of Burke's account of the particular "delight" one has in tragic representations makes, on the face of it, a rather unusual claim. Literature does not reside in the conscious reflection on objects; in fact, it does not reside in cognition at all. Literary experience is, rather, "physical." The recourse to Burke fashions an anti-Johnsonian version of literary autonomy founded on sensation, on the passions' prevailing over the understanding. "The business of ratiocination is laid aside"; "the understanding enters into a compact, as it were, to keep holiday, while the passions are amusing themselves within the ordinary bounds of sentiment" (376). In its broadest assumptions, Kenrick's polemic is not entirely novel; it restates theses argued not just by Burke but, in different ways, by Smith, Hume, Addison, and Shaftesbury. The novelty of Kenrick's argument stems, rather, from the lengths to which the engagement with Johnson's theory of fictionality and consciousness takes the theory of sensation. Attacking Johnson's version of incredulous delight in fiction with a notion of credulous delight in sensation, Kenrick is pushed to assert that literature flies so far below the understanding that our reaction to it ceases to count as thinking. He strains aesthetic discourse to yield as much of an anti-Johnsonian argument as it can muster, and to do so in the guise of literary rigor. Johnson's recourse to "consciousness of fiction" is an indolent refusal to investigate what makes literature literary. In contrast, an un-wavering theory of the literary commences with the negation of consciousness, commences, that is, with the body.

Soon after the *Monthly Review* articles appeared, Kenrick published *A Review of Doctor Johnson's New Edition of Shakespeare: in which the ignorance or inattention of that editor is exposed, and the poet defended from the persecution of his commentators* (1765). This pamphlet effectively con-tinued the earlier reviews, moving from the preface to the notes and considering the manner in which Johnson handled textual problems and engaged previous editors. Editorial questions, as we have seen in previous chapters, could often lead to heated and bitter debates, and such was the case here. Kenrick's caustic pamphlet (and the second pamphlet that followed in its "defense") not only continued this tradition of philological disputation but also raised more directly institutional and political issues. The narrowly "literary" matters of the *Monthly Review* transformed in the pamphlet into an *engagé* denunciation of the imperious Dr. Johnson.

Kenrick begins the pamphlet by likening his assault on the Johnsonian monument to several lines from *Macbeth*. When the story of the Kenrick–Johnson debate is retold, readers will remember that "'An Eagle, tow'ring in his pride of place, / Was, by a mousing owl, hawk'd at and kill'd'" (v). The figure serves both as a metaphor and analogy. Kenrick happily suggests that, in the pages to follow, Johnson's towering pride will be toppled by the diligent labors of a low-flying unknown. The analogy is, as it were, within this metaphor: the "place" of the Eagle well describes the "place" of the critic because the latter is analogous to the literal places given to Church and Government leaders. The argument works by a mock philology:

> For tho', Dr. Johnson having neither preferment in the church, nor post in the state, the word *place* may seem to want that strict propriety the critics require; yet, if we reflect how nearly *places* and *pensions* are allied, there is not one of Shakespeare's commentators who would make any scruple of substituting one word for the other, reciprocally, and alternately, as he thought the case might require. There is no doubt also that, on this occasion, the word pension would be preferred; as a pension must be universally allowed, *caeteris paribus*, to be better than a place, to a man so fond of doing but little; as it is apprehended the reader will think is the case with Dr. Johnson. (v)

This analogy is a favorite of Kenrick's; its nuanced and varied repetition fills the pages of the pamphlet and the defense. The essential substance will be familiar from Huggins and elsewhere: Johnson has accrued to himself a charismatic power that both exceeds what is due to his particular acumen and deforms the republic of letters, a power that is like that of tyrannical prelates, monarchs, and nobles.

The pamphlet takes the *Monthly*'s theory of literary autonomy in a dramatically new direction. The freedom of literature from morality and politics alike is, paradoxically, political:

> The republic of letters is a perfect democracy, where all being equal, there is no respect of persons, but every one hath a right to speak the truth of another, to censure without fear, and to commend without favour or affectation. Nor is the *literary* community of less dignity than the *political*. Popularity and influence indeed may be obtained, for a while, by sinister means in both; but though birth and wealth may confer eminence and power in the one, not the descent of an Alexander, nor the riches of Croesus, confer prerogative or authority in the other. (x)

The limpid economy of this prefatory statement rivals any image of the literary republic in eighteenth-century critical discourse. The statement carries with it the weight of the century-long sifting out of politics from literature, each of which rises to the surface here as fully abstracted and semi-detached categories. The separating out of literature from politics is so achieved by the moment of this utterance that the one may serve easily as a model for the other. But, Kenrick insists, this reciprocal mirroring remains imperfect; the literary community is a pure democracy, while the political community is corrupted by birth and wealth. Literature looks like what politics ought to look like.

For as much as Kenrick invests the literary republic with a sort of compensatory democracy he also writes out of a sense of the impending dissolution of that republic by authoritarian critics like Johnson:

Is it, by the way, then, to be wondered at, that a private individual, like Samuel Johnson, should be even preposterously elated at finding that homage paid to him, which has been in vain solicited by sovereigns, and is refused even to the King on his throne? Graduated by universities, pensioned by his prince, and surrounded by pedagogues and poetasters, he finds a grateful odour in the incense of adulation; while admiring booksellers stand at a distance, and look up to him with awful reverence, bowing to the knee to Baal; and holding in fearful remembrance the exemplary fate of Tom Osborne. (xi)

Here Kenrick rises to one of his more evocative descriptions of the problem of Johnson's charisma. A singular individual, whose private interests should be dissolved into the common interests of the republic, Johnson has become the fetish object of the literary world. Devotion, honors, ritual obeisance swirl and stink around him. The rhetorical flourish is owing to the underlying institutional critique: Johnson's charisma is a figure of literary tyranny, of political corruption entering the purity of literature. Even the rational avatars of print-democracy, the booksellers, are in awe of Johnson's magnificence. Kenrick's terms deliberately transpose earlier conceptions of literary fame as a kind of odor. From Dryden through the late contortions of Huggins, critics distanced themselves from the indelicacy of the market by casting it as a fetid and excremental stench. Kenrick adopts and inverts this model: commerce is infected by the foul smell of a critical aristocracy. Cleansing the literary republic means taking on Johnson: "if the interests of our literary state require it, it cannot be doubted that the mere gratification of an individual ought to be given up for the good of the whole community" (xii). And taking on Johnson means endowing the reading public with an authority allegedly taken from them: "WE are all Doctors, Dr. Johnson" (52). Here Kenrick rejects the authority of critical commissars, the imperious strength and baleful charisma of Johnson, and

"Doctors" the public, cedes to them the territory of literary evaluation. "WE" refers both to the plenum of abused critics, the monthly
reviewers and minor writers, *and* to the public at large. "How *dare* Dr.
Johnson treat *that public* with so much *contempt* . . . How dare he
behave to that public with such imparallel'd ingratitude?" (55). The
answer to these questions lies in Johnson's despotic separation from
the democratic will of assembled readers; hence Kenrick's double
adjective "the self-sufficient, the arrogant Dr. Johnson" (55).

The Doctoring of the public is a tactical move in the effort to
dethrone or defrock Johnson. The public garners more authority at
the same pace that Johnson becomes more of a pariah. It is in this
sense, then, that we may understand Kenrick's nationalism: the
more that the "republic of letters" swells to displace its "political"
analogue, the more it endows a nation of readers, hence "the
pleasure, which it is presumed every true Englishman will feel, at
[the pamphlet's] attempt to do justice to his favourite poet" (xii).
What distinguished the public from the nation in Johnson was the
passing of literary historical time, the sliding of reading into an
immemorial past. Kenrick's nationalism exhibits a dialectical complement to Johnson's: reading slides back from the eternal past
through the present to the imagined future. The nation of readers
give their trust to Shakespeare, who becomes an icon and image of
the community of readers. The cause of the "republic of letters"
binds itself to "the cause of Shakespeare" (111). Kenrick's love of
Shakespeare is a love of his countrymen; his passion for readers,
"the zeal with which the very name of Shakespeare inspires me"
(55). The "outrage committed on Shakespeare" (ix) by Johnson's
edition is, in contrast, a heretical degradation of the icon into which
the nation has poured its collective faith: "he should not have
presumed to think that his public, tasteless and ignorant as he may
suppose it, could ever be prevailed on to grace his waving noddle
with a wreath, irreverently torn from the brows of Shakespeare!"
(55). Against Johnson's heresy, Kenrick declares a highly charged
reverence: "Away, therefore, with all such trifling, and revere THE
TEXT OF SHAKESPEARE" (24). For whom, then, is Shakespeare an icon?
In the first pamphlet, Kenrick uses the terms public and nation more
or less interchangeably. The slide from the one to the other is
nevertheless revealing. The success of the national model for him
relies on the shared worshipping of Shakespeare defeating the
critical tyranny of Johnson.

The varied meanings of public, nation, and market are further revealed by the next installment of the debate. Kenrick's anti-Johnsonian tract received the negative attention for which it most likely was designed.[25] Among the often heated responses, James Barclay's *An Examination of Mr. Kenrick's Review of Mr. Johnson's Edition of Shakespeare* (1766) is particularly notable. An Oxford student and would-be clubman, Barclay begins his *Examination* by placing Johnson in the position Kenrick established for Shakespeare: "A deference is certainly due to established fame, and decorum to those members of the community who have been honoured with the public approbation: IT IS A DOWNRIGHT AFFRONT TO NATIONAL APPROBATION, TO STIGMATISE THAT MAN WITH IGNORANCE, WHO HAS BEEN SELECTED FROM THE COLLECTIVE LEARNED AS PECULIARLY DESERVING THEIR FAVOURS" (iv). Like Kenrick's Shakespeare, Barclay's Johnson achieves national iconicity because he springs from collective reading. And, like Kenrick's Johnson, Barclay's Kenrick is now the apostate of the nation's taste. The deliberate syntactical transposition breaks down, however, with the introduction of a new and hitherto absent qualification. It is not, as in the *Review*, the assembled generality of readers that elevates Johnson to icon, but rather the "collective learned." In the repetition of Kenrick's charge, Barclay makes two changes: the community that has lent its collected approbation to a singular cultural icon is the nation (a word which Kenrick uses but not in the exact sentence Barclay quotes); that nation is comprised of the "learned." Barclay's revisions are thus at apparent odds with each other; the dilation of the republic into the nation leads at once to a constriction to the intelligentsia. Kenrick is a pariah of the national will *and* of the critical ministry. The assault is on an officialdom tacitly consented to by the nation of readers; it follows, then, that Kenrick's assault is that of an impudent stranger: "It was a natural question in every reader . . . Who is this W. Kenrick? What works have proceeded from his pen sufficient to countenance this unaccountable charge? To these interrogatories, few, very few, could make a satisfactory answer, and the world was apt to conclude, THAT A MAN THAT NO BODY KNEW HAD ATTACKED A MAN WHOM EVERY BODY KNEW" (v). Barclay here echoes the pronouncement Boswell ascribes to Johnson: Kenrick's literary labor is unknown; it has yet to ascend the hierarchy of literary achievement. The plea for openness and democracy in the republic of letters is met with a stalwart reiteration of tradition and

hierarchy; "he is of the leveling tribe; he wants to reduce every one
to his standard of learning and criticism" (*Examination*: 49). This
political reading of the literary community remains within Kenrick's
terms, or squares their circle; in the guise of defending Johnson, it
ends up agreeing with the account of his charisma.

The accusation of "leveler" finds in Kenrick the example and
herald of unruly cultural democracy. This democracy has two
interrelated causes. In typical fashion, true learning and critical
authority are imperiled by the universal leveler of the cash-nexus, in
this case, the profitability of scandal. The ever present specter of the
market bears a particular stamp in Barclay's critique, however. And
here he cannily discovers the fulcrum of Kenrick's project: responding to the accusation that Johnson is a "blockhead" because
he objects to the disappearance of the hermit in *The Merchant of
Venice*, Barclay opines that this is: "*à la mode d'un journalist sçavant,
n'est ce pas*, Mons. Kenrick?" (41). The nomination of Kenrick,
writer for the *Monthly Review*, as a "journalist" and the switch to
French are both important. While the idea of the newspaper was
relatively settled by the 1760s, "journalist" as a name for a
professional writer for the periodical press was still in its infancy.
The word lagged behind the concept. Johnson's definition in the
*Dictionary* is simply "a writer of journals," which he follows with no
citations. (This is why, then, "journalist" appeared in English well
before "journalism"; the coining of the latter term requires that the
former already signifies a professional identity.)[26] Barclay switches
to French not just to strike an elegant pose against the ill mannered
Kenrick but also to find an adequate name for a new and equivocal
identity.[27]

The change in language is symptomatic of the difficulty that "the
manner of a clever journalist" introduces into critical discussion.
Barclay musters an entire arsenal of available obloquy; Kenrick is a
commoner and pedant at once, an impertinent leveler and a
"mouldy inmate of libraries and moth of manuscripts" (51);
"nothing can be more nauseous to the man of sense" (76). His
precise location is impossible to pinpoint:

The author of the pamphlet before me, is a mere *Galimatia* in reading;
nothing comes amiss to him, French, English, Latin, Greek, Dutch, Italian,
of each he gives us a spice: To these I suppose upon occasion he could add
the *gibberish* of the Hottentots. Nor are his abilities as a writer less
multifarious than his merits as a linguist. He is a critick and hypercritick,

an haberdasher of words, and a lexicographer, a politician, a patriot, a poet, and a freethinker; he is – what is he not?" (77)

The specification of Kenrick's identity as a "journalist" brings about a spiraling confusion over what that identity entails. Barclay's final switch from the epistemic (*who* is Kenrick?) to the ontic (*what* is Kenrick?) turns the question into its own answer, "what is he not?" The symptom whose name is Kenrick can not be wished away so much as diagnosed: the writer for the periodical press is as plural as the print market itself; he embodies the flattening of values into uniform objects of exchange, from French to Italian, from a lexicographer to a freethinker.

As befits an irksome Proteus, Kenrick responded to his critics in spirited haste. Written under the pseudonym of a partial compatriot, his *A Defense of Mr. Kenrick's Review of Dr. Johnson's Shakespeare: Containing a Number of Curious and Ludicrous Anecdotes of Literary Biography, By a Friend* (1766) extended the analysis of the literary republic and added a novel description of literary professionalism as a kind of labor. Kenrick's "friend" asserts a fantasy of literary redemption by means of political language: "I take up the pen to defend his cause and assert the right of every citizen in the Republick of Letters to think and write freely" (3). The conception of this republic is considerably darkened. A "literary Junto" rules over a cowering nation (2). At the top of the junto sits Dr. Johnson.

There are those who condemn both [Mr. K] and his Review, without seeing or knowing any thing of either, except what is told them by Dr. Johnson's partisans. Nay, several of these *candid* and *impartial* gentry began to rail openly in the public news-papers, at the sight of Mr. K's advertisement only. The terms of this, truly were highly indecent; it was a kind of high-treason, a species of impiety, even to imagine Dr. Johnson could be *ignorant* or *inattentive*. One would have thought him placed at the head of literature, as the Roman pontiff is at the head of his church, and with the same pretensions to infallibility. Every body, forsooth, was expected to kiss pope Johnson's toe, even at the hazard of having their fore-teeth kicked out by his holiness's brutality. (43)

This evocative portrait serves to rebuke the nominally democratic overtures of Johnson's idea of audience. Johnson's wrapping himself in ages and generations of readers is merely a cloak for an imperious design on the servile republic. The national audience enjoys its dictatorial critic, abandoning sacred Shakespeare for the idol Johnson. Even the "public news-papers" have fallen sway to the dominion of a gentry elite hostile to commoners like Kenrick. The subsequent analogy to papal tyranny means to suggest that literature ought to have no infallible head, just as the church ought to have no pontiff. And, just as the Pope deformed the Christian church, the literary pontiff has deformed English literature. Yet the call for a literary-critical Reformation – "I take up the pen to defend his cause and assert the right of every citizen in the Republick of Letters to think and write freely" (3) – as it is articulated once more in the second pamphlet, seems wearied of the modern nation: "To this [defense] I am particularly incited also, from a due sense that such freedom is become absolutely necessary to support the present interests of literature; which are daily dropping under the dead weights of indolence, partiality, and prepossession" (3). The story is told in the familiar terms of descent. Describing "our literary character," Kenrick writes

> We degenerated from our forefathers; from the wits and philosophers of those ages which produced a Shakespeare . . . whom instead of imitating, we exert all our little abilities to depreciate, and level with the diminutive standard of the present times . . . We are now-a-days so far from having the *virtues* of great men, that we have not even their vices; everything . . . is little, mean, and pitiful among us. (4)

This lament shares a certain affinity with dominant strains of midcentury criticism: literary history charts a decline in achievement after the seventeenth century. Yet the terms of this crisis emerge differently in Kenrick; the baleful charm of the market that so worries the Wartonian school returns as the charisma of the master critic. The very solution to crisis – critical mastery – ends up accelerating the career of descent.

The shared coordinates between these two lines of descent extend beyond the mordant sense of literary infirmity. Like Upton, Kenrick genders this decline. Johnson's "junto" are yesterday's aristocratic connoisseurs, reborn as feminized men of refinement with ill designs on the cultural product:

> If any of Dr. J's partisans think they can defend him, in the late outrage he hath committed against the memory and reputation of Shakespeare, let them stand forth boldly, and they shall be received like men. But this, it seems, is not enough for the refined and elegant writers of the present age: they must be treated with *tenderness*, with *gentility*, with sweetmeat and sugar-candy I warrant ye, like fine ladies and peeking children – Out upon such a pack of finicking fribbles; with hearts in their bellies no bigger than pins

heads; and those even minnikins; mere dealers in frippery in the rag-fair of Literature! It is certainly a wonderful instance of a man's self-sufficiency to think himself able to encounter such diminutive opponents as these! Here, as Falstaff says, is no vanity. (39)

This portrait of literary rectitude expresses an obverse affinity to historicism. The scholar's disavowal of the public's ignorance has turned into the journalist's zealous avowal of the nation's reading, but this criss-crossing of critical lines yields once more a stalwart male tradition defending the literary past against an onslaught of effete readers. As the attitude toward the public turns on its head, the scholar's arrogation of "literature" passes intact into the journalist's appropriation of the nation's taste; each projects a common, Shakespearean masculinity.

Johnson's otiose grandeur is an index and symptom of cultural effeminacy and literary descent. One ought to ask, Kenrick writes, "whether imbecility and indolence be really good-nature and benevolence; and whether, in an age of less ceremony and greater sincerity, the magisterial supineness, affected by Dr. J. would not be frankly called *pride* and *idleness*" (14). Sloth traverses Johnson's disinclination to discuss the passions – *and* the splendor of his reign. "Supine" meets "magisterial" by way of a shared ignorance of the literary nation, which is structured without hierarchy and built out of passions. "Dr. J"'s torpid arrogance is preeminently a failure to satisfy "the faithful discharge of the common duties of his profession or calling" (14). And here, in the closing pages of the debate over Johnson's edition, Kenrick executes his principal charge. The manifold dangers of Johnson's practice coalesce in a single error: a lack of professionalism. Kenrick's version of professionalism amounts neither to philological expertise nor to aesthetic rarefaction, but rather to practical labor. In the endeavor to understand how the charisma of Johnson has beguiled the community of Shakespeare lovers, Kenrick switches to a largely economic model of the literary community and the critical profession.

The economic model is put forth in a pair of small essays that conclude the *Defense*, "On the Modesty of Men of Letters" and "On Literary Knowledge." This discussion shows Kenrick's sharpest break, not only from Johnson, but also from the tradition of cultivated modesty that extends from Shaftesbury to Huggins. His account is worth quoting in full:

I must own I cannot help thinking that such writers debase themselves greatly, whenever they affect the false modesty of unexperienced tyros, or designing ignorants. There is a species of assurance in men of real knowledge, which may be said, without impropriety, to be consistent with the modesty becoming their character, as they could not possibly divest themselves of it without evident hypocrisy and affectation. As to authors by profession, they must necessarily either display their assurance by insisting on their own merit, or, in fact, confess themselves bunglers, or impostors. And indeed why should they not? If an artist discover any mode of mechanical operation, or execute a piece of mechanism, which is an improvement on what others have done before him, or what nobody can execute but himself, who charges him with want of modesty in boldly asserting his own pre-eminence? Why then should a critick, a philosopher, an historian, or a poet, be thought too assuming in laying publick claim to that merit, which they actually possess? What should we think of an artisan or manufacturer, who should, in his advertisements and shop-bills, *modestly* affect a diffidence of being able to give his customers satisfaction, having himself a mean opinion of his own abilities? Yet how common is it to meet with authors, who have been many years *in trade*, ridiculously affecting to think meanly of productions, which they nevertheless importunately obtrude on the public, and make us pay for at as high a price as possible? Yet many of these writers have the character of being modest men. In my opinion, however, I think it an instance of very great *impudence*, to say no worse of it, for a man to offer me a commodity at a great price, and to tell me at the same time he thinks it good for little. For what is this, in fact but to tell me that he thinks I am as great a fool as he confesses to be a knave. (50–51)

This rather candid admission of writing as a vocation, criticism as labor, and both as artisanal commodities, skills that one performs for a wage, seeks to overturn the cult of affected modesty by disclosing the real relations that sustain the cultural marketplace. By means of this disclosure, the professional critic replaces the scholar and the man of taste alike. The argument is at once analogical and structural. "Literary knowledge" is similar to a trade, having a guild-like protocol and convention, and one element of a larger division of labor, having a market price and cultural value. Modest pretensions to disinterest have, in contrast, a secret interest in gouging the price of their cultural commodity, inflating its nominal value, paradoxically, by disclaiming authorial labor. What brings together these two sides of Kenrick's argument is an inversion of the typical relations of the cultural economy, or rather a turning of that economy back on its feet. If the cultural field is typically "an economic world reversed," it is in Kenrick's model an *economic world reverted*, in which value is folded back into the market as a function of work, of the quantum of skill and socially necessary labor contained in a given cultural product. Johnson and Kenrick's models are, in this respect, two halves that do not quite add up to a whole: the one turns on the abstraction of consumption as the motor of literary endurance, the other on the abstraction of production as the agent of value. The rational grounding of the literary profession in the division of labor is thus, for Kenrick, at one with a certain plea for the professional standard of criticism as a secular calling; it is a travesty, Kenrick proffers, that "if a writer were to use the same arguments in the preface of his book, to set off his works to advantage, as an artizan or manufacturer is allowed to do his, in his shop or warehouse, he would of course be condemned for want of *modesty*" (52). The critical trade is ideally located in periodical journalism, the medium closest to the print market. He claims to be surprised that his colleagues at the *Monthly Review* did not throw themselves entirely behind his review of Dr. Johnson's edition; why, he asks, "find fault with the tools of another artizan, whose work you do not seem to disapprove so much as his manner of executing it?" (58). In Kenrick's account of the "wholesale branch of criticism" that is "fabricated or vended in [a] workshop or warehouse," what usually passes for heteronomy (the market) is actually professional autonomy, while what usually passes for autonomy (disinterested modesty) is actually political or religious heteronomy (57). "What can we think of those writers," Kenrick asks, "who after being long hackneyed in the ways of men, and of their profession; who, after setting themselves even at the head of that profession, pretend *to tremble while they write, to bow down with reverential awe to superior learning, to kiss the rod of correction, &c, &c*" (52). The market asks not of one's birth and bows to no idols. The argument that politics should stay out of literature is here an argument for the maximal *economizing* of the literary, for a cultural *laissez-faire*; "Mr. K. detests all *combinations* in literature, as much as he despises the *monopolists* of fame" (35).

The *Defense* closes by representing Kenrick and Johnson as the twin poles of this cultural market. Johnson is happy to take a pension and so have his congenital languor given concrete form in a spurious wage. The real value of his criticism reflects the dearth of his labor; consequently, he cannot rely on the price allotted by the market itself and must fall back on the intervention of the state. In contrast,

Kenrick throws in his lot with the public of purchasers, who reward his work with fame:

The *Reviewer of Dr. Johnson's Shakespeare*, indeed, hath too long and too successfully laboured in the literary vineyard, to need now, by any servile or sinister means, to solicit his [majesty's] reward. No: the small portion of literary fame, to which Mr. K. hath at any time made, or hereafter may make, pretensions, he claims, with proper deference to the publick, not as a *favour* but as his *due*. He thinks it not less disgraceful to *beg* of the multitude than of an individual; and as he would not willingly *give* undeserved applause to *others*, he scorns to *accept* it *himself*. His demands are few, and his expectations *moderate*; but, such as they are, he hath sufficient reason to think they will be complied with; for, in spite of artifice and cabal, sooner or later, the PUBLICK *will be* JUST." (67–68)

The request here for fame confirms the earlier defense of anonymity; both proceed from the critic's work. In this reverted economy, where economic and aesthetic value rejoin in the concept of labor, fame is not so much cultural capital as cultural wages, the esteem Kenrick expects to get from his criticism, as it were, a fair day's pay for a fair day's work. The justice of the public rests in its capacity to adjust price to labor. In spite of the influence of political cabals, the market will ultimately reward the efficient expenditure of critical work. Kenrick's redemption is displaced into the future as the inevitable working out of the market's logic, not just the flattening out of values into a democracy of access, but also the final adequation of price, wage, and socially necessary labor. That Johnson is "magisterial" and "supine" expresses the consummate inversion of economic logic – the disjunction of profit from labor – or from another vantage, simply the maximal functioning of the cultural field as an economic world reversed. Kenrick's fatality is that the market cannot adjust itself to the rational allotment of cultural wages; it has invested far too much cultural capital in Johnson, as the reception of the *Review* indicates.

How are we to assess the economizing of literature? Modernity's famous prizing apart of aesthetic from exchange value has been a recurrent problem and motif in many of the critics we have read. The reuniting of art and the market in Kenrick is not entirely removed from this larger complex, as the return of literature to the economic fold presupposes their definitive separation. This presupposition is most dramatically born out, however, in the mediation which the economy itself is taken to perform. The dreamt-of

adequation of wage, price, and labor that closes the *Defense* turns on
the need for the critic's work, not just the reflection of popularity by
consumption, since spending can always be temporarily deceived by
the charismatic interdiction of master critics, but the social necessity
of that labor. Yet how does cultural labor provide a social need?
There is, of course, no cultural equivalent to social utility, and it is
here that Kenrick betrays the insuperable break between aesthetic
and economic discourse. He turns the problem into its own solution;
good Shakespeare criticism is the attunement of labor to need. The
secular calling of literary labor serves the public undefiled. It gives
them canonical works.

## III

The *Monthly Review* closed its critique of Kenrick's pamphlet by
asking that their former colleague "moderate his wrath against a
fellow countryman and brother author" so as not to endanger "the
honour of letters in general, and British literature in particular" (III:
no. 42, 467). Kenrick's argument, in this analysis, runs the risk of
disturbing the national tradition it so stalwartly defends. The animus
of accusation terminates in a kind of irretrievable particularism;
Kenrick founders, according to the *Monthly*, in what is precisely the
negation of national interest, namely, the interest of the individual
critic in the defamation of his "brother." By the end of the 1760s, the
problem of mounting a generalizable literary culture around Shakespeare had become rather pronounced, as evidenced not just by the
case of Kenrick but also by one of the more bracing attempts at a
national synthesis, Elizabeth Montagu's *An Essay on the Writings and
Genius of Shakespear, Compared with the Greek and French Dramatic Poets,
with Some Remarks upon the Misrepresentations of Mons. de Voltaire* (1769).
As the title suggests, Montagu's treatise sought to defend the leading
poet of the English canon against the cultural battalions of a nation
with whom the English had just concluded a seven year war.
Montagu takes up where Johnson left off, in the excursus on the
unities, to defend the English taste for Shakespeare against the
French charge that the uncouth playwright bespeaks his nation's
barbarous philistinism. Yet Montagu's fortification of Shakespeare is
no simple chauvinism. Rather, it takes chauvinism, in the form of
parochial interest, customary prejudice, local tradition, and the like
to be the central problem and obstacle to the defense of Shake-

speare's greatness. In this sense, Montagu's response to Voltaire is a rejoinder to Kenrick as well, working out at a different level of emphasis the problem of critical labor and cultural wages. Whose interest is served by the critic? From where does fame arise?

Montagu begins by paying a debt to her critical predecessors. Now that Shakespeare has been "elucidated by them," the road "lies open to a thorough enquiry into the genius of our English classic."[28] "Elucidation" nicely bridges the aesthetic and historicist projects, referring either to the text's beauty or difficulty and allowing Montagu to act as if she comes after this debate has completed its course. But the new consensus leads to a different problem: our perhaps over-indulgent "consecration" of Shakespeare (2). While Montagu argues that Voltaire is, of course, wrong to accuse the English of philistinism and Shakespeare of monstrosity, she does welcome the accusation as an opportunity to meet the problem of *national* taste square on, the sense in which "English" does not so much signify a uniform condition as a particular experience.[29] When Montagu asks if our predilection for Shakespeare is caused only by "ignorant credulity and national prepossession" – "the prejudice of a particular nation" – she clarifies an issue which we can now see had preoccupied earlier critics shaping a vernacular canon on the model of classical antiquity, namely, the apparent particularity of the English nation, whose customary forms and individual traditions are hard pressed to approximate the perennial appeal of the classics (2). Is it the case, she asks, that Shakespeare is the consummate example of local color? The answer is a complicated "no," the force of which is to resituate much of the earlier discussion of Shakespeare and Spenser's unique status in the canon. From this new perspective, the various revivals of lyrical compression or spectral enchantment are so many attempts to mediate a community bound by geography, language, and tradition into a transcendent order, an order whose particular expressions encode the continuity of England and its literature.

One term for this mediation is the sublime. On this matter, Montagu is both quite typical and rather emphatic: "Great indulgence is due to the errors of original writers, who, quitting the beaten track which others have traveled, make daring incursions into unexplored regions of invention, and boldly strike into the pathless sublime" (8). Shakespeare's sublime boldness soon proves to bear a particular nationality. Comparing the bard's roughness to the more refined productions of the French, Montagu implores, "let not example teach us to fetter the energy, and enervate the nobler powers of the British muse, and of a language fit to express sublimer sentiments" (42). Shakespeare's *British* sublime tenaciously performs the self-correction of particularity into generality, the tendency for the concrete to become the universal. "As the misfortunes of nations as well as of individuals often arise from their peculiar dispositions, customs, prejudices, and vices, these home-born dramas are excellently calculated to correct them" (58). Montagu answers Johnson's worry about the particular's refrigerating hold on the spectator by arguing that only a thorough grounding in the customary and prejudicial can serve as a vehicle for the abstracting arts of the general. (Hence not only Shakespeare over Corneille, but also, Montagu mentions in aside, Shakespeare over the less rustically inclined Jonson.) Shakespeare is more refined the more he is "hurly burly" (71). Local color self-abstracts the national forms it both epitomizes and incubates. It is on the basis of the particular's reversal into the general, then, that "Shakespeare redeems the nonsense, the indecorums, the irregularities of his plays" (79).

Montagu's concern with generalizing the particular, transcending the immanent, leads her to embark on a lengthy excursus on the literary history of enchantment. In arguably the most original section of the *Essay*, "On the Praeternatural Beings," she moves the defense of Shakespeare to his "peculiar felicity, in those fictions and inventions, from which poetry derives its highest distinction, and from whence it first assumed its pretensions to divine inspiration, and appeared the associate of religion" (133). Shakespeare's "felicity" expresses an English genius bound up with native tradition:

While there is any national superstition which credulity has consecrated, any hallowed tradition long revered by vulgar faith; to that sanctuary, that asylum, may the poet resort. – Let him tread the holy ground with reverence; respect the established doctrine; exactly observe the accustomed rites, and the attributes of the object of veneration; then shall he not vainly invoke an inexorable or absent deity. Ghosts, fairies, goblin, elves, were as propitious, were as assistant to Shakespeare, and gave as much of the sublime, and of the marvelous, to his fictions, as nymphs, satyrs, fawns, and even the triple Geyron, to the works of ancient bards. (137)

Citing the argument of "a celebrated writer in his letters on chivalry," Montagu distinguishes between Hellenic and English enchantment, and like Hurd finds the homespun gothic to be a worthy adversary of its classical precursor. For both critics, gothicism is the means by which national literary history can step out from under the shadow of Greece and Rome. England's gothic romance is not a diminutive version of a classical precursor; it is rather the singular achievement of native culture. Yet the victory of the moderns over the ancients takes its toll on modernity. The literary monuments of the gothic nation are lodged in a vernacular antiquity against which modern English now pales.

The gothic romance grew out of a singular and passing moment. As with Hurd, Montagu argues that the origins of popular belief are to be found in the peculiarities of English history. "Climate, temper, modes of life, and institutions of government seem all to have conspired to make the superstitions of the Celtic nations melancholy and terrible" (143). Following the dissolution of this originary scene, she continues, the praeternatural lifeworld of the Celts subsisted in folk belief: "The church of Rome adopted many of the Celtic superstitions; others, which were not established by it as points of faith, still maintained a traditional authority among the vulgar . . . After the consecrated groves were cut down, and the temples demolished, the tales that sprung from thence were still preserved with religious reverence in the minds of the people" (144). The "traditional authority" of demotic belief carved poetry's numinous pathways:

The poet found himself happily situated amidst enchantments, ghosts, goblins; every element supposed the residence of a kind of deity; the genius of the mountain, the spirit of the floods, the oak endued with sacred prophecy, made men walk abroad with a fearful apprehension . . . The reader will easily perceive what resources remained for the poet in this visionary land of ideal forms . . . that awe of the immediate presence of the deity . . . as here diffused over every object. They passed trembling though the woods, and over the mountain, and by the lakes, inhabited by these invisible powers; such apprehensions must indeed . . . give fearful accents to every whisper of the animate or inanimate creation, and arm every shadow with terrors. (146)

Montagu's image of enchantment rivals that of Hurd in its baleful portrait of what comes before the modern, what issues into rationality, what we have lost. As with Hurd, the libidinal tumult of Montagu's vision, in which the recesses of the national landscape secrete dread and portend divinity, sets the stage for her favorite poet by leading the reader to wonder who walks the earth after enchantment. For Hurd, enchantment's legatee is Spenser, who holds on to the meaning-laden world through the device of allegory. For Montagu, in contrast, the heir of enchantment is Shakespeare, who inscribes his closer proximity to the vulgar belief by means of a formal predilection; "our Gothic bard employs the potent agency of *sacred fable*, instead of the mere *amusive allegory*" (147).

The difference between fable and allegory proves to be rather important for Montagu's literary history:

When the world becomes learned and philosophical, fable refines into allegory. But the age of fable is the golden age of poetry; when the beams of unclouded reason, and the steady lamp of inquisitive philosophy, throw their penetrating rays upon the phantoms of imagination, they discover them to have been mere shadows, formed by ignorance . . . All the poet's spells are broken, his charms dissolved: deserted on his own enchanted ground, he takes refuge in the groves of philosophy; but there his divinities evaporate in allegory in which mystic and insubstantial state they do but weakly assist his operations . . . Allegory, the daughter of fable, is admired by the fastidious wit, and abstruse scholar, when her mother begins to be treated as superannuated, foolish, and doting; but however well she may please and amuse, not being worshipped as divine, she does not awe and terrify like sacred mythology, nor ever can establish the same fearful devotion, nor assume such arbitrary power over the mind. (148)

This recitation of the narrative of disenchantment remains within Hurd's terms while also departing from them in a subtle and important manner. Both critics write of reason's shackling a vibrant imagination to the cold chains of philosophy. The difference between their accounts lies in the literary form and corresponding institution that best exploits the transition to enlightenment. In Montagu's narrative, Shakespeare is placed before Spenser, as closer to the national superstition. Spenser takes the elite route of allegory, whose figural evocation of the old enchanted world bespeaks its own disenchantment. Shakespeare's choice of fable, in contrast, shows his fidelity to the popular lifeworld of the nation. That "our poet never carries his praeternatural beings beyond the limits of the popular tradition" is both the excuse for his animated landscape and the condition of its sublimity (137). "Shakespeare, in the dark shades of Gothic barbarism, had no resources but in the very phantoms that walked the night of ignorance and superstition," and, Montagu adds, "his management of them [was] so masterly, that he will be admired in all times" (150). Mastery of superstition expresses itself in the formal rejection of allegory: "Shakespeare disdained these quaint devices . . . He contented himself with giving dramatic manners to history, sublimity and its appropriated powers and charms to fiction; and in both these arts he is unequaled" (151). "Shakespeare has the advantage" over Spenser "in the more solemn, gloomy, and mysterious airs of his national superstitions" (158). As distinct from Spenserian allegory, Shakespearean fable affords an aesthetic pleasure in the rustic manners and demotic beliefs of premodernity. The formal distinction is the basis for a social distinction, a distinction between works suited for a minority of scholarly experts and works "admired in all times" by the assembled community of readers.

In Montagu's redaction of Hurd's tale, two kinds of English canons come together only to split once more on rather different terms. By now the aesthetic appropriation of allegedly popular forms, already implicit in the making "English" of the Longinian sublime, is well underway. In this vernacularizing of the sublime, Montagu turns to Hurd on gothic animism and enchanted poetry, but disagrees with him on allegory, preferring fable as the meridian point between enchantment and rationality (opting, that is, for Shakespeare over Spenser). This minor quarrel seeks, as it were, to vernacularize the vernacular, to make popular what is in Hurd a rather abstruse pleasure. Hence the subjoining of national to super-stition as "national superstition." The disagreement sheds light on the lability of literary nationalism during the mid-eighteenth century. Hurd and Montagu both write of an English literary tradition distinct from the tradition of the classics. They likewise share an emphasis on the generative foundation of this tradition in the demotic belief forms of feudal culture. Yet the meaning of literature and nation alike are importantly varied between them. For Hurd, canonical works grow out of a vulgar belief system which they also transfigure. Literature is not the spontaneous emanation of popular feeling so much as it is the figural evocation of that feeling. The winnowing of national culture into the elite form of the trope (paradigmatically in Spenser's allegory) is twice reflected in the status of Spenser's audience, first in the sixteenth-century *literati* able to enjoy a skeptical pleasure in matters of rustic belief, second in the "few lettered and curious men" of the eighteenth century able to read Spenser at all. The nation is preserved by scholars who also, as it happens, compose that nation. In contrast, Montagu narrows the cleft of transfiguration and widens the ambit of nationality. Literature is not the fragile troping of popular culture so much as it is the instinctive eliciting of that culture. "Gothic" means the spirit of indigenous English expressed in the works of the country's preeminent fabulist. The wider compass of the gothic in Montagu's formulation conforms to a deliberately extensive view of audience as a nation held under the "arbitrary power" of shared, "sacred" fables.

Montagu's preference for the vulgar fables of Shakespeare over the more recondite allegory of Spenser aims to expand Hurd's "few lettered or curious men" into the nation at large and so to solve the problem of particularity that had both vexed the gothic account of feudalism and led Johnson to subsume gothicism into the stable rhythms of human permanence. In the guise of "national superstition," particularity turns into the very condition of generality and, since "a sublime genius, in all its operations, sacrifices little things to great, and parts to the whole," of transcendence (274). Yet if sublime nationality, or literary Englishness, amounts to a dialectical transformation of the particular into the general, that dialectic is less completed than left as a pivotal dilemma for future literary historians, the dilemma of the part and the fragment, say, or that of realism and character. *Macbeth*, for example, shows that while Shakespeare's fable is of comprehensive appeal – its praeternatural landscape the vehicle of a generalizable, human character – the liaison between the general and the particular remains in a state of unresolved tension:

It appears to me that the character of Macbeth was . . . represented less particular and special, [so] that his example might be of more universal utility. He has therefore placed him on that line on which the major part of mankind may be ranked, just between the extremes of good and bad; a station assailable by various temptations, and which stands in need of the guard of cautionary admonition. The supernatural agents, in some measure, take off our attention from the other characters, especially as they are throughout the piece, what they have a right to be, predominant in the events. They should not interfere but to weave the fatal web, or to unravel it; they ought ever to be the regents of the fable and artificers of the catastrophe, as the witches are in this piece . . . With all the powers of poetry he elevates a legendary tale, without carrying it beyond the limits of vulgar faith and tradition . . . It seizes the heart of the ignorant, and communicates an irresistible horror to the imagination of even the more informed spectator.. (196–197)

The personality of Macbeth represents the overcoming of "particular dispositions" by a venerable "constancy of character" (196). Shakespeare purchases this constancy neither by repressing "particular and special" traits, nor by elevating praeternatural enchantment, but rather by opposing the two to each other. Macbeth's constancy and "universal utility" depend upon the attention we pay to the various "supernatural agents." The "irresistible" allure of "vulgar faith and tradition" draws our notice away from the clutter and interference of minor characters and allows for Macbeth's universal humanity to hold our gaze. At the same time, however, Macbeth's constancy is the cipher through which the praeternatural machinery "weaves the fatal web," his inimitable humanity the occasion for poetry to unleash its numinous charm. Shakespeare neither consumes tradition into Macbeth, nor sacrifices Macbeth to the supernatural. Rather, the characterlogical general and the praeternatural particular each project the other as an irreconcilable opposite.

Herein lies much of the symptomatic importance of Montagu's *Essay* for the critical development we have been tracing. The former opposition between aesthetics and historicism reappears as one between "the human" and "national superstition." But to say that the opposition reappears is to acknowledge that it has fundamentally transformed. If "national superstition" occupies the place of historicism and "the human" that of aesthetics, each contains the other as a constitutive antithesis. Each term in the new pair includes a fully mediated unity between previously antithetical parts. Philology and the sublime have passed together into the gothic ("national superstition"), just as taste and historical recession have combined into the human generality. The impasse at the end of Montagu's *Essay* is that these two separate resolutions join into a contradiction. By this point, Montagu has already developed the human *and* the national as tendential settlements to the aesthetics/historicism quarrel. We have seen how the spectral forms "acknowledged and revered by the national superstition . . . augment our pleasure" (164). Of equal importance to Montagu's defense is Shakespeare's appeal to our sense of ourselves. Describing the "persistence . . . of Shakespeare's plays" over their modern descendants, she argues that "nature, which speaks in Shakespeare, prevails over them all." Generations of readers find in his characters a reflection of themselves, of the transcendently human:

Shakespear's dramatis personae are men, frail by constitution, hurt by ill habits, faulty and unequal. But they speak with human voices, are actuated by human passions, and are engaged in the common affairs of human life. We are interested in what they do, or say, by feeling every moment, that they are of the same nature as ourselves. Their precepts therefore are an instruction, their fates and fortunes an experience, their testimony an authority, and their misfortunes a warning. (81)

As with Johnson, humanity describes the adamantine survival of Shakespeare through the shades of ages. A nation of readers finds itself reflected in the human travails of Shakespeare's characters. Montagu repeats Johnson's trick: masculine constancy is the agent of human permanence, depersonalized from the particulars of time and situation and abstracted into the eternal medium of print. The diversity of gender, social status, and local idiom are sublimated into common humanity. Yet Montagu's essay is no less adamant that Shakespeare expresses the antique, rustic ardor of old-England. As with Hurd, national superstition describes the falling backward into earlier ages of sublime enchantment. The particulars of England's feudal past – baronial rule and demotic lure, strange emanations and enchanted groves – lie beneath the permanent appeal. Humanism meets gothicism and inclines it to widen its conception of antique nationality. Montagu does not so much integrate these newly formed antitheses as fully exploit their tension.

## IV

The formation of the English canon comes to a stopping point at the midcentury, then, not with a composed synthesis but with a new tension. The opposition of historicism and aesthetics transforms into one between "the nation" and "the human," each of which contains the other as a defining contrast. Rather than follow this tension into its later manifestations, I will end this chapter, and this study, by freezing the development of the canon at one of its more important moments of transition. Johnson's equanimous "general" and ever-lasting "human" join together in the concept of the reader, whose commonality overcomes the particulars of time and place and whose rational taste ensures the survival of classics. Abstract reading is both the ticket to, and the incarnation of, the immemorial nation. Common reading and conscious fictionality are both overturned by William Kenrick, who understands the enormity of Johnson's critical effort as a baleful politicizing of the cultural field, a violation of aesthetic autonomy. His rejoinder is at once theoretical and institutional: literature affects the passions and not the understanding (the seat of Johnson's "consciousness"); rigorous critical labor is practiced by the anonymous drudges of periodical criticism, whose value will be amply rewarded, in an ideal republic of letters, by a fair cultural wage. To this identifying of the cultural field with literary labor and social utility, Elizabeth Montagu responds with a prolonged consideration of the dialectic of generality and particularity, and this as it is importantly borne out in national culture building. Montagu's argument that the particular has a tendency to become the general, that the seeds of abstract nationality are to be found in the detritus of vernacular lore and ritual, works also in countermotion; the general's concrete mediation and singular instruments are tradition, belief, enchantment, and the like. Within this neatly reflexive movement, a significant recombination of critical lines of affiliation occurs. The antithetical unity of a historicist sublime, to which we post-Romantics are so accustomed as, perhaps, to find rather obvious, takes shape as a stable entity called "national superstition" and finds its newly opposite number in the equally antithetical joining of taste and antiquity into the "human." With this emergent contradiction, we may better understand not only the complicated situation of Johnson's criticism, still too often studied in isolation from the thick of its cultural moment, but also the historical process that gave rise to the English canon.

# Afterword: the present crisis

The foregoing pages end their chronicle well before the teaching of English literary history in the national universities.[1] Mid-eighteenth-century criticism had an uneven and uncertain footing: half scholarly, half public, each viewed through the looking glass of the other. The institutional instability of our origins can tell us something about our present. A view taken from the eighteenth to the twenty-first century reveals a deceptive symmetry. Mawkish tributes to literary tradition and stringent efforts to update cultural study once more for the next millennium are not hard to come by. But both seem to testify to a pervasive and wide-ranging crisis: diminished expectations, organizational downsizing, wide-spread anti-intellectualism, educational defunding. The eighteenth century came up with literary tradition as a way to think about the market, the division of labor, and the public. To argue that these institutions later dissolved the idea of the canon to which they gave birth would be a conservative tautology. It is safer to say, I think, that the modernity of tradition has once more become antique. The canon debate now takes place within an increasingly reduced sense of its own importance. Pressed by straitened circumstances, an initially curricular argument has in recent years widened into a discussion of the very rationales and futures of the discipline. (How should, for example, literary study represent itself to its publics?) This new debate has the potential to open ground between the methods of literary analysis and the institutions in which they reside, if not also to inflate mistakenly our sense of influence on a world with little room left for the humanities. Literary study and its publics have a history worth considering in this forbidding context.

Against the backdrop of national skepticism about academic labor, eighteenth-century quarrels over the location and provenance of literary criticism take on fresh salience. A central concern of this

237

study has been the tension between the emergent public sphere and the academy, between conversation and expertise, commerce and the aesthetic. In the eighteenth century, public culture was dialectically bound to privacy. Initially, the worldly medium of the periodical press defined itself against the chill philology of the academy; later, public criticism discovered that it too contained a private cadre of experts, while the academy itself grew concerned with the national, public culture. The often heated discussion occurred within an overall pattern of institution building, the uneven development of the national literature and its caretakers. Today, the relation between official literary study and the public sphere is similarly conspicuous, if drawn on a downward sloping curve. It is a matter of common concern that the academy has faired poorly in the current economic climate.[2] The largely in-house discussions of canonicity that dominated the nineteen-eighties have given way to somber estimations of the job market and budgets.[3] Academic criticism is again marginal to a society that regards it either with derision or with neglect.[4] In the mirror of our past, we see an image of our future.

The crisis of the university at the close of the twentieth century has led me toward an analysis of the beginnings of literary study different from some of my predecessors. Altered times call for new histories. In this spirit, I have attempted to revise the account that locates the beginnings of criticism comfortably within the rise of the public sphere. I have emphasized rather the combined evolution of publicity and expertise. The critical landscape of the eighteenth century was shaped less by a consensus over national and literary norms than by an ongoing debate over what those norms might be. This seems, today, a more fitting image of our origins than the narrative with which we are often presented. We are often told that criticism grew out of periodical journalism, as the emergent public sphere took arms against the restricted culture of the aristocracy and the state.[5] Criticism then was still a public affair, one not yet confined to the seminar room or the learned essay. Whether the subject was *Paradise Lost* or the waters at Bath, critics imagined themselves in dialogue with the whole of the reading public, and the public imagined itself in a struggle with political power.

How did we get from this origin in bourgeois journalism to the present moment of academic criticism? From the mid-nineteenth century onward, so it is often said, English slowly coalesced as a modern discipline and a university department.[6] Once the middle classes learned to find their cultural expression in bureaucratic rationality and the techno-sciences, English became more and more an affair for academic reading and antiquarian research. Criticism was no longer an indictment of political power or an assertion of class ethics; it was, rather, a means to tenure and a route to self-promotion, a practice of a guild cut off from the concerns of society. On this account, the present crisis finds a simple remedy. Criticism should, as it were, republicize its practice, shed its priestly cast and take on the concerns of this world in a language recognizable to the laity. Hence the prominent and laudable attempt to rethink the category of the public intellectual as the mediator between the academy and the press. The desire for publicity imagines a reunion between two halves of a fatally dissevered whole. To end our self-damaging futility, we should return to an origins of instrumental culture building, reconcile with the medium from which we have been unhappily divorced.[7]

How successful has our attempt been to explain our work as a public activity? Considering the response of the "public" one might say not very. Yet the question itself seems to me to misunderstand the historical relation between the public sphere and the literature faculty. For if the faculty looks to journalism as the imaginary reparation of its break with the public, journalism looks to the faculty as nothing less than a scandal, a scandal that we now know as "political correctness" (a term that continually resists its inevitable antiquity). There is no accounting for this updated form of anti-intellectual name calling within the terms of the literary critical narrative as I have recounted them, unless one supposes that journalism defensively accuses the faculty of treading onto a public territory that is properly its own. (Even this argument, however, fails to account for the re-emergence of the oldest of anti-intellectual obloquies: societal uselessness, pedantry, quasi-aristocratic languor, and so forth.) I would hope, then, that this book has revised the story of our origins in such a way that might shed light on this dilemma. Literary study did not begin simply with journalism. Rather, our origins lie in an antagonism between bourgeois journalism and the official literary faculty. Both laid claim to the cultural product. Here we are returned inevitably to the inaugural moment of Addison and Steele. "I shall be ambitious to have it said of me that I have brought philosophy out of closets and libraries, schools and colleges, to dwell

in clubs and assemblies, at tea-tables and in coffee-houses"
(Addison, *Spectator*, no. 10). In this founding declaration, the ambition
to make public the discussion of vernacular culture already imagined
an intellectual enemy from whom the national literature must be
rescued: the malicious pedant, with eyes trained on the tedious
particulars of language and culture. To describe this enemy as the
aristocracy or the state is to misrecognize the nature of cultural
struggle during the originary moment of our practice. It would be
more fitting to call this enemy, in the Gramscian idiom, "traditional
intellectuals."[8] I do not mean to say, therefore, that the academic foe
of the journalists represented the interests of the *ancien régime*.
Nothing more typifies the crime of "traditional" study than its
violation of genteel decorum. Rather, the antithetical position of
traditional study in the eighteenth century grew out of ongoing
dialectic with nominally public modes of reading. Traditional study
was both real and imagined. It was real, insofar as critics like
Addison and Steele situated their public against the already established institutions of higher learning, namely, Oxford, Cambridge
and the Church. It was imagined insofar as these traditional institutions were continuously reinvented as the negative counterpart of
the public sphere. Grasping this duality gets us to the heart of the
matter of our origins. "Closets and libraries, schools and colleges"
serve to define the contrasting space of open and rational dialogue,
the space of instrumental and assimilable culture.

Literary study was born of a moment as anti-intellectual as our
own. Here is a sketch of this history: as journalism established norms
of public culture it both confronted and invented the hostile specter
of the academy, an establishment that blocked the program to
disseminate polite learning. Anti-intellectualism formed much of the
literary theory of early periodical criticism. According to periodical
criticism, the philological and historical practice of the academy
both required a knowledge of ancient languages and literatures and
failed to describe the aesthetic value of cultural goods. Recall
Addison's "Tom Folio," the "learned idiot." In such figures we saw
the necessity of the intellectual pariah in the building of public
culture. The "men of deep learning without commonsense," as
Addison puts it, impede the dissemination of literature to a nation
poised for its reading. What Addison understands to be the method
of the clergy and the academy is bereft of the open and worldly
language of the periodical and the salon. For the future looking

critics of periodical journalism, literary intellectuals seem overly bound to the detritus of the past. Hence the two-fold accusation against them. Their backward looking historicism fails to appreciate the ever-unfolding progress of the bourgeois public. Their philology is too particular to please the general taste of that public. When, for example, Thomas Warton declined to remark on the beauty of *The Faerie Queen* and chose instead to focus on source material – chose, in his words, "explanation" over "encomiums" – he provoked this response from William Huggins: "What harm is there in marking beauties, in their various light, turns, and methods? Is paper so valuable? Or is the time of the peruser so important? There is something open and communicative in such a step; it is ever entertaining to many [and] may be improving to all." The academy's refusal to comment on the beauty of works illustrates its cloistered irrelevance for a nation of readers, the "innate vanity and known malevolence," in Huggins's words, of an institution bereft of social meaning (*Observer Observed*: 53–54). To this leave-taking of aesthetic judgment and the public sphere, the critic responds as an "honest, fair disquisitor," "*a friend to society.*" Then as now, forsaking aesthetic appreciation formed the core of the public's accusation against the academy.

Over the course of the eighteenth century, the baleful example of the pedant became increasingly important for the self-definition of the public sphere. The figure is hauntingly recognizable to us as the otiose scholar, shorn from the concerns and manners of society and caught in the endless circuit of his own research. Looking back at the attacks on the academy leveled by early-periodical critics one is struck by the recoiling attention they pay to the idea of the past, even as it is the past that they are so busy constructing. "Explanations" merely root texts in their time and place while "encomiums" avail texts to the community of readers. And here we can perhaps catch the early glimmerings of what makes our own work appear so invidious. The opprobrium in which traditional intellectuals are steeped is, in John Oldmixon's words, a "gothic darkness" in the prehistory of the modern public. Scholarship is guilty of blocking the self-recognition of the public sphere, of failing to assimilate the past to the instrumental culture of the present, of focusing on lost and irredeemable negativity.

Public-minded critics argued that their work was best suited to the amiable task of bringing together readers by way of shared taste and the collective experience of beauty. The academics and pedants, for their part, responded that critical reading required diligent training in older customs and language. Examining the collective position of these scholars has, I hope, given a more complete sense of our own past. The intellectual arrogation of English literature was coincident with the emergence of a periodical based criticism that found it anathema. Two models of professional reading grew together as an antithetical unity, each deriving its sense of its vocation through the contrasting model of the other. Now, it would certainly be gauche to throw in one's lot with the intelligentsia and the shamelessly elitist circuits of restricted culture, just as it would be quaint to suggest that this intelligentsia still has a powerful influence on the public's self-understanding. Yet we might wish to risk considering what is recoverable in the imagination and practice of early English scholarship. One problem with the public sphere, the scholars argued, was that it tended to simplify the difficulty of older works, to update their unassimilable alterity for the genteel habits of the modern age. There is something recognizably academic, and even contemporary, about this insistence on historical specificity, on the repugnance of anachronism and aestheticism alike. In the defense of professional norms against the incursions of commodity culture, lies for us an important lesson. The recourse to expertise resists making literature serviceable to polite society and the emergent middle classes. Here we see the skeptical and negative practice that is as much our own as the public and the instrumental, that is, the insistence on what is irrecoverable and not useful for modernity.

Having said all that, we shouldn't lose sight of the correlative example of the press's appeal to an aesthetics of amiable judgment. Today, our desire for public influence is matched only by our need for public support. Our beginnings yield no simple moral. The intimacy between the public and criticism during the eighteenth century was preeminently concerned with the dissemination of taste. At its utopian limit, eighteenth-century anti-professionalism sketches a commendable picture of egalitarian knowledge, in which the aesthetic is the relevant medium of social cohesion and culture building. In so doing, it also set the precedent for modern anti-intellectualism, for the menacing demand that the academy drop its silly jargon, let go of its interest in historical arcana, and make literature consumable once again. The public, like expertise, comes to us from the past as a vexed desire. In this fateful twinning dwells a riddle worth pondering. We have not been lacking in attempts to reconceive the public sphere or revisit the category of the public intellectual. Yet, this addresses only one side of the problem. To rethink the public is necessarily to rethink expertise and perhaps to imagine a future that could accommodate both.

It is testimony to the difficulty of imagining such a future that recent attempts to make criticism sociable again have been roundly dismissed as a political degradation of literary pursuits. As we have seen, this accusation was coeval with the emergence of criticism itself. Yet its coordinates were precisely reversed. The idea of literary expertise in the eighteenth century went hand in hand with the complaint that public modes of reading were too utilitarian, too bound up with the practicalities of social refinement. The accusation of "political correctness" was first made *by* the academy *against* the public. The intellectuals found in engaged journalism an unwarranted harnessing of literature for political ends, ends prosecuted in the worldly domain of class society. The journalists, for their part, found that the intellectuals weren't political *enough*. What are we to make of this reversal, in which journalism learns to accuse the academy of the political intemperance of which it was once guilty? For one, I would hope that it would draw attention to, as it were, the "politics" of political criticism within the larger society it inhabits. By this I mean no more than the obvious: that the assignation of "politics" does not refer to an intrinsic set of activities or desires but to the meaning of the term in the context of its articulation. We might turn here to no less an authority on the matter of intellectual politics than Gramsci: "The most widespread error of method seems to me that of having looked for this criterion of distinction in the intrinsic nature of intellectual activities, rather than in the ensemble of the system of relations in which these activities (and therefore the intellectual groups who personify them) have their place within the general complex of social relations" (8). Following Gramsci, I would suggest that the long history of anti-intellectualism and "politics" might be explained by something like an historical sociology of academic labor. In our present context, it is rather telling of the deprived conditions of this labor that many humanities professors have found ways to dignify the activity of their work day with the compensatory weight of the political. The luck to work on "culture" in a moment of "cultural politics" turns out to be the misfortune of teaching literature in a moment of economic downsizing. Likewise, the misfortune of teaching literature in a moment when its founding rationale has been called into radical doubt turns out to be confirmed by the assault on "political correctness." Hence for a public grown weary of the official study of culture, claims made for the importance of what we do are simply political hectoring, while the only way to imagine the teaching of literature is in the most banal sense of appreciation.

The accusation of political correctness is at once nothing new and also a compelling turnaround in the long history of anti-intellectualism and public culture. It has compelled us, for instance, to explain our work to an often hostile public. In the place of such an explanation, allow me now to conclude with some reflections on our history. It has not been tremendously difficult for criticism to find redemptive value in an origins of engaged journalism. The challenge remains to find utopian imaginings in an avowedly elitist and reclusive clerisy, in engaged scholarship. Despite this difficulty, it hardly seems appropriate at this post-historical moment to abandon the concept of the past, a past that has shaped a present which it continues to frustrate. "For every image of the past that is not recognized by the present as one of its concerns," cautions Walter Benjamin, "threatens to disappear completely . . . Only that historian will have the gift of fanning the spark of hope in the past who is firmly convinced that *even the dead* will not be safe from the enemy if he wins."[9] To confine cultural study to the present is to condemn it to a downsized emptiness, in which the contemporary itself ceases to have meaning as it slips into the dimness of yesterday. Likewise, to yearn for the public, without an understanding of its history, is to miss precisely the context of the present crisis. For the public to which we turn and which reproaches our appeal no longer exists, at least not as a stable and unified entity. An historical sense of the famous "structural transformation of the public sphere," the gradual penetration of public debate by the twin forces of commodity exchange and the state, might give us a better understanding of who lays claim to our work. The public that I am thinking of comprises not just cynical journalism but also university bureaucracies, state legislatures, tuition-paying parents and the like. Each of these mini-publics has its own goals, and each has reacted with varying degrees of austerity to corporate downsizing and the end of deficit spending. Another way of putting this is that the dissolution of the public has led the various mini-publics to turn on their antithetical twin, the faculty, with unmatched vengeance. The faculty and its publics, considered thus, are lodged at the end of a dialectic grown corrosive in its finality. It is unlikely that the idea of public engagement will ever loose its hold on literary criticism, nor is it desirable that it should. Certainly one would want to imagine a world in which the fact of specialization and the will of the public formed an integral unity. Still, in the present moment, our obligation to the past's incomplete or unfulfilled passages may be what hangs in the balance.

# Notes

## INTRODUCTION: THE MODERNITY OF THE PAST

1 Joseph Warton, *An Essay on the Writings and Genius of Pope* (London, 1756), xi.
2 I encourage readers interested in the social history of reading and print-capitalism during the eighteenth century, however, to examine the footnotes to chapter one, where I discuss the lively and extensive historical literature.
3 Jürgen Habermas, *The Structural Transformation of the Public Sphere*, trans. Thomas Burger (Cambridge, Mass.: MIT Press, 1989).
4 Largely unremarked in the eighteenth-century studies reception of Habermas, his English evidence comes from Richard Altick's *The English Common Reader: A Social History of the Mass Reading Public, 1800– 1900* (University of Chicago Press, 1957), Arnold Hauser's *Social History of Art*, vol. III, trans. Stanley Goldman (New York: Vintage, 1951), and Ian Watt's *The Rise of the Novel: Studies in Defoe, Fielding and Richardson* (London: Chatto and Windus, 1957). In the first and last case, a familiar and older paradigm takes on a ghostly afterlife via the uneven temporality of translation.
5 Also unremarked, Habermas's debt to Theador Adorno and Max Horkeimer's *Dialectic of Enlightenment*, trans. John Cumming (New York: Continuum, 1988) is manifest in this early work, which grounds the paradoxical birth of instrumental reason out of commodity exchange in the print market. Adorno and Horkeimer's mordant story becomes in Habermas's retelling a lengthy meditation on the generative limits imposed on rational debate by the uneven distribution of print, literacy, and power.
6 Terry Eagleton, *The Function of Criticism: From the "Spectator" to Post-Structuralism* (London: verso 1984).
7 Benedict Anderson, *Imagined Communities: Reflections on the Origin and Spread of Nationalism*, rev. edn (London: Verso, 1991).
8 Anderson, *Imagined Communities*, 11.
9 See, in particular, "The Field of Cultural Production, or: the Economic World Reversed" and "The Market of Symbolic Goods," in Pierre

Bourdieu, *The Field of Cultural Production*, ed. Randal Johnson (New York: Columbia University Press, 1993) 29–74, 112–43.

10 Bourdieu, *The Field of Cultural Production*, 123

11 For an extended reflection on the precedent to our culture wars in seventeenth- and eighteenth-century France, see Joan DeJean, *Ancients against Moderns: Culture Wars and the Making of a Fin-de-Siècle* (University of Chicago Press, 1997).

12 For a cogent reflection on gender and canon formation see John Guillory's *Cultural Capital: the Problem of Literary Canon Formation* (University of Chicago Press, 1993). Guillory argues for revising the problematic of "exclusion" by thinking of it less as a conspiratorial expulsion of a large body of writers than as a mediation of the social relations of literacy and education.

## I  THE STRUCTURAL TRANSFORMATION OF LITERARY HISTORY

1 As J. C. D. Clarke has pointed out eighteenth-century *pedagogy* maintained a tacit hierarchy of Latin over Greek, the former the language of genteel learning, the latter the language of pedantry. Hence the accusations against Pope's shabby translation of Homer were in a sense self-defeating. Nevertheless, this hierarchy of linguistic learning did not ramify within the category of "ancient" as a canonical unit. Homer might be more sublime than Virgil, Virgil more regular than Homer, but neither definitively superior to the other. See J. C. D. Clarke, *Samuel Johnson: Literature, Religion, and English Cultural Politics from the Restoration to Romanticism* (Cambridge, 1994).

2 Studies that have been important for my sense of this process include Guillory, *Cultural Capital*; Lawrence Lipking, *The Ordering of the Arts in Eighteenth-Century England* (Princeton University Press, 1970), Douglas Patey, "The Eighteenth Century Invents the Canon," *Modern Language Studies*, 18.1 (1988): 17–37; Trevor Ross, "The Emergence of 'Literature': Making and Reading the English Canon in the Eighteenth Century," *ELH* 63 (1996): 340–365; Earl Wasserman, *Elizabethan Poetry in the Eighteenth Century* (Urbana, ILL.: University of Illinois Press, 1947); Howard Weinbrot, *Britannia's Issue: the Rise of British Literature from Dryden to Ossian* (Cambridge, 1993); René Wellek, *The Rise of English Literary History* (New York: McGraw-Hill, 1941). Wellek's study remains in some sense the only book-length treatment of literary history as an emergent practice in the eighteenth century. The present study intends to widen the ambit in which we might consider this emergence. In chapter four in particular I dissent from Wellek's account of Thomas Warton's Spenser project.

3 For a recent and thickly documented account of the quarrel between the ancients and the moderns in England, see Joseph Levine, *The Battle of the Books: History and Literature in the Augustan Age* (Ithaca, N.Y.: Cornell

University Press, 1991). I address Levine's account of the hermeneutical context of much of the debate in chapter two. For an account of the quarrel in France, see DeJean, *Ancients Against Moderns*. Although focused exclusively on France, DeJean's emphasis on the cultural origins of European modernity and the epochal importance of late seventeenth century's culture wars is directly relevant to the present study in two respects: firstly, in the importance it places on the "modern," which enters into British critical discourse in the domestication of the "quarrel" and second in its reading of enlightenment culture against the antecedent formulations of the fin de siècle. DeJean's own quarrel with Habermas is provocative, and compelling in its demand for empirical evidence. Still, it seems to me that Habermas's account of the epochal invention of the public sphere (first for literature, later for politics) is enriched, ultimately, by DeJean's complaint, in particular her emphasis on the female salon, which has an English analogue in the overall emphasis placed on female literacy in what DeJean calls the "invention of a public for literature." Interestingly, DeJean does not address Habermas's *The Philosophical Discourse of Modernity* (Cambridge, Mass.: MIT Press, 1987), which grounds his theory of modernity as an "unfinished project" in the very "quarrel between the ancients and the moderns" that is DeJean's topic.

4 Gerard Langbaine's *An Account of the English Dramatick Poets, or, some Observations and Remarks on the lives and writings of all those that have publish'd comedies, tragedies, tragi-comedies, pastorals, masques, interludes, farces or opera's in the English tongue (1668)*, republished as *The Lives and Characters of the English Dramatic Poets* (London, 1691).

5 Sir William Temple, *Miscellanea*, 2 vols. (London, 1692) II: p. 325.

6 Thomas Rymer, *A Short View of Tragedy*, in *The Critical Works of Thomas Rymer*, ed. Curt Zimanksi (New Haven, Conn.: Yale University Press, 1956), p. 127.

7 Consider also the vision of literary history given in the young Joseph Addison's *An Account of the Greatest English Poets* (1694): "Old Spenser next, warm'd with poetick rage, / In ancient tales amus'd a barb'rous age, / An age that yet uncultivate and rude, / Where-'er the poet's fancy led, pursu'd" (lines 17–20). Of more importance to the progressive unfolding of "British rhymes" "from Chaucer's days to Dryden's times" is the ease of meter and diction exemplified by Waller: "But now my Muse a softer strain reherse, / Turn ev'ry line with art, and smooth thy verse; / The courtly Waller next commands thy lays: / Muse tune thy verse, with art to Waller's praise" (86–89).

8 John Dryden, Preface, *Fables Ancient and Modern, Of Dramatic Poetry and other Critical Essays* (New York: Everyman, 1962) 271. All references are to this edition.

9 John Dennis, *The Advancement of Modern Poetry* (London, 1701) vii.

10 Important precursors to Bysshe's volume include George Puttenham's

*Arte of English Poesie, Contrived into three Bookes: the First of Poets and Poesie, the Second of Proportion, the Third of Ornament* (1589). A century later, Puttenham's idea of the poet as a wily courtier, who advances himself through flattery and deception (as they are both effected by the *trope*) has become Bysshe's polite versifier, who makes smooth sounding verse for a genteel audience of readers. For a text bridging the two, see Josua Poole's *The English parnassus: or, A help to English poesie. Containing a collection of all the rhyming monosyllables, the choicest epithets and phrases. With some general forms upon all occasions, subjects, and themes, alphabetically digested* (1655).

11 Edward Bysshe, *The Art of English Poetry* (London, 1702) iii.

12 As in Alexander Pope, in *An Essay on Criticism* (1715): "praise the easy vigour of a line, / Where Denham's strength, and Waller's sweetness join."

13 For the history of the English book trade see *inter alia* John Feather, *The Provincial Book Trade in Eighteenth-Century England* (Cambridge University Press, 1985); C. Y. Ferdinand, "Local Distribution Networks in Eighteenth-Century England," *Spreading the Word: the Distribution Networks of Print 1550–1850*, eds. Robin Myers and Michael Harris (Detroit, Mich.: St. Paul's Bibliographies Winchester, 1990); Michael Harris, "A Few Shillings for Small Books: the Experiences of a Flying Stationer in the 18th Century," *Spreading the Word*; F. A. Mumby, *Publishing and Bookselling: from the Earliest Times to 1890* (London: Jonathan Cape, 1930); eds. Robin Myers and Michael Harris, *Development of the English Book Trade, 1700–1899* (Oxford Polytechnic Press, 1981) and *Economics of the British Book Trade 1605–1939* (Cambridge: Chadwyck-Healy, 1985); Marjorie Plant, *The English Book Trade, an Economic History of the Making and Sale of Books*, 3rd edn. (London: Allen and Unwin, 1974); and R. M. Wiles, *Serial Publication in England Before 1750* (Cambridge University Press, 1957).

For the political context, see Jeremy Black, *The English Press in the Eighteenth Century* (Philadelphia, Penn.: University of Pennsylvania Press, 1987); Alan Downey, "The Growth of Government Tolerance of the Press to 1790," in *English Book Trade*, eds. Myers and Harris, pp. 36–65; and Frederick S. Siebert, *Freedom of the Press in England, 1476–1776: the Rise and Decline of Government Control* (Urbana, Ill.: University of Illinois Press, 1965).

On the importance of copyright laws, see John Feather, "The Publishers and the Pirates: British Copyright Law in Theory and Practice, 1710–1775," *Publishing History* 22 (1987): 5–32; Mark Rose, *Authors and Owners: the Invention of Copyright* (Cambridge, Mass.: Harvard University Press, 1993); Trevor Ross, "Copyright and the Invention of Tradition," *Eighteenth-Century Studies* 26:1 (1992): 1–27; Martha Woodmansee, *The Author, Art, and the Market: Rereading the History of Aesthetics* (New York: Columbia University Press, 1994); Ross's article is especially important for the concerns of this book, as it situates the rise of the idea of national literary tradition in the context of legal disputes over reprinting and literary property.

For speculative readings on the historical importance of "printing technology" see Elizabeth Eisenstein, *The Printing Press as an Agent of Change*, 2 vols. (Cambridge, 1979) and "Some Conjectures about the Impact of Printing on Western Society and Thought," *Journal of Modern History* 40 (1968): 1–56; and Alvin Kernan, *Samuel Johnson and the Impact of Print* (Princeton University Press, 1987). Eisenstein and Kernan both presuppose a fundamental historical and theoretical model derived from Marshall McLuhan, *The Gutenberg Galaxy: the Making of Typographic Man* (University of Toronto Press, 1962) which finds – in its highly eclectic manner – the whole of modernity as an exfoliation of typographic technology. For a critique of the McCluhanite model, see Michael Warner, *The Letters of the Republic: Publication and the Public Sphere in Eighteenth-Century America* (Cambridge, Mass.: Harvard University Press, 1990) 1–33. Warner's dismissal of technological determinism is presupposed by the present study.

As for the question of reading and literacy, it is a commonplace that eighteenth-century England witnessed "the rise of the reading public." And like all commonplaces, this one has undergone its due share of revisionist debunking. Ground clearing challenges to received wisdom are always productive in one way or another, but I would caution against any revisionism that sets its targets on models of social change as such. In any event, the history of literacy has steadily defied empirical measurement. The only quantifiable index of literacy in the early modern period is the ability to sign one's name, which is available for historians in the archives of legal depositions and marriage records, both of which present sociologically and regionally varied data. Unmeasurable, however, is the ability to read, which most but not all historians claim precedes the ability to write. In either case, the numbers of the literate exceed the empirically measurable; this is especially the case among women and lower class men, who might achieve enough rudimentary education to learn to read without ever learning to write (Defoe's Moll Flanders, for instance, learns to read at around seven, which she recalls as unusual for someone of the lower classes but not remarkable. It is her learning to write at age fourteen, however, that signals her ensuing upward mobility). David Cressy argues that while "almost 70 percent of English men and 90 percent of English women of the mid-seventeenth century could not write their own name . . . the proportions had changed to 40 percent and 60 percent a century later," "Literacy in Context: Meaning and Measurement in Early Modern England," in *Consumption and the World of Goods*, eds. John Brewer and Roy Porter (New York, Routledge, 1993) 303–320. See also, Cressy, "Levels of

Illiteracy in England, 1530–1730," and Margaret Spufford, "First Steps in Literacy: the Reading and Writing Experiences of the Humblest Seventeenth-Century Spiritual Autobiographers," in *Literacy and Social Development*, ed. Harvey J. Graff (Cambridge University Press, 1981); Robert DeMaria, "Samuel Johnson and the Reading Revolution," *Eighteenth-Century Life* (November, 1992): 86–102; R. S. Schofield, "The Measurement of Literacy in Pre-Industrial England," *Literacy in Traditional Societies*, ed. Jack Goody (Cambridge University Press, 1968); and Robert Stone, "Literacy and Education in England, 1640–1900," *Past and Present* 42 (1969): 98–112. For a slightly different historical model see François Furet and Jacques Ozouf, *Reading and Writing: Literacy in France from Calvin to Jules Ferry*, trans. Rupert Swyer (Cambridge University Press, 1982). Spufford would like to rescue a notion of empowered, female reading without writing, while Furet and Ozouf argue that without writing, reading is inert and passive. For an elaborate sociological reflection on the shifting variables of literacy and politics see Brian Street, *Literacy in Theory and Practice* (Cambridge University Press, 1984). Cressy and Scholfield's figures suggest that the community of readers was by and large composed of the upper stratum of society; more to the point, perhaps they confirm the postulate that literacy corresponds to social rank and the levels of schooling thus attained. See on this matter Nicholas Hans, *New Trends of Education in the Eighteenth Century* (London: Routledge and Kegan Paul, 1951); M. G. Jones, *The Charity School Movement* (Cambridge University Press, 1933).

The "rise of the reading public" thesis, from its early elaboration in Altick and Watt onward, makes frequent reference to the importance of circulating libraries, the primary means by which the public circumvented the high price of books. For a recent discussion of the library revolution in eighteenth-century England see James Raven, "From Promotion to Proscription: Arrangements for Reading and Eighteenth-Century Libraries" in James Raven, Helen Small, and Naomi Tadmore, eds., *The Practice and Representation of Reading in England* (Cambridge University Press, 1996) 175–201. See also, Hilda Hamlyn, "Eighteenth-Century Circulating Libraries in England," *The Library*, 5th Ser., 1 (1947): 197–218 and Paul Kaufman, *Libraries and their Users* (London: Library Association, 1969).

Finally, for a recent and vivid summary of the historical literature on eighteenth-century print culture, see John Brewer, *The Pleasures of the Imagination: English Culture in the Eighteenth Century* (New York, N.Y.: Farrar Straus Giroux, 1997), 125–197.

14 See Anderson, *Imagined Communities*, chapter one.
15 See Habermas *Structural Transformation*, Eagleton *Function of Criticism*, Richard Altick, *The English Common Reader* and Watt, *Rise of the Novel*. The dispersion of reading institutions during the period has become

something of a truism of eighteenth-century studies, one which this book attempts to complicate, in part by paying attention not just to the anxieties which allegedly wide-spread reading attended, but also the uneven manner in which the perception of such reading came about.

16 Habermas, *Structural Transformation.*

17 See *inter alia*, in the English context, Elizabeth Heckendorn-Cook, *Epistolary Bodies: Gender and Genre in the Eighteenth-Century Republic of Letters* (Stanford University Press, 1996), in the French context, Joan Landes, *Women and the Public Sphere in the Age of the French Revolution* (Ithaca, N.Y.: Cornell University Press, 1988), and in the American context, see Warner, *Letters of the Republic.*

18 Habermas, *Structural Transformation*, 31–43 and passim.

19 Joseph Addison, *Spectator*, no. 10, *The Spectator*, ed. Donald Bond, 5 vols. (Oxford: Clarendon Press, 1965) I, 44. All subsequent references are to this edition.

20 See, for example, *Spectator*, no. 15 on female sociability (I: 66–69) and no. 37 on female learning (II: 52 no.59). For a sustained reflection on this problem, see Kathy Shevelow, *Women and Print Culture: the Construction of Femininity in the. Early Periodical* (New York: Routledge, 1989).

21 See in particular Addison's *Spectator*, no. 419 on "the faerie way of writing" (a term he takes from Dryden). The term "gothic" is often Addison's preferred term of abuse for antique forms of culture, especially as they persist into the present.

22 Anthony Ashley Cooper, the Third Earl of Shaftesbury, *Characteristicks of Men, Manners, Opinions and Times*, 2nd revised edn, 3 vols. (London), III: 150. All references are to this edition.

23 Anon. *The Present State of the Republic of Learning*, no. 1 (1728): ii-ii.

24 The historiographical literature on consumption and the "consumer revolution" has grown particularly rich. See, *inter alia*, the essays collected in *The Birth of a Consumer Society*, eds. Neil McKendrick, John Brewer, J. H. Plumb (Bloomington, Ind.: Indiana University Press, 1982); Paul Langford, *A Polite and Commercial People: England 1727–1783* (Oxford University Press, 1989); Roy Porter, *English Society in the Eighteenth Century* (London: Penguin, 1982); Lorna Weatherhill, *Consumer Behavior and Material Culture in Britain 1660–1760*, 2nd edn (New York: Routledge, 1996); and the essays collected in the omnibus *Consumption and the World of Goods*, eds. John Brewer and Roy Porter (New York: Routledge, 1993). For a sharp dissection of the neoclassical economic theory lurking behind the historiography of consumption and of the very real tensions between McKendrick's analysis of consumerism and Marxist categories of commodification see Ben Fine and Ellen Leopold, "Consumerism and the Industrial Revolution," *Journal of Social History* 15 (1988): 150–175. For a discussion of McKendrick's "consumer revolution" thesis with reference specifically to debates engendered by and

surrounding the book trade, see James Raven, *Judging New Wealth: Popular Publishing and Responses to Commerce in England 1750–1800* (Oxford: Clarendon Press, 1992).

25 For the question of literacy see note 13 above.

26 See Walter Benjamin's seminal essay "The Work of Art in the Age of Mechanical Reproduction," trans. Harry Zohn, ed. Hannah Arendt, *Illuminations* (New York: Schocken, 1968). Benjamin's analysis of the simultaneous destruction and reinvention (in the displaced arena of aesthetics) of the aura by reproduction conforms to the present analysis in three respects: firstly in pointing to the historicity of mass culture around printing, secondly, in suggesting how the dissolution of the aura prompts critics to elevate older texts against the depredation of the market, and lastly in suggesting that mechanical reproduction bears a relation to the secularized aura of aesthetic value.

27 Dryden's "To My Dear Friend Mr. Congreve on his Comedy, Call'd The Double-Dealer" begins:
    Well then; the promised hour is come at last,
    The present age of wit obscures the past:
    Strong were our syres; and as they fought they writ,
    Conqu'ring with force of arms, and dint of wit;
    Theirs was the gyant race, before the flood;
    And thus, when *Charles* return'd, our empire stood.
    Like James he the stubborn soil manur'd,
    With rules of husbandry the rankness cur'd:
    Tam'd us to manners, when the stage was rude;
    And boisterous English wit, with art indu'd.
    Our age was cultured thus at length;
    But what we gained in skill we lost in strength." (lines 1–12)
    *The Works of John Dryden*, ed. H. T. Swedenberg (Berkeley, Ca.: University of California Press, 1974) IV: 432.

28 John Oldmixon, *An Essay on Criticism* (London, 1728) 46.

29 Philip Skelton, *The Candid Reader: Or A Modest Yet Unanswerable Apology For All Books That Ever Were Or Can Be Wrote, The Works of the Rev. Philip Skelton*, 9 vols. (Dublin, 1770) V: 227–245.

30 *The World*, no. 214 (September 4, 1755), in *The British Essayists*, 46 vols. (London, 1816) XVII: 151. All references (except Warton references later) are to this edition.

31 Alexander Pope, *Peri Bathous, or Of the Art of Sinking in Poetry*, in *Poetry and Prose of Alexander Pope*, ed. Aubrey Williams (Boston, Mass.: Houghton Mifflin, 1969) 369.

32 The preceding paragraph makes reference to Bourdieu's historical sociology of the aesthetic in general and, in particular, to two articles in his recent collection, *The Field of Cultural Production*, ed. Johnson, "The Field of Cultural Production, or: the Economic World Reversed," 29–74, and "The Market of Symbolic Goods," 112–143.

33 Anon. *A Letter to the Society of Booksellers* (London, 1738) 8.

34 Henry Fielding, *Joseph Andrews*, ed. Martin C. Batteston (Middletown, Conn.: Wesleyan, 1967) 90–91.

35 Anon. *Reflections on Various Subjects Relating to Arts and Commerce* (London, 1752) 15–16.

36 Dustin Griffin's *Literary Patronage in England, 1650–1800* (Cambridge University Press, 1996), for example, complicates the familiar narrative of the decline of patronage by examining the varied range of patron-client practices, their early crises and sturdy persistence. See also, Paul Korshin's incisive "Types of Eighteenth-Century Literary Patronage," *Eighteenth-Century Studies* 7 (1973–1974): 453–473.

37 See Shevelow, *Women and Print Culture*.

38 Clara Reeve, *The Progress of Romance Through Times, Countries, and Manners*, 2 vols. (London, 1785) II: 7.

39 Anon. *The Present State of the Republic of Learning*, no. 6 (1730) 450–454.

40 See Naomi Tadmor, "Even My Wife Read to Men: Women, Reading and Household Life in the Eighteenth Century," in eds. Raven *et al.*, *Practice and Representation of Reading*, 162–174. In *Origins of the English Novel, 1600–1740* (Baltimore, Md.: Johns Hopkins University Press, 1987), Michael McKeon levies a brief but trenchant critique of the equation of women, romance, and the rise of reading: "From Dante on, the fear that women's morals will be corrupted by reading romances is quite conventional, and its articulation may provide evidence less of the rise of the reading public than of the persistence of anxiety about women" (52). One need not claim that the anxiety about domesticity, leisure, and the romance were entirely novel to argue that they nonetheless took on a new urgency and shape during the eighteenth century. In the chapters below, I shall be concerned with both the feminization of elite culture, predominantly in the guise of aesthetic sociability *and* with the compensatory re-masculination of the past and the sublime.

41 *The World*, no. 19 (Thursday, May 10, 1752), in *British Essayists*, ed. Chalmers, XVI, 83.

42 For a discussion of the professionalization of criticism in response to a perceived relaxation of national taste, see Frank Donoghue's analysis of the *Monthly* and *Critical Review, The Fame Machine: Book Reviewing and the Making of Literary Careers* (Stanford University Press, 1996). While I agree with Donoghue's fundamental argument, that midcentury criticism was "an important battleground on which the war to determine refined taste in a consumer society was waged" (4), I would also point to the ways in which the contours of this ground were shaped by battles earlier in the century, and, even, by the ur-battle itself, the "battle of the books."

43 In fact, the narrative of descent that takes over from the narrative of refinement has a precursor and antecedent in the discussion of the

ancients. In *An Enquiry into the Writings of Homer* (1736), for example, Thomas Blackwell discusses how the Greeks

> lived naturally, and were governed by the *natural poesie* of the passions, as it is settled in every human breast. This made them speak and act, without other restraint than their own native apprehensions of *good* and *evil, just*, and *unjust*, each as he was prompted from *within*. "These manners afford the most *natural* pictures, and proper words to paint them." They have a peculiar effect upon the language, not only as they are ingenious and *good*. While a nation continues simple and sincere, whatever they say receives a *weight* from *truth*: Their sentiments are strong and honest, which always produce fit *words* to express them: Their passions and sound are genuine, not adulterated or disguised, and break out in their own phrase and affected style. They are not accustomed to the prattle, and little pretty *forms* that enervate a polished speech: nor are they over-run with quibble and sheer-wit, which makes into appearance late in every country, and in Greece came long after Trojan ties. And *this* I like to be the reason 'why most nations are so delighted with their ancient poets': Before they are polished into flattery and refined into falsehood we feel the *force* of their *words*, and the *truth* of their *thoughts*. (55–56)

44 Joseph Warton, *Adventurer*, no. 139 in *The British Essayists*, ed. A. Chalmers, 25 vols. (London, 1823) XXI: 289–290; all Warton references are to this edition of *British Essayists*. Warton wrote two essays on *The Tempest* (nos. 93 and 97) and three on *King Lear* (nos. 113, 116, 122).

45 See Raymond Williams, *Marxism and Literature* (Oxford University Press, 1977).

46 See Trevor Ross, "The Emergence of 'Literature'," 340–365 and Guillory, *Cultural Capital*, especially chapter two. For a far-reaching analysis of "literature" and national culture building, see Greg Laugero, "Infrastructures of the Enlightenment: Road-Making, the Public Sphere, and the Emergence of Literature," *Eighteenth-Century Studies* 29 (1995): 45–68. For an argument that the category preexists the eighteenth century see Richard Terry, "The Eighteenth-Century Invention of Literature: a Truism Reconsidered," *British Journal for Eighteenth-Century Studies* 19 (1996): 47–62.

47 Adam Ferguson, *An Essay on the History of Civil Society* (New Brunswick: Tavistock, 1980) 174. All further references are to this edition.

48 The *Connoisseur*, no. 24 (July 11, 1754), *British Essayists*, ed. Chalmers, XXVI: 179.

49 As in, also, the *World*, no. 152 (November 28, 1755), where a satirical letter written by "neo-academicus" celebrates the dilution of learning and the leveling of knowledge brought about by literacy and the book trade:

> "the main business I am upon is to congratulate the great world on that diffusion of science and literature, which, for some years, has been spreading itself abroad upon the face of it, a revolution this, in the kingdom of learning, which has introduced the leveling principle, with much better success than ever it met with in politics. The old fences have been happily broken down, the trade has been laid open, and the old repositories, or storehouses, are now no longer necessary or useful for the purpose of managing or conducting it." (199)

The leveling agent is here the commodity: "In short, it has fared with learning, as with our pine-apples. At their first introduction amongst us, the manner of raising them was a very great secret, and little less than a mystery. The expenses of compost, hot-house, and attendance, were prodigious; and at last, at a great price, they were introduced into the tables of a few of the nobility and gentry. But how common are they grown of late!" (199). Commodification, the letter continues, has transformed the scope and nature of reading " . . . those exuberant groups of readers as well as writers. The idea of being a reader, or a man given to books had heretofore something very solemn and frightful in it. It conveyed the notion of severity, moroseness, and unacquaintance with the world. But this is not the case at present. The very deepest of our learning may be read, if not understood, by the men of dress and fashion; and the ladies themselves may converse with the abstrusest of our philosophy with great ease" (201). The qualification "if not understood" suggests the difference between this essayist's position and that of Addison. For Addison, "understanding" was much less at stake than the imaginative pleasure brought about by reading as such, which disencumbered learning from its priestly entombment and placed it in the hands of the public. For this writer, publicity has turned its back on learning and become a new form of ignorance.

50 Oliver Goldsmith, *New Fashions in Learning*, in *The Collected Works of Oliver Goldsmith*, ed. Arthur Friedman, 5 vols. (Oxford: Clarendon Press, 1961) III: 161. See also Donoghue, *Fame Machine*, 86–124.

51 See John D. Scheffer, "The Idea of Decline in Literature and the Fine Arts in Eighteenth-Century England," *Modern Philology* 24 (1936): 155–178.

52 John Brown, *An Estimate on the Manners and Principles of the Time* (London, 1757) 25–26. Brown's estimate went through six editions in the first year.

53 Warton, *Essay on Pope*, xi.

54 Goldsmith, *An Enquiry into the Present State of Polite Learning in Europe* (1758) in ed. Friedman, *Oliver Goldsmith*, vol. I: 258.

55 Warton, *Essay on Pope*, vii.

2  THE MODE OF CONSECRATION: BETWEEN
AESTHETICS AND HISTORICISM

1 I use the term aesthetics as a shorthand for the discussion of "taste" and the "sublime, beautiful and picturesque"; see, *inter alia*, Peter de Bolla, *The Discourse of the Sublime: History, Aesthetics and the Subject* (Oxford: Basil Blackwell, 1989); Frances Ferguson, *Solitude and the Sublime: Romanticism and the Aesthetics of Individuation* (New York: Routledge, 1992); Peter J. McCormick, *Modernity, Aesthetics, and the Bounds of Art* (Ithaca, N.Y.: Cornell University Press, 1990) esp. 35–60; Michael McKean "The Politics of Discourses and the Rise of the Aesthetic," in *Politics of*

*Discourse: the Literature and History of Seventeenth-Century England*, eds. Kevin Sharpe and Steven Zwicker (Berkeley, Calif.: University of California Press, 1987) 35–51; Ronald Paulson, *Breaking and Remaking: Aesthetic Practice in England 1700–1820* (New Brunswick: Rutgers University Press, 1989); and R. G. Saisselin, "Critical Reflections on the Origins of Aesthetics," *British Journal of Aesthetics* 4 (1964): 7–21.

2 See, in particular, Howard Caygill, *Art of Judgment* (Oxford: Basil Blackwell, 1989) and Terry Eagleton, *The Ideology of the Aesthetic* (Oxford: Basil Blackwell, 1990).

3 The important category of the "imagination" is, as it were, inserted in between the understanding and sensations by theorists writing after Locke. Of paramount importance to Addison, the "imagination" amounts to a dilation of Locke's category of "memory." See John Locke, *An Essay Concerning Human Understanding*, ed. P. H. Nidditch, (Oxford University Press, 1975) 149–155.

4 Shaftesbury, *Characteristicks*, I: 111–112.

5 This trajectory underlies Eagleton's suggestive claim that "aesthetics is born as a discourse of the body," *Ideology*, 13. My debt to and disagreement with Eagleton's project are discussed briefly below. See also, Guillory, *Cultural Capital*, 269–340 and Jerome Stolnitz, "On the Importance of Lord Shaftesbury in Modern Aesthetic Theory," *Philosophical Quarterly* 2 (1961): 97–113.

6 See Caygill, *Art of Judgment*, 34–63 and Eagleton's synopsis of Caygill, *Ideology of the Aesthetic*, 31–67.

7 See Eagleton, *Ideology*, 31–70.

8 For a discussion of the class politics of Shaftesbury's aesthetic see Robert Markley, "Sentimentality as Performance: Shaftesbury, Sterne and the Theatrics of Virtue," *The New Eighteenth Century*, eds. Laura Brown and Felicity Nussbaum (New York: Methuen, 1987).

9 Cf. Shaftesbury, *Characteristicks* III: 168–169 and III: 184–185.

10 It is on the basis of statements like these that Shaftesbury's aesthetics have recently been read in terms of what J. G. A. Pocock calls "civic humanism." See J. G. A. Pocock, *The Machiavellian Moment* (Princeton: Princeton University Press, 1975). Of significance to the appropriation of Pocock's work by cultural studies has been the distinction between civic and civil humanism, the discourse of land and commerce, public and private, respectively. See Pocock, "Virtues, Rights and Manners" and "The Mobility of Property and the Rise of Eighteenth-Century Sociology" in *Virtue, Commerce and History* (Cambridge University Press, 1986). For a suggestively "Pocockian" reading of Shaftesbury, see Lawrence Klein, *Shaftesbury and the Culture of Politeness* (Cambridge University Press, 1992). For an application to aesthetic philosophy, in particular, see John Barrell, *The Political Theory of Painting from Reynolds to Hazlitt: "The Body of the Public"* (New Haven, Conn.: Yale University Press, 1986) and the essays collected in his *The Birth of Pandora and the*

*Division of Knowledge* (Philadelphia, Penn.: University of Pennsylvania Press, 1992). For a critique of this model see Ronald Paulson, *Beautiful, Novel, and Strange: Aesthetics and Heterodoxy* (Baltimore, Md.: Johns Hopkins University Press, 1995).

11 For Klein, Shaftesbury's cultural politics turn on his republicanism; for Eagleton, Shaftesbury's aesthetic is an attempt to think about agrarian social relations at an important moment of their transformation.

12 For the importance of Shaftesbury's aesthetics in the development of the discourse of "disinterest" see Jeremy Stolnitz, "On the Origins of 'Aesthetic Disinterestedness'," *Journal of the Aesthetics and Art Criticism* 20 (Winter, 1961): 131–143. The notion that an elite audience, with a cultivated and disinterested relation to the arts, is the proper readership for literary works does not begin with Shaftesbury, of course, although he may be said to set the critical terms for many theorists who followed. Bysshe's description in *Art of English Poetry* (1702) of the "many excellent qualifications" [for] "the making of a good judge of poetry" begins, for instance, that "a man must be of an elevated mind, founded on a great compass of knowledge, on a generous education, on reading of the best authors, and on a conversation with men of the first rank and fortunes: all of which must concur to give him that readiness and clearness of apprehension, that fine and just taste of what is natural and great, that elegance and depth of thought; in a word, that happy turn of soul and race of judgment, which distinguish him from the vulgar in every thing he speaks and acts" (ii).

13 See John Barrell, *English Literature in History 1730–1780, an Equal Wide Survey* (London: Hutchinson and Co., 1983), especially the first chapter on the authority of "the gentleman."

14 The origin of this truism is, of course, to be found in Michel Foucault's influential essay, "What is an Author?", where he writes that "since the eighteenth century, the author has played the role of the regulator of the fictive, a role quite characteristic of our era of industrial and bourgeois society," *The Foucault Reader*, ed. Paul Rabinow (New York: Pantheon, 1983) 119. For wide-ranging studies of authorship in the eighteenth century, see Nancy Armstrong and Leonard Tennenhouse's *The Imaginary Puritan: Literature, Intellectual Labor, and the Origins of Personal Life* (Berkeley, Calif.: University of California Press, 1992) and Catherine Gallagher, *Nobody's Story: The Vanishing Acts of Women Writers in the Marketplace 1670–1820* (Berkeley, Calif.: University of California Press, 1994).

15 For Addison's celebration of trade, and elevation of it to a position of moral equivalence with land, see especially *Spectator*, no. 69. Terry Eagleton conceives the "major impulse" of the "English bourgeois public sphere," and the *Spectator* particularly, as "one of class-consolidation, a codifying of the norms and regulating of the practices whereby the English bourgeoisie may negotiate an historic alliance with its social

superiors." Eagleton, *Function of Criticism*, 10. For an intelligent engagement with the "pre-dialectical moralism" of Eagleton's corpus, see
Richard Aczel, "Eagleton and English," *The New Left Review* 154
(November/December 1985): 113–123. Aczel's argument that Eagleton
never really broke from Leavis is certainly evident in this book, where
Leavis is in some sense the last heir to Addison and Steele's brand of
publicly engaged criticism.

16 On the relation between reading, textuality, and the aesthetic in
Addison, see Neal Saccamono, "The Sublime Force of Words in
Addison's 'Pleasures'," in *ELH* 58 (1992): 88–106.

17 The importance of Addison's series on the "pleasures of the imagination" in the history of aesthetics was first theorized by Samuel H.
Monk in *The Sublime: A Study of Critical Theories in Eighteenth Century
England* (New York, N.Y.: Modern Language Association, 1935), who
credits Addison with having displaced the rhetorical sublime with the
natural sublime, and so to have paved the way for Kant. My argument
has to do, however, with the persistent importance of reading and
textuality for Addison's understanding of the aesthetic. See also,
William H. Youngren, "Addison and the Birth of Eighteenth-Century
Aesthetics," *Modern Philology* 79 (1982): 267–283.

18 As early as Hutcheson a dozen years later: "Pleasure does not arise
from any knowledge of the principles, proportions, causes, or of the
usefulness of the object; but strikes us first with the Idea of Beauty: nor
does knowledge increase this pleasure of beauty," a pleasure which,
Hutcheson continues, is a "passive power of receiving ideas of beauty
from all objects in which there is uniformity within variety." Francis
Hutcheson, *An Enquiry into the Original of our Ideas of Beauty and Virtue*
(London, 1725) 82, emphasis mine. In a recent discussion of Hutcheson's aesthetics, David Paxman makes the point that Hutcheson is
aiming to describe a kind of second degree of knowledge which can
qualify as such. David Paxman, "Aesthetics as Epistemology, or Knowledge Without Certainty," *Eighteenth Century Studies* 26 (1992–1993):
285–306.

19 On the social transvaluation of the aesthetic in Addison's work, see
Mary Poovey, "Aesthetics and Political Economy in the Eighteenth
Century: The Place of Gender in the Social Constitution of Know-
ledge," *Aesthetics and Ideology*, ed. George Levine (New Brunswick:
Rutgers University Press, 1994) 79–105.

20 For a wide-ranging model of agrarian capitalism in early-modern
England, see Ellen Meiksins Wood, *The Pristine Culture of Capitalism*
(London: Verso, 1991) and Perry Anderson, "Figures of Descent," in his
*English Questions* (London: Verso, 1993).

21 Consider, for example, the following pronouncement from the *Connoisseur*, no. 120 (Thursday, May 13, 1754): "Taste is at present the darling
idol of the polite world and the world of letters; and, indeed, seems to

be considered as the quintessence of almost all the arts and sciences. The fine ladies and gentlemen dress with taste; the architects, whether Gothic or Chinese, build with taste; the painters paint with taste; the poets write with taste; critics read with taste; and, in short, fiddlers, players, singers, dancers, and mechanics themselves are all the sons and daughters of taste. Yet, in this amazing superabundancy of taste, few can say what it really is, or what the word itself signifies." (no. 26: 307)

22 John Gilbert Cooper, *Letters Concerning Taste* (London, 1755).

23 The joining of landscape, ideology, and the aesthetic in this manner is pronounced in the picturesque, which, by the end of the century, achieves a certain stability as the image of unity within (social and natural) variety. See John Barrell, *The Idea of the Landscape and the Sense of Place* (New York: Cambridge University Press, 1980) and Ann Bermingham, *Landscape and Ideology: the English Rustic Tradition 1740–1860* (London: Thames and Hudson, 1987).

24 See Ferguson, *Solitude and the Sublime.*

25 For the midcentury equation of women with refinement see C. J. Barker-Benfield, *The Culture of Sensibility: Sex and Society in Eighteenth-Century England* (University of Chicago Press, 1991). For the midcentury rethinking of sensibility see also John Mullan, *Sentiment and Sociability: The Language of Feeling in the Eighteenth Century* (Oxford: Clarendon Press, 1988).

26 David Hume, "Of the Standard of Taste" in *Essays Moral, Political, and Literary*, ed. Eugene F. Miller (Indianapolis, Ind.: Liberty Press, 1985) 227.

27 The midcentury's transformation of the sublime from a term of rhetorical embellishment to a category of aesthetic experience is well known. For a suggestive rethinking of this transformation see de Bolla's *Discourse of the Sublime*. De Bolla's argument is concerned, specifically, with the connections among the seven years war, the sublime, and the national debt. These form for him a cluster of discourses which produce what de Bolla calls the "autonomous subject."

28 Edmund Burke, *A Philosophical Enquiry into the Origin of our Ideas of the Sublime and Beautiful*, ed. James T. Boulton (University of Notre Dame Press, 1958) 42–43. Further references are to this edition.

29 Addison, *Spectator*, no. 279, no. 285, and no. 417, in *The Spectator*, ed. Bond, vols. II and III.

30 For the importance of "obscurity" and "difficulty" in the elaboration of the Burkean sublime see Angus Fletcher, *Allegory: The Theory of a Symbolic Mode* (Ithaca, N.Y.: Cornell University Press, 1964) 220–278.

31 But see also Ferguson's reworking of the gender binarisms of Burke's *Enquiry* in *Solitude and the Sublime*, 53 ff.

32 Ferguson, *Solitude and the Sublime*, 41.

33 Henry Home, Lord Kames, *Elements of Criticism* (Edinburgh and London, 1762).

34 Eagleton, *Ideology of the Aesthetic*, 3.

35 For an interesting revisiting of the problem of intellectual labor, see Armstrong and Tennenhouse, *The Imaginary Puritan*. I am interested in the status group of intellectuals during the period (with, that is, "scholars," "scholiasts," "professors," "pedants," the "learned," "philologers," and so on), and the way in which some writing is coded as specifically intellectual (often negatively so) over and against other forms of writing, namely, the "public" forms of open and general conversation and the "common" forms of mass culture.

36 See Wasserman, *Elizabethan Poetry*; Wellek, *Rise of Literary History*; Lipking, *Ordering of the Arts*; and Joseph Levine, *Humanism and History: The Origins of English Historiography* (Ithaca, N.Y.: Cornell University Press, 1987). For a more speculative discussion of historicist thinking in the early-modern period, see Michel de Certeau, *The Writing of History*, trans. Tom Conley (New York: Columbia University Press, 1988) esp. 115–205.

37 Levine, *Battle of the Books*.

38 See C. O. Brink, *English Classical Scholarship: Historical Reflections on Bentley, Porson and Housman* (Cambridge University Press, 1985); E. J. Kinney, *The Classical Text: Aspects of Editing in the Age of the Printed Book* (Berkeley, Calif.: University of California Press, 1974); and Rudolf Pfeiffer, *History of Classical Scholarship from 1300 to 1850* (Oxford: Clarendon Press, 1976).

39 See Levine, *Battle of the Books*, 47–84.

40 Richard Bentley, *A Dissertation Upon the Epistles of Phalaris, with an Answer to the Objections of The Honourable Charles Boyle, esq.* (London, 1699), 198.

41 "Regularity" is an important category in Elizabeth Eisenstein's widely influential account of print culture in early modern Europe. My use of the term here is meant to describe how the idea of stable typeface made earlier texts appear to be dubious and in need of experts. I do not mean, as does Alvin Kernan, that eighteenth-century print technology suddenly ordered and rationalized all texts. See Eisenstein, *Printing Press* and "Conjectures," *Journal of Modern History* 40: 1–56; and Kernan, *Impact of Print*.

42 For a discussion of anti-pedantry in seventeenth-century science, see Steven Shapin, *The Social History of Truth: Civility and Science in Seventeenth-Century England* (University of Chicago Press, 1994). Shapin's argument that the "authority of the gentleman" was important for the making of trust in scientific experiments bears an analogous relation to parallel developments in the literary culture. For a discussion of anti-pedantry with particular reference to Shakespeare criticism, see Simon Jarvis, *Scholars and Gentlemen: Shakespearean Textual Criticism and the Representation of Scholarly Labour 1725–1769* (New York: Oxford University Press, 1995).

43 Joseph Addison, *Tatler*, no. 158, *The Tatler*, 3 vols., ed. Donald Bond (Oxford: Clarendon Press, 1987) 1: 184–187.

44 Here is Shaftesbury: " a good poet ... may afford learning for a gentleman. And such a one, whilst he reads these authors as his diversion, will have a truer relish of their sense, and understand 'em better than a pedant with all his labours, and the assistance of volumes of commentaries" (*Characteristicks*: 1: 122).

45 For more detailed accounts of practices and debates among eighteenth-century Shakespeare editors than what is below, see, inter alia, Michael Dobson, *The Making of the National Poet: Shakespeare, Adaptation and Authorship, 1679–1769* (Oxford: Clarendon Press, 1993); Colin Franklin, *Shakespeare Domesticated: The Eighteenth-Century Editions* (New York: Scholar Press, 1990); Margreta de Grazia, *Shakespeare Verbatim: The Reproduction of Authenticity and the 1790 Apparatus* (New York: Oxford University Press, 1991); Jarvis, *Scholars and Gentlemen*; R. B. McKerrow, "The Treatment of Shakespeare's Text by his Early Editors, 1709–68" (1933) reprinted in *Studies in Shakespeare: British Academy Lectures*, ed. Peter Alexander (New York: Oxford University Press, 1964); Arthur Sherbo, *The Birth of Shakespeare Studies: Commentators from Rowe (1709) to Boswell-Malone (1821)* (East Lansing, Mich.: Michigan State University Press, 1986); Gary Taylor, *Reinventing Shakespeare: a Cultural History from the Restoration to the Present* (New York: Weidenfeld and Nicolson, 1989); and George W. Williams, "The Publishing and Editing of Shakespeare's Plays," in *William Shakespeare: his World, his Work, his Influence*, ed. John F. Andrews (New York: Scribners, 1985).

46 See Levine, *Battle of the Books*, 245–263.

47 See Leslie E. Moore, *Beautiful Sublime: The Making of Paradise Lost 1701–1734* (Stanford University Press, 1990).

48 See Richard Foster Jones, *Lewis Theobald: His Contribution to English Scholarship with some Unpublished Letters* (1919; reprinted New York: AMS Press, 1966) and Peter Seary, *Lewis Theobald and the Editing of Shakespeare* (Oxford University Press, 1990).

49 Lewis Theobald, Preface, *Shakespeare's Works* (1733, 1740) reprinted in Beverly Warner, *Famous Introductions to Shakespeare's Plays by the Notable Editors of the Eighteenth Century* (New York: Dodd, Mead, and Co., 1906) 71.

50 Pope's suppression of Theobald is uncannily repeated by contemporary accounts of eighteenth-century Shakespeare studies, such as de Grazia's *Shakespeare Verbatim*, which make scant reference to the importance of Theobald or of classical philology in the editorial construction of his works. Jarvis's *Scholars and Gentlemen* is an important exception to this tendency.

51 Alexander Pope, "Preface to Shakespeare," *Alexander Pope*, ed. Williams, 462.

52 Pope's sense of social history is expressed in his practical handling of the text. That the Folio was edited by actors and the Quartos were, to Pope's mind, closer to the authorial hand, is the central reason why Pope claims that the latter are more reliable.

53 John Upton, *Critical Observations on Shakespeare* (London, 1748) v.
54 Richard Bentley, *Proposals for Printing a New Edition of the Greek Testament and St. Hierom's Latin Version* (London, 1721) 2.

3 NOVEL TO LYRIC: SHAKESPEARE IN THE FIELD OF CULTURE, 1752–1754

1 See Jonathan Bate, *Shakespearean Constitutions: Politics, Theatre, Criticism, 1730–1830* (Oxford: Clarendon, 1989), Dobson, *Making of the National Poet*, and Gary Taylor, *Reinventing Shakespeare*.

2 Precursors to Dodd's anthology include Bysshe's *Art of English Poetry* and Charles Gildon's *Complete Art of Poetry* (London, 1743). Dodd's anthology was the first to focus exclusively on Shakespeare, however, in fact Bysshe pointedly avoids "good Shakespeare" because the "garb" of his language "is now become so out of fashion" (4).

3 On anthologies and canon formation see Barbara Benedict, *Making the Modern Reader: Cultural Mediation in Early Modern Literary Anthologies* (Princeton University Press, 1996).

4 A sense of the encroaching banalization of this passage, even in the eighteenth century, is given in Joseph Warton's lampooning of the cult of poetic poverty:

> I can easily conceive, that a mind overwhelmed with the weight and immensity of its own conceptions, "glancing" with astonishing rapidity "from heaven to earth, and from earth to heaven" cannot willingly submit to the dull drudgery of examining the justness and accuracy of a butcher's bill.
>
> *Adventurer* no. 59, *British Essayists*, ed. Chalmers, xxi: 105.

5 William Dodd, *The Beauties of Shakespeare, regularly selected from each play. With a general index, digesting them under proper heads. Illustrated with explanatory notes, and similar passages from ancient and modern authors* (London, 1752) v.

6 The most influential account of the separation of "art" and "religion" in the modern division of knowledge begins with Max Weber: "religion [was] an inexhaustible spring for artistic creation [which] is evident from the existence of idols and icons." With the dawn of reformation and modernity, however, "art tends to acquire its own set of constitutive values, which are quite different from those obtaining in the religious and ethical domain." (Weber, *Economy and Society*, 2 vols., ii: 608.) Even as Protestant religion exerts "an increasingly rational influence upon the conduct of life," including a systematic "devaluation of art," it also forces a "sharp contrast between the aesthetic attitude and religio-ethical norms," that is, between "spiritualistic and mystical virtues," on the one hand, and "the distinctive form producing values of art" on the other (ii: 609–10). Protestant iconoclasm is paradoxically the condition of the first separating out of the aesthetic from the religious (in the effort to purge the latter of the former). Weber's narrative describes the

conditions under which Dodd might imagine the sublime to be a medium of collective meaning, if not "faith" itself, a "sacred" form whose power is imagined to unite the poet and the reader through "imagination" and "transport." "Literature" in this case is that secular form of meaning sundered from "religion" and given its own "constitutive values." The displacement of "religion" by "literature" happens when the print market structures an imaginary relation between "Shakespeare" and the (notionally) identical plenum of readers. As a theory of modernity, this account brings together Weber's *The Protestant Ethic and the Spirit of Capitalism* (1921) and Marx's analysis of "commodity fetishism." Karl Marx *Capital Volume 1*, trans. Ben Fowkes (New York: Vintage, 1977) 163–177. But see also Theador Adorno, "Theses upon Art and Religion Today," *Notes to Literature II*, trans. Shierry Weber Nicholsen (New York: Columbia University Press, 1992) 292–298. Adorno's skepticism in this regard is sobering: "The exalted unity of art and religion is, and always was, highly problematic in itself. Actually it is largely a romantic projection into the past of a desire for organic, nonalienated relations between men, for doing away with the universal division of labor" (293). For an historical discussion of the "secularization thesis" see C. John Sommerville, *The Secularization of Early-Modern England: from Religious Culture to Religious Faith* (Oxford University Press, 1992). Anderson's analysis of the emergence of nationalism, in *Imagined Communities*, makes a great deal of the secularization narrative, proposing the nation as the reenchanted form of spiritual feeling, the supplementary medium for securing continuity from inevitable finality. McKeon's analysis of the origins of the novel (*Origins of the English Novel*) is the most extensive application of the thesis of secularization to cultural study. See also his article, "Politics of Discourses," in *Politics of Discourse*, eds. Sharpe and Zwicker, 35–51. In Hans Blumenberg's spirited critique, "secularization" entails a reoccupation of spaces once occupied by religious categories not a "*transposition* of authentically theological contents into a secularized alienation from their origin," *The Legitimacy of the Modern Age*, trans. Robert M. Wallace (Cambridge, Mass.: MIT Press, 1992) 65.

7 See Anderson, *Imagined Communities*: "The very possibility of imagining the nation only arose historically when and where three cultural conceptions lost their axiomatic grip on men's minds. The first of these was the idea that a particular script-language offered privileged access to ontological truth, precisely because it was an inseparable part of that truth" (36).

8 I rely here on *Dictionary of National Biography* (London: Oxford University Press, 1917) v: 1060–1062.

9 Lennox criticism has tended to focus on *The Female Quixote*. Recent work on that novel that has been important for my understanding of *Shakespeare Illustrated* includes: Catherine A. Craft, "Reworking Male

Models: Aphra Behn's *Fair Vow-Breaker*, Eliza Haywood's *Fantomina*, and Charlotte Lennox's *Female Quixote*," *Modern Language Review* 84 (October, 1991): 821–838; Gallagher, *Nobody's Story*; Laurie Langbauer, "Romance Revised: Charlotte Lennox's *The Female Quixote*," *Novel: a Forum on Fiction* (Fall, 1984): 29–44; James J. Lynch, "Romance and Realism in Charlotte Lennox's *The Female Quixote*," *Essays in Literature* (Spring, 1987): 51–74; Ronald Paulson, *Satire and the Novel in Eighteenth-Century England* (New Haven, Conn.: Yale University Press, 1967); Deborah Ross, "Mirror, Mirror: The Didactic Dilemma of *The Female Quixote*," *Studies in English Literature 1500–1900* 27 (1987): 455–473; Patricia Meyer Spacks, "The Subtle Sophistry of Desire: Dr. Johnson and *The Female Quixote*," *Modern Philology* 85 (1988): 532–542; and Helen Thompson, "Charlotte Lennox's *The Female Quixote*: A Novel Interrogation," in *Living by the Pen: Early British Women Writers*, ed. Dale Spender (New York and London: Teachers College Press, 1992) 113–125.

10 For Lennox's biography see Miriam Rossiter Small, *Charlotte Ramsay Lennox: An Eighteenth Century Woman of Letters* (New Haven, Conn.: Yale University Press, 1935) and Kathryn Shevelow, "Charlotte Lennox," in *A Dictionary of British and American Women Writers 1660–1800*, ed. Janet Todd (Totowa, N.J.: Rowman and Littlefield, 1987) 196–198.

11 Small and other Lennox critics (see note 16 below) have suggested that her major precursor in this practice is Gerard Langbaine's *Account of English Dramatick Poets* (London, 1691). Langbaine accounts for the source of a dozen plays, but does not reprint or translate them as does Lennox's larger survey, nor does he focus exclusively on Shakespeare.

12 Samuel Johnson, *The Letters of Samuel Johnson*, ed. Bruce Redford (Princeton University Press, 1992) 62. On Thursday, July 9, 1752, Johnson wrote to Lord Orrery that "I hope I shall always rejoice when I am the Occasion of good, and therefore congratulate myself upon the accident by which I introduced Mrs. Lennox to your Lordship. She tells me with how much historical information you have pleased to honour her, but thinks she has not clearly explained her plan which comprise[s] . . . translations, and extracts from such writers as he [Shakespeare] appears to have made use of." In fact, Lennox's anxiety had already been discussed and cleared with Orrery, as his May 9, 1752 letter indicates: "you are entirely right, Madam, to translate, and not to epitomize or imitate" (*The Letters of Samuel Johnson*: 62).

13 Charlotte Lennox, *Shakespeare Illustrated: Or, The Novels and Histories on which the Plays of Shakespeare are Founded, Collected and Translated from the Original Authors, with Critical Remarks in Three Volumes, by the Author of The Female Quixote*, 3 vols. (London 1753, 1754) 1: 89.

14 Thomas R. Lounsbury, Miriam Rossiter Small, and Margaret Doody at various points this century have all claimed that Lennox's criticism is somehow anachronistic, that it looks back to the heyday of early

eighteenth-century neoclassicism. Lounsbury was the first to call Lennox's criticism anachronistic in *Shakespeare as a Dramatic Artist with an Account of his Reputation at Various Periods* (New York: Scribners, 1901). Both Small and Doody cite and accept Lounsbury's verdict, even if the latter would like to see the resurgence of such "Restoration" theory as "advancing upon" Shakespeare, understood as a monument of patriarchal culture. See Small's *Charlotte Ramsay Lennox* (184–228), and Margaret Doody, "Shakespeare's Novels: Charlotte Lennox Illustrated" *Studies in the Novel* 19 (Fall, 1987): 296–310. My reading, by contrast, attempts to place Lennox in the context of midcentury criticism.

15 Whereas criticism once assumed that Lennox was burlesquing the "romance" (understood in the restricted sense as the tradition of "extravagant" French narratives by Scudery and so forth), recent feminist studies have pointed to Lennox's complex and ambivalent relation to this critique. The romance's attention to the etiquettes of courtship, according to Craft, "Reworking Male Models," and Thompson, "Charlotte Lennox's *The Female Quixote*," represented to women readers something of a utopian alternative to the misogynist realities of the eighteenth century. Lennox's understanding of Arabella's library hence records the loss of this domain of female literariness to the harsh necessities of real life. Langbauer "Romance Revised," makes the Derridean point that even as an "anti-romance" it is predicated on, and contaminated by, that which it subordinates and refuses, namely the "romance" but also "the feminine" and "writing" which are in her argument tantamount to the same thing. Spacks, "Subtle Sophistry of Desire," suggestively discusses the twin generic modes of romance and anti-romance as matters of reader response or "desire." I shall argue below that *Shakespeare Illustrated* might be understood on a different set of terms having to do with the novel's relation to "effeminate" culture and with Lennox's coordinate understanding of the regulative value of female character.

16 As we shall see, Lennox's sense of the term is well in advance of Johnson's, whose definition in the *Dictionary* is "a small tale, generally of love." Samuel Johnson, *A Dictionary of the English Language in which the words are deduced from their originals and illustrated in their different significations by examples from the best writers to which are prefixed a history of the language, and an English grammar* (London: Robinson, 1828) 800.

17 Doody's argument, in "Shakespeare's Novels," that *Shakespeare Illustrated* expresses Lennox's commitment to the romance is, in this sense, mistaken. Lennox prefers the sources precisely because they are less romantic than Shakespeare. Romance is the sign of premodern epistemological and narrative instability. See McKeon, *Origins of the English Novel*, which explains the stigmatized meaning of "romance" as a touchstone in the dialectic of "naive-empiricism" and "extreme skepticism"; according to this account, "romance" emerges as such in this

"open ended reversal" of literary and social polarities, thus enclosing otherwise random and disparate texts and discourses in a single, complex unit, or "simple abstraction" (25–65).

18 The one time Johnson uses the term "fiction" in the dedication to *Shakespeare Illustrated* it is as a pejorative "Shakespeare's excellence is not the fiction of the tale, but the representation of life" (x). Lennox's discussion of the history plays distinguishes her account of the novel from Fielding's too. Since *Tom Jones* is called a "history" and defended on these grounds, Fielding cannot make Lennox's neo-Aristotelian defense of the novel as the genre which has taken over from poetry as the countervailing form to history; thus he writes, "It is by falling into fiction, therefore, that we generally offend against this rule, of deserting probability, which the historian seldom if ever quits, till he forsakes his character, and commences a writer of romance" (305). According to Catherine Gallagher, Lennox's commitment to fiction is an early and important example of the novel's ability to promote sympathetic identification with professedly invented characters; see *Nobody's Story*.

19 See Douglas Lane Patey, *Probability and Literary Form: Philosophic Theory and Literary Practice in the Augustan Age* (Cambridge University Press, 1984). For more general accounts of "probabilistic" discourse in the eighteenth century, see Ian Hacking, *The Emergence of Probability: A Philosophical Study of Early Ideas about Probability, Induction, and Statistical Inference* (Cambridge University Press, 1975) and Barbara J. Shapiro, *Probability and Certainty in Seventeenth-Century England: A Study of the Relationship between Natural Science, History, Law, and Literature* (Princeton University Press, 1983).

20 Even those who write directly on *Shakespeare Illustrated*, like Margaret Doody, have assumed that Lennox's interest in the history plays is not "careful," merely a contractual necessity bearing the marks of boredom and haste ("Shakespeare's Novels": 299). Doody assumes that Lennox is only interested in "romances" and "comedies," because these are somehow more essentially "female," an assertion which would have difficulty explaining how the history plays are clearly Lennox's favorite; she reserves some of the highest praise in the whole work, for example, for *Henry VI* where "the poet has given us the finest picture of true heroism, paternal tenderness, and filial love" (III: 144) and for *Henry VIII*, which is full of "pathetic eloquence," "propriety," and "inexpressible grace and beauty" (III: 177).

21 In any case, this suspect conflation of gender and genre would have difficulty explaining the enthusiasm in which some women critics read Shakespeare's plays (most notable in this regard is Elizabeth Montagu, whose *Essay on the Genius and Writings of Shakespeare* (1769), discussed in chapter five, out performs Johnson in its nationalist bardolatry) and the skepticism in which others read the "romance."

22 For a richly historicized account of the emergence of this ideology of

female propriety and its connection both to the novel and to social structures in the eighteenth century, see Mary Poovey, *The Proper Lady and the Woman Writer: Ideology as Style in the Works of Wollstonecraft, Shelley, and Austen* (University of Chicago Press, 1984). Poovey argues that ideologies of female conduct emerge out of the "complex social role that actual women played" during the eighteenth century, on the one hand as ballast in familial property structures (the "settlement" and transfer of estates and moneys) and on the other as a totem for the "political and economic triumph of the middle classes" (15, 10, and passim). Although thematically linked, Poovey's account of the emergence of the "proper lady" over the long course of the eighteenth century is at implicit odds with Nancy Armstrong's *Desire and Domestic Action: a Political History of the Novel* (Oxford University Press, 1986), insofar as Poovey understands ideologies of conduct as *effects* of larger historical structures and transformations, while Armstrong sees them as *causes*.

23 See Doody, "Shakespeare's Novels", 305–306 and Lennox, *Shakespeare Illustrated*: II: 85–87.

24 Small and Doody's reading of critical anachronism in Lennox's work is redoubled as social anachronism as well. (See Small, *Woman of Letters*; Doody, "Shakespeare's Novels").

25 In Lennox's case, any personal identification with the aristocracy can only be at the level of class longing. Her own position was precarious throughout her entire life. See Small, *Woman of Letters, Charlotte Ramsay Lennox* and Shevelow, "Charlotte Lennox."

26 Fredric Jameson, *The Political Unconscious: Narrative as a Socially Symbolic Act* (Ithaca, N.Y.: Cornell University Press, 1981) 141.

27 At some point during the writing of *Shakespeare Illustrated,* Johnson wrote to an apparently ill Lennox that "I hope you take care to observe the Doctor's prescriptions, and take your physick regularly, for I shall soon come to inquire. I should be sorry to lose criticism in her bloom. Your remarks are I think all very judicious, clearly expressed, and incontrovertibly certain. When Shakespeare is demolished your wings will be full summed and I will fly you at Milton; for you are a bird of prey, but the bird of Jupiter." Johnson, *Letters*, ed. Redford, I: 71. The editor's dating of the letter as May, 1753 because of the *Shakespeare Illustrated* reference (which was published that month) seems to me to be erroneous, since Johnson is clearly referring to work in progress. It is for my mind undecidable whether or not Johnson privately enjoyed Lennox's work but found it necessary to discount it in public, or if his initial response changed as he continued to read, or simply if he is consoling a sick friend. For whatever reason, however, Johnson never sent Lennox after Milton.

28 Samuel Johnson, *Rambler*, no. 4, in *Yale Works of Johnson*, eds. Bate and Strauss, vols. 3–5: III: 21.

29 Johnson's edition of Shakespeare, for instance, leaves the final adjudication of textual problems to the "reader." His notion of the "common reader" is famously trumpeted years later in the life of Gray, where he "rejoices to concur with the common reader" in enjoying the "Elegy"; this occurs however in a different conjuncture than our present concern, namely, the appearance of Bell's mass-marketed editions of "English Poets."

30 The eighteenth-century conduct book is essential to both Armstrong's and Poovey's account of the "rise of the novel." See Armstrong, *Desire and Domestic Fiction*, 28–96, and Poovey, *The Proper Lady and the Woman Writer*, 3–48.

31 "An admirable writer of our own time, has found the way to convey the most solid instructions, the noblest sentiments, and the most exalted piety, in the pleasing dress of a novel, and, to use the words of the greatest genius of the present age, 'has taught the passions to move at the command of virtue'." Charlotte Lennox, *The Female Quixote* (New York: Oxford University Press, 1982) 377. The novel writer and "the greatest genius" in this passage, Lennox tells us in her own footnotes, are Richardson and Johnson.

32 *The Gentleman's Magazine* awaits critical analysis, although it is for my mind a crucial instrument not only in the long-term structural transformation of the public sphere in the direction of mass-produced commodity journalism, but also in the related history of the division and dissection of discourses and knowledge, which their categorization of new publications at once records and instances. Carl Carlson's *The First Magazine: a History of the Gentleman's Magazine* (Providence, R.I.: Brown University Press, 1938) remains the only extensive study of the magazine.

33 *Gentleman's Magazine*, no. 23 (1753), 250.

34 Carl Carlson, *The First Magazine*, title page and passim.

35 Samuel Johnson, *A Dictionary of the English Language*, 404.

36 *Gentleman's Magazine*, no. 24 (1753), 256.

37 Johnson, *Letters*, ed. Redford, 1: 67–68. The *Adventurer* was designed initially by John Hawkesworth and Johnson (whose role in the serial was larger then he here lets on); it ran twice a week between November, 1752 and March, 1754 for a total of 140 issues.

38 Joseph Warton, *Odes on Various Subjects* (London, 1746) A2.

39 See Joan Pittock, *The Ascendancy of Taste: the Achievement of Joseph and Thomas Warton* (New York: Routledge and Keagan Paul, 1973). Pittock claims that the Warton brothers constitute "a revolution in taste" (3). For as much as I would dissent from the particular terms of Pittock's contextualization of the Wartons in midcentury aesthetics, her argument that their work must be understood as a response to "a loosening and decentralizing of cultural authority" is in broad conformity with the claims of this book, as is her intention to situate the Wartons in the

specificity of midcentury culture, rather than as a proleptic instauration of romanticism. The reading of Joseph Warton's poetry and criticism as "preromantic" dates back to Edmund Gosse's "Two Pioneers of Romanticism: Joseph and Thomas Warton," *Proceedings of the British Academy* 7 (1915): 145–163, and was made programmatic in Arthur O. Lovejoy's inclusion of Joseph Warton in his critique of the concept of "romanticism" in "On the Discrimination of Romanticism," *PMLA* 39 (1924): 229–253. Marshall Brown's recent and suggestively revisionist resuscitation of the term "Preromanticism" includes scant reference to Warton, however, *Preromanticism* (Stanford University Press, 1991).

40 For the larger poetic context of the nationalist Ode – especially as it is established over and against antiquity – see Howard Weinbrot, *Brittania's Issue: The Rise of British Literature from Dryden to Ossian* (New York: Cambridge University Press, 1993).

41 See John Sitter, *Literary Loneliness in Mid-Eighteenth-Century England* (Ithaca, N.Y.: Cornell University Press, 1982). Sitter describes Warton's disavowal of the public sphere as a "flight from history," because his poetry rejects the Popean habit of addressing the political and social concerns of the day. Warton flies from history, I would argue, only if we define history as topicality, that is, as the present. Warton may be said to fly *from* the topical *to* the historical if we consider the historical to refer to the past, especially the literary past. See also, William Dowling, "Ideology and the Flight From History in Mid-Eighteenth-Century Poetry," *The Profession of Eighteenth-Century Literature: Reflections on an Institution*, ed. Leo Damrosch (Madison, Wis.: University of Wisconsin Press, 1993) 135–153.

42 For a decisive meditation on how the lyric evinces a social statement by means of its refusal to make statements see Theador Adorno, "On Lyric Poetry and Society," trans. Weber Nicholsen, *Notes to Literature I* (New York: Columbia, 1991).

43 Warton, *Adventurer*, no. 93, XXI. Warton wrote two essays on *The Tempest* (93 and 97) and three on *King Lear* (113, 116, 122).

## 4 THE CULTURAL LOGIC OF LATE FEUDALISM: OR, SPENSER AND THE ROMANCE OF SCHOLARSHIP, 1754–1762

1 Although I have followed the convention of adopting Spenser's spelling when referring to the poem at large, I have also retained in citation the individual and highly various spellings used by the critics.

2 A synoptic account of eighteenth-century Spenserianism may be found in Jewel Wurtsbaugh, *Two Centuries of Spenserian Scholarship* (Baltimore, Md.: Johns Hopkins University Press, 1936). See also Greg Kucich, *Keats, Shelley, and Romantic Spenserianism* (University Park, Penn.: Pennsylvania State Univ. Press, 1991) 11–64; and Richard C. Frushell, "Spenser and the Eighteenth-Century Schools," *Spenser Studies* 7 (1986): 175–198.

3 Ben Jonson, *Timber, or Discoveries: Made upon Men and Matter as They Have Flowed Out of His Daily Readings or Had Their Reflux to His Peculiar Notion of the Times*, in *Ben Jonson's Literary Criticism*, ed. James D. Redwine Jr. (Lincoln, Nebr.: University of Nebraska Press, 1970) 19.

4 Johnson's position here in *Rambler* no. 37 is on the Pastoral generally and Spenser's practice of it particularly. I discuss Johnson's position more fully in chapter five below. For Johnson's relation to Spenser and Spenserianism, see Maxine Turnage, "Samuel Johnson's Criticism of the Works of Edmund Spenser," *Studies in English Literature 1500–1900*, 10 (1970): 557–567; and Eithne Henson, *"The Fictions of Romantick Chivalry": Samuel Johnson and Romance* (Rutherford, N.J.: Fairleigh Dickinson University Press, 1992).

5 My understanding of the politics of romantic revival is indebted to two definitive works: Jameson's chapter "Magical Narratives: on the Dialectical Use of Genre Criticism" from *The Political Unconscious*, 103–150, and McKeon's *Origins*, 25–64, 131–270, passim. Jameson's argument that "genre is essentially a socio-symbolic message, or in other terms, that form is immanently and intrinsically an ideology in its own right" I take to be apodictic (141). What is particularly compelling about Jameson's elaboration of this with respect to the romance is the description of how "such forms are reappropriated and refashioned in quite different social and cultural contexts" (141). In Warton and Hurd's rehabilitation of Spenser, the romance is "reappropriated" in the guise of a nostalgic recollection of feudal premodernity. I distinguish this argument slightly from Jameson's by noting that in midcentury criticism feudalism is less a "sedimented" than an actively constituted form (see note 36 below). In this vein, I rely throughout on McKeon's account of the emergence of the "romance" as a "simple abstraction" in the early modern period. McKeon's analysis of the dialectical constitution of the category of the romance can hardly be done justice in a footnote. I would only stress that the constitution of romance as it were after the fact – as its implicit generic doxa was challenged by the antiromance – is recapitulated in the critical texts I examine in this chapter by the analogous category of "feudalism." See also, Arthur Johnston, *Enchanted Ground: The Study of Medieval Romance in the Eighteenth Century* (London: Athlone Press, 1964). On the question of epic unity see Herbert F. Tucker, Jr., "Spenser's Eighteenth-Century Readers and the Question of Unity in *The Faerie Queene*," *University of Toronto Quarterly* 46 (1977): 322–341.

6 John Hughes, *The Works of Edmund Spenser*, 3 vols. (London, 1715) 1: x.

7 Here I disagree with Wellek's argument in *Rise of Literary History* that Warton's *Observations* was simply a commonplace book piece of juvenilia that bore its fruit only in the later *History of English Poetry.*

8 Anon. *An Impartial Account of Mr. Upton's Notes on the Fairy Queene* (London, 1759) 1.

9 See John A. Vance, "Samuel Johnson and Thomas Warton," *Biography: An Interdisciplinary Quarterly*, 9 (Spring, 1986): 95–111

10 "To Thomas Warton, July 16, 1754" in *Letters*, ed. Redford, 1: 81.

11 Thomas Warton, *Observations on the Fairy Queen of Spenser*, 2 vols. (London, 1754, 1762; New York: Greenwood Press, 1968) 1, pp. 87–88. All citations are to this edition. Not wanting to seem a "pedant" myself, I have spared readers a discussion of the difference between the initial *Observations* and the later two volume set. Suffice it to say that the intervening years show the influence of Richard Hurd's understanding of the gothic discussed below.

12 See John A. Vance, *Joseph and Thomas Warton* (Boston, Mass.: Twayne, 1983), and Joan Pittock, "Thomas Warton and the Oxford Chair of Poetry," *English Studies: A Journal of English Language and Literature*, 62 (January, 1981): 14–33.

13 This investment in the University as the site of serious scholarship need not, according to the argument I am making, bear a relation to what actual "research" went on at Oxford and Cambridge during this time, which in the customary account is rather nugatory. It is difficult to extract, however, the element of "truth" in this account from the ideological charge of pedantry. See A. L. Rowse, *Oxford in the History of England* (Oxford University Press, 1975).

14 See Franklin Court, *Institutionalizing English Literature: the Culture and Politics of Literary Study, 1750–1900* (Stanford University Press, 1992), 12–13. This point is crucial for Court's narrative because he is concerned with a genealogy of academic criticism wed to pedagogy. Hence his eighteenth-century materials are primarily Scottish. For my purposes, the *idea* of the academy in eighteenth-century critical culture is finally more important than actual pedagogical practices. In this vein, Warton fits the bill more than Adam Smith or Hugh Blair (Court's important figures).

15 Dowling argues that such gothic revival, in particular the recourse to the myth of Scottish liberty and enchantment, represents the mid-century's aestheticizing of Augustan country ideology. See "Ideology and the Flight from History," *The Profession of Eighteenth-Century Literature*, ed. Leo Damrosch, 135–153.

16 This argument is amplified in the 1762 edition but already present in the 1754 volume.

17 The source Warton gives for this anecdote is Luigi Riccoboni's *Historia de Theatro Italiano* (London, 1728).

18 The quotation is Gianvincenzo Gravini's *Della Ragion Poetica* (Naples, 1716).

19 The spellings of *The Faerie Queene* and of Spenser are Huggins's (or his printer's).

20 For an interesting discussion of Huggins's relation to the Wartons and Johnson see James Clifford, *Dictionary Johnson: Samuel Johnson's Middle*

*Years* (New York: McGraw-Hill, 1979) 128–133. See also, L. F. Powell, "William Huggins and Tobias Smollett," *Modern Philology* 4 (1936): 179–190.

21 *The Observer Observ'd: or Some Remarks on a Curious Tract, intitled, Observations on the Faerie Queene of Spencer. By Thomas Warton, A.M. &c.* (London, 1756) 3, emphasis in original. The attribution of this unsigned pamphlet is discussed in Powell, "Huggins and Smollett."

22 The imaginary relation of Huggins's notion of pedantry to the real university named Oxford may be sensed in this specific utterance by the fact that this gentleman who, in fact, graduated from Oxford may claim to be without "the honor of a university education."

23 Quoted in Powell, "Huggins and Smollett," 181.

24 For an account of the eighteenth-century public sphere as an effort to police the borders between the upper and lower body, cognition and defecation, purity and filth, see Peter Stallybrass and Allon White, *The Politics and Poetics of Transgression* (Ithaca, N.Y.: Cornell University Press, 1992).

25 See the discussion of "entertainment" with reference particularly to the novel and *The Gentleman's Magazine* in chapter three.

26 John Upton, Preface, *Notes on the Fairy Queen*, ed. John Radcliffe (New York: Garland Press, 1987) xx. All references are to this edition.

27 John Upton, "A Letter Concerning a New Edition of Spenser's Fairy Queene" (London, 1752) 50.

28 The concluding section of Longinus's treatise was a common topos in the alignment of poetic exuberance with political liberty during the eighteenth century. The nature of that liberty, as we shall see, can vary according to ideological predisposition. For the *locus-classicus*, see Longinus, *Peri Hypsos*, trans. G. M. A. Grube (Cambridge, Mass.: Hackett, 1957) 56–58; and Michael Meehan *Liberty and Poetics in Eighteenth-Century England* (London: Croom Helm, 1988).

29 See Meehan, *Liberty and Poetics*, 64–78.

30 James Boswell, *The Life of Samuel Johnson LL.D.* (New York: Random House, 1954) 1033–1034.

31 The important texts here are Bolingbroke's *The Craftsman* (1726–1735) including the twenty-four papers written between 1730–1731 that comprised his later *Remarks on the History of England* (1735), Lord Lyttleton's *Letters from a Persian in England to a Friend in England* (1737), and Bolingbroke's *Idea of a Patriot King* (1740). Lyttleton's Elizabethan panegyric, for instance, sets the stage for Hurd's later investment in the period. Lyttleton writes in Letter 60: "the period when the English nation enjoyed the greatest happiness, after the Norman invasion, was under the influence of a woman . . . [for] it was not till the reign of Queen Elizabeth that the government came to an equal balance, which is the true state of perfection." George Lyttleton, *Letters from a Persian in England to a Friend in England*, in *Select British Classics: Containing The*

*Rambler, by Dr. Johnson and Lord Lyttleton's Persian Letters* (London, 1796) 61. But as we move from Lyttleton to Hurd we notice two important developments. First, while Lyttleton describes the period as the waning of feudalism – "the bonds of vassalage were broke or lightened; the barons were by different laws encouraged and enabled to part with their lands; the weight of property was transferred to the people" (61) – Hurd's view is decidedly ambivalent, or inconsistent, on whether or not feudalism was at this point extinct. Second, while Lyttleton celebrates the religious condition as properly reformed, "free from the dominion of superstition, *the worst of all slavery,*" Hurd in turn longs for "superstition" as such (61). In both of these respectively social and epistemological cases, then, Hurd may be said to amplify the case for premodernity.

32 Hurd's literary historical narrative is essentially Tory even as Hurd himself is apparently a Whig, hence Johnson's antipathy according to Boswell.

33 Indeed, connections between Johnson and Hurd's understanding of the past are easier to detect in Johnson's "London" (1738) where his lament about "these degenerate days" (line 35) leads to a recollection of Elizabeth:

> Struck with the seat that gave Eliza birth,
> We kneel, and kiss the consecrated earth;
> In pleasing dreams the blissful age renew,
> And call Britannia's glories back to view;
> Behold her cross triumphant on the main,
> The guard of commerce, and the dread of Spain,
> Ere masquerades debauched, excise oppressed,
> Or English honour grew a standing jest. (23–30)

These lines are the subject of J. C. D Clarke's argument (*Samuel Johnson*) that Johnson held, at heart, Jacobite sympathies. This has become a topic of much controversy among Johnsonians.

34 Hurd announces on the title page of the *Letters* that they are designed to expound on the themes of the *Dialogue*. Richard Hurd, *Letters on Chivalry and Romance with the Third Elizabethan Dialogue*, ed. Edith Morley (1911; reprint, New York: AMS Press, 1976) 77. References are all to this edition.

35 Hurd here refers to Sir Kenelm Digby (1603–1665).

36 Here I would distinguish my understanding of the romance from Jameson's theory of "sedimentation" in *Political Unconscious*. While Jameson casts romantic revivals as traces of feudalism *as such* – however buried or sedimented they may be within the political unconscious – I am arguing for the constitution of the *category* of "feudalism" during the eighteenth century. This is not to make the familiar nominalist point, I hasten to add, that modes of production are simply discursive entities, nor is it to dispute Jameson's brilliant narrative of cultural forms. It is, rather, to suggest that if feudalism is "sedimented" in this text, it also and preeminently constituted as what

Jameson calls (following Levi-Strauss) "an ideological resolution to a real contradiction," a resolution in this case to the crisis which subsumes on the one hand the reading public and the problem of mass culture, and on the other hand secularization and the waning of "belief." Feudalism here amounts to what Raymond Williams calls a "traditional formation," "an intentionally selective version of a shaping past and a preshaped present, which is then powerfully operative in the process of social and cultural definition and identification." Jameson seems to have in mind something closer to what Williams calls a "residual formation," that which is "effectively formed in the past, but . . . still active in the cultural process, not only and often not at all as an element of the past, but as an effective element of the present." (Williams, *Marxism and Literature*, 115 and 122.) Considered from this perspective, the Jamesonian concept of "sedimentation" is a necessary complement to the argument advanced in these pages, as it arrives from a different angle (that of the historical structure of the feudal mode of production, rather than the later ideological constitution of that structure) to a similar set of questions.

37  Hurd responds to this point later in the *Letters* by quoting Pope's "Epistle to Cobham": "Nature once known, no prodigies remain" (90). Hurd's citation of Pope changes the meaning. In Pope's poem, "nature" refers to the "ruling passion" of individual men; in Hurd's criticism, by contrast, "nature" refers to the historico-literary context of the writer and hence to the "systematic" derivation of all that may appear to be *sui generis*.

38  See Perry Anderson, *Lineages of the Absolutist State* (London: Verso, 1974) 113–142.

39  Edmund Spenser, *The Faerie Queene*, in *Spenser: Poetical Works*, eds. J. C. Smith and E. De Selincourt (New York: Oxford University Press, 1912) v: 11, 5–7. All references are to this edition.

40  Cf. Anderson, *Lineages*, "when the Absolutist States were constituted in the West, their structure was fundamentally determined by the feudal regroupment against the peasantry, after the dissolution of serfdom; but it was secondarily *over-determined* by the rise of an urban bourgeoisie which after a series of technical advances was now developing into pre-industrial manufactures on a considerable scale" (22–23).

41  For eighteenth-century gothicism, see Samuel Kliger, *The Goths in England: a Study in Seventeenth- and Eighteenth-Century Thought* (Cambridge, Mass.: Harvard University Press, 1952) and Johnston, *Enchanted Ground*.

42  Robert Markley's suggestion of a simple continuum between Shaftes-bury's "aristocratic snobbishness" and later "bourgeois" cultural norms is thus rather dubious. Hurd's response to Shaftesbury suggests, rather, that Shaftesburian elitism is dialectically transformed, that is, extended *and* reversed, by the midcentury to an "anti-bourgeois," or Gothic conservatism. See Markley, "Sentimentality and Performance."

43 Richard Hurd, *Dissertation on the Idea of Universal Poetry*, in *The Works of Richard Hurd, D. D. Lord Bishop of Worcester*, v. ii (London, 1811 reprinted New York: AMS Press, 1811) 19.

44 Wellek, *Rise of Literary History*, 10.

45 Here I mean preromantic in the sense of simply an early version of what will later flower in Wordsworth and Coleridge, not in Brown's powerfully genealogical revitalizing of the term in *Preromanticism*. For Brown, "preromantic" means what will develop into romanticism not what is already romantic, cut off from its age and so forth. Hence Collins and the Wartons give way in his study to Goldsmith and Sterne.

5    SHAKESPEARE'S NATION: THE LITERARY PROFESSION AND
       "THE SHADES OF AGE"

1 *Rambler*, no. 23 in *Yale Works of Johnson*, eds. Bate and Strauss, vols. 3–5: III: 128–129.

2 See William K. Wimsatt, *Samuel Johnson's Prose Style* (New Haven, Conn.: Yale University Press, 1947).

3 *Idler*, no. 60, *The Idler and the Adventurer*, in *Yale Works of Johnson*, eds. Bate, Ballet and Powell, II: 186.

4 This point is taken up with considerable nuance in Thomas Reinert, *Regulating Confusion: Samuel Johnson and the Crowd* (Durham, Duke University Press, 1996) and Deidre Lynch, "'Beating the Track of the Alphabet': Samuel Johnson, Tourism and ABCs of Modern Authority." *ELH* 57 (1990): 357–405.

5 On blockage and the sublime, see Neil Hertz, *The End of the Line* (New York: Columbia University Press, 1985).

6 Samuel Johnson, *The History of Rasselas*, in Donald Greene, ed., *Samuel Johnson* (Oxford University Press, 1984) 351–352.

7 *Preface*, to *A Dictionary of the English Language, in which the words are deduced from their originals and illustrated in their different significations by examples from the best writers*, in Greene, ed. *Samuel Johnson* (New York: Oxford University Press, 1984) 318.

8 Samuel Johnson, "Preface," *The Works of Shakespeare, The Yale Edition of the Works of Samuel Johnson*, ed. Arthur Sherbo (New Haven: Yale University Press, 1968) VIII: 59.

9 For the importance of time in Johnson's corpus, see Paul Alkon, "Johnson and Time Criticism," *Modern Philology* (May, 1988): 543–557; Regina Hewitt, "Time in Rasselas: Johnson's Use of Locke's Concept," *Studies in Eighteenth-Century Culture* 19 (1989): 267–276; and Thomas Reinert, "Johnson and Conjecture," *SEL* (Summer, 1988): 483–496.

10 See Leo Damrosch, *Fictions of Reality in the Age of Hume and Johnson* (Madison, Wis.: Wisconsin University Press, 1989) and Adam Potkay, "The Spirit of Ending in Johnson and Hume," *Eighteenth-Century Life*

(November, 1992): 103–121. "Suffrage of futurity" is from the *Preface* to the *Dictionary*, 311.

11 According to Wellek, Johnson's pragmatist apostasy is that he "treats art as life," René Wellek, *A History of Modern Criticism 1750–1950* (Cambridge University Press, 1955) I: 79. Eagleton's argument that, in Johnson, "the act of literary criticism inhabits no autonomous aesthetic sphere but belongs organically with 'general ideology'" thus oddly repeats a commonplace dating back at least to Hazlitt (if not, as I shall argue below in my discussion of William Kenrick's response to Johnson, to Johnson's day), *Function of Criticism*, 20. For an extensive rebuttal to this understanding of Johnson, see Morris Brownell, *Samuel Johnson's Attitude toward the Arts* (Oxford: Clarendon Press, 1989). Brownell directs his recovery of Johnson's deep involvement in the eighteenth-century art world against the caricature of, in his words, "a bull in the china shop of taste" (1).

12 See Shirley White Johnston, "From Preface to Practice: Samuel Johnson's Editorship of Shakespeare," *Greene Centennial Studies: Essays Presented in the Centennial Year of the University of Southern California*, eds. Robert Allen and Paul Korshin (Charlottesville, Va.: University of Virginia Press, 1984); Gwin Kolb and Robert DeMaria, "Thomas Warton's *Observations on the Fairy Queen of Spenser*, Samuel Johnson's 'History of the English Language', and Warton's *History of English Poetry*: Reciprocal Indebtedness?" *Philological Quarterly* (Summer, 1995): 45–59; and Peter Seary, "The Early Editors of Shakespeare and the Judgments of Johnson," in *Johnson after Two Hundred Years*, ed. Paul Korshin (Philadelphia, Penn.: University of Pennsylvania Press, 1986): 175–186.

13 See Fredric V. Bogel, *The Dream of my Brother: an Essay on Johnson's Authority* (University of Victoria Press, 1990) and Lynch, "'Beating the Track of the Alphabet.'"

14 The status of philological particulars evidently changed over the course of the Shakespeare project. Johnson noted in the early *Proposals* that literary works, as they recede in time, accrete a certain "obscurity": "When a writer outlives his contemporaries, and remains almost the only unforgotten name of a distant time, he is necessarily obscure. Every age has its modes of speech, and its cast of thought; which, though easily explained when there are many books to be compared with each other, become some times unintelligible, and always difficult, when there are no parallel passages that may conduce to their illustration." (*Yale Works of Johnson*: VII: 52) The method is blandly historical: "When . . . any obscurity arises from an allusion to some other book, the passage will be quoted. When the diction is entangled, it will be cleared by a paraphrase or interpretation. When the sense is broken by the suppression of part of the sentiment in pleasantry or passion, the connection will be supplied. When any forgotten custom is hinted, care will be taken to retrieve and explain it. The meaning assigned to doubtful words will be supported by the authorities of other

writers, or by parallel passages of Shakespeare himself" (56–57). Printed two years after his letter to Thomas Warton celebrating the method of *Observations on The Fairy Queen of Spenser*, this passage succinctly expresses Johnson's commitment to historicist annotation. Whereas textual obscurity provided for Warton a relation to the past bound up with his understanding of the sublime and to a literary history charting a rueful descent from sublimity, however, Johnson's thinking through of these questions in the years between the *Proposals* and the edition leads to an important self-revision in which the particular becomes the baleful agent of canonical blockage.

15 For a suggestive discussion of this note and its relation to the history of the sublime, in particular *vis-à-vis* Romanticism, see Jonathan Arac, "The Media of Sublimity: Johnson and Lamb on *King Lear*," *Studies in Romanticism* (Summer, 1987): 209–220.

16 Johnson's weariness of singularities stretches back to the *Rambler*; two pertinent essays here would be no. 47 on melancholia (understood to be a domination of lost objects) and no. 137 which balances the pursuit of knowledge with the consolation of sociability.

17 See Paulson, *Breaking and Remaking*, 149–202.

18 For a reading of Johnson in this manner see Barrell's chapter on the *Dictionary* in *English Literature in History: An Equal Wide Survey* (London: Hutchinson, 1983).

19 I would contrast my reading of Johnson, in this respect, to that of Kernan in *Johnson and the Impact of Print*, who finds him the democratic avatar of print's universality. See also Walter Ong, "Samuel Johnson and the Printed Word," *Review* 10 (1988): 97–112.

20 In this respect, Johnson develops the notion of the "common" already in the *Dictionary* in terms of "common speech," which studiously avoids the "many terms of art and manufacture," words "which being not admitted into general use stand yet as candidates or probationers, and must depend for their adoption on the suffrage of futurity" (313). See Robert DeMaria's "The Politics of Johnson's Dictionary," *PMLA*: 104, I, (1989): 64–74; and Barrell, *An Equal Wide Survey*.

21 See Black, *English Press* and Michael Harris, "London Printers and Newspaper Production during the First Half of the Eighteenth Century," *Journal of Printing Historical Society* 12 (1977–1998): 33–51. For the political context of midcentury journalism see Leslie Hanson, *The Government and the Press, 1695–1763* (Oxford University Press, 1967); Robert Harris, *A Patriot Press: National Politics and the London Press in the 1740s* (Cambridge University Press, 1988) and Robert Rea, *The English Press in Politics, 1760–1774* (Lincoln, Nebr.: University of Nebraska Press, 1963)). For antecedent developments see Joseph Frank, *The Beginnings of English Newspapers 1620–1660* (Cambridge, Mass.: Harvard University Press, 1961) and James Sutherland, *The Restoration Newspaper and its Development* (Cambridge University Press, 1986).

22  See Donoghue, *The Fame Machine.*

23  William Kenrick, *Monthly Review, A Literary Journal* (October 1765) no. 33, 286.

24  Nearly two hundred years later F. R. Leavis reads the same lines of Johnson's preface and makes the same accusation as Kenrick: "Johnson cannot understand that works of art *enact* their moral valuations. It is not enough that Shakespeare, on the evidence of his works, 'thinks' (and feels), morally; for Johnson a moral judgment that isn't *stated* isn't there. Further, he demands that the whole play shall be conceived and composed as a statement. The dramatist must start with a conscious and abstractly formulated moral and proceed to manipulate his puppets so as to demonstrate and enforce it." F. R. Leavis, *The Common Pursuit* (New York University Press, 1952) 110–111. Leavis represents this failure as "an essential tendency of the Augustan tradition," a tradition with which he is otherwise quite sympathetic (111). That this critique was already articulated by Johnson's contemporaries can tell us something about the tensions that inhabited the critical profession at the moment of its emergence and about the different models of literature contained within "the Augustan tradition."

25  In addition to pamphlets such as *A Candid Review of Mr. Kenrick's Review of Dr. Johnson's Edition of Shakespeare*, responses came from *The Critical Review, The London Chronicle*, his own erstwhile organ the *Monthly Review*, and elsewhere.

26  The OED dates the first use of "journalism" as 1833 in the *Westminster Review*.

27  The OED dates the first use of the term "journalist" in 1693 to the satire "Humours Town," which includes "Epistle writers or journalists." The OED's first entry for a writer for the press is 1733, but usage seems to have remained that of one who wrote journals well through the century.

28  *An Essay on the Writings and Genius of Shakespear, Compared with the Greek and French Dramatic Poets, with Some Remarks upon the Misrepresentations of Mons. de Voltaire* (London, 1769) 1.

29  This, interestingly, from a woman whose cultural identity was that of a consummate cosmopolitan, well known in the salons in Paris as well as London. See Reginald Blunt, *Mrs. Montagu, "Queen of the Blues": Her Letters and Friendships from 1762 to 1800* (Scribners: New York, 1923). For the larger context of a so-called "age of cosmopolitanism," see Gerald Newman, *The Rise of English Nationalism: a Cultural History, 1740–1830* (New York: St. Martins, 1987) 1–47.

## AFTERWORD: THE PRESENT CRISIS

1  For the history of English literary pedagogy see Chris Baldick's *The Social Mission of English Studies, 1848–1932* (Oxford University Press,

1983), the first chapter of Terry Eagleton's *Literary Theory: An Introduction* (Minneapolis, Minn., University of Minnesota Press, 1983), and D. J. Palmer's *The Rise of English Studies* (Oxford University Press, 1965). For an interesting revisionary account, see Franklin Court's *Institutionalizing English: The Culture and Politics of Literary Study, 1750–1900* (Stanford University Press, 1992). Arguing against the narrative that focuses exclusively on Matthew Arnold, Court's book recovers the many debates that went into the establishment of English as an academic discipline. Centrally concerned with the nineteenth century, Court's genealogy stretches back to Adam Smith and Hugh Blair's fledgling attempt to institute something like a course of English in the Scottish university system. I would place greater emphasis than Court on *criticism* as an institution during the eighteenth century. In this light, I would also argue that, as the official institutions of higher learning and thus of "pedantry" and "scholarly" reading, Oxford and Cambridge had a greater effect on critical discourse in the eighteenth century than the more pedagogically advanced schools in the north.

2 See for example the report prepared by the "Council for Aid to Education." A subsidiary of the RAND corporation, the council's committee was composed largely of CEOs and University Presidents, a strategic alliance of corporate America and academic management. The closing words of the report's preamble are ominous: "The business community has a direct interest in the outcome of educational reform and broad experience in the kind of strategic thinking and internal restructuring that will be required of American colleges and universities." Joseph Dionne, Thomas Kean *et al.*, *Breaking the Social Contract: The Fiscal Crisis in Higher Education* (Santa Monica, Calif.: Rand, 1996) 3. The meaning of terms like "internal restructuring" in the argot of late-nineties managerial culture is not very mysterious. The report means to suggest that universities should pursue the kind of streamlining that corporations have successfully implemented to compete in the global marketplace. As we can see in note 3 below, these cost-cutting strategies have begun to shape the future of literary study.

3 Here is a very recent report from the Modern Language Association, sent to all members: "Higher Education in the fields that our organization represents has reached a crisis that has been building for a long time . . . On the one hand, the cost of providing higher education has been going up at a rate notably greater than that of inflation, while funding for institutions has failed to keep pace. On the other hand, despite the manifest need for post secondary teachers to serve a growing student population, there are far more candidates for professorial jobs in higher education than there are tenure-track positions to be filled." Sandra Gilbert *et al.*, *MLA Committee on Professional Employment* (New York: MLA, 1998). See also the essays collected in *Higher Education*

*Under Fire: Politics, Economics, and the Crisis of the Humanities,* eds. Cary Nelson and Michael Bérube (New York: Routledge, 1994).

4 I refer not just to the ritual skewering of the MLA by the press, but also to such books as Paul Gross and Norman Levitt, *Higher Superstition: The Academic Left and its Quarrel with Science* (Baltimore: Johns Hopkins University Press, 1994), which uses literary criticism as the synecdoche for the "academic left" and which, in a moment of reverie, imagines the science faculty (closer as it is to the pragmatic norms of public responsibility) commandeering and teaching the courses of the literature faculty (243–244).

5 This is the moral of the story in Eagleton's *Function of Criticism,* which concentrates on the aspects of decline within Habermas's narrative in order to indict the feckless criticism of the modern age.

6 See Palmer, *Rise of English Studies* and Court, *Institutionalizing English.*

7 The argument that criticism has declined from a prior unity with the public sphere and can only be redeemed by a return to that unity is available to all sides of the political spectrum. Before Eagleton's *Function of Criticism* after all there was John Gross's *The Rise and Fall of the Man of Letters: A Study of the Idiosyncratic and the Humane in Modern Literature* (New York: Macmillan, 1969). For a recent version of the narrative of decline see Cary Nelson's *Manifesto of a Tenured Radical* (New York University Press, 1997).

8 Antonio Gramsci, *Prison Notebooks* (New York: International, 1971). "Since these various categories of traditional intellectuals experience through an '*esprit de corps*' their uninterrupted historical continuity and their special qualification, they thus put themselves forward as autonomous and independent of the dominant social group. This self-assessment is not without consequences in the ideological and political field, consequences of wide-ranging import" (7).

9 Walter Benjamin, "Theses on the Philosophy of History," in *Illuminations,* ed. Arendt, 255.

# Index